200 WATERFALLS

IN
CENTRAL & WESTERN
NEW YORK

A Finders' Guide

REVISED AND UPDATED

Rich & Sue Freeman

Burford Books

Cover Design by Lynch Graphics and Design (www.bookcoverdesign.com)

Maps by Rich Freeman
Pictures by Rich & Sue Freeman
Cover Photos by Rich Freeman
Front Cover Photo is of a waterfall at Sugar Creek Glen

Every effort has been made to provide accurate and up-to-date route descriptions in this book. Hazards are noted where known. Users of this book are reminded that they alone are responsible for their own safety when on any outing and that they use the routes described in this book at their own risk.

If you find inaccurate information or substantially different conditions (after all, things do change), please send an email detailing your findings to info@burfordbooks.com.

Printed in the United States of America.

10 9 8 7 6 5 4 3 2 1

Library of Congress Cataloging-in-Publication Data is on file with the Library of Congress.

200 WATERFALLS

IN
CENTRAL & WESTERN
NEW YORK

A Finders' Guide

Waterfall Locations by Number

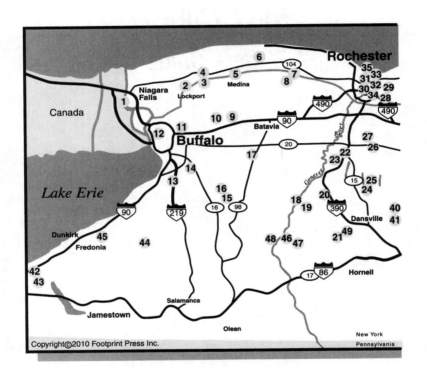

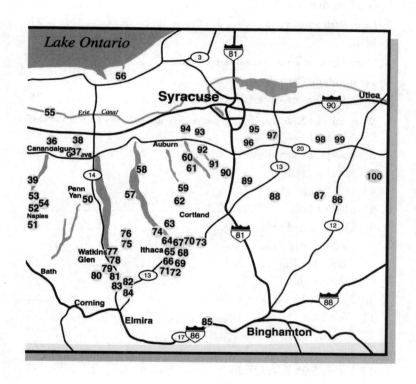

Contents

Acknowledgments

The research, writing, production, and promotion of a book such as this is never a solitary adventure. *200 Waterfalls in Central and Western New York* came into being because of the assistance of many wonderful people who freely shared their knowledge, experience, resources, thoughts, and time. We extend our heartfelt thanks to them all. Each in his or her own way is responsible for making central and western New York a better place to live and, most of all, a region rich with the spirit of collaboration for the betterment of all. This is what ensures quality of life. Thank you, each and every one.

Adirondack Mountain Club, Onondaga Chapter: Mary Coffin
Adventure Calls Outfitters, Inc.: Terry Shearn
Allens Creek/Corbett's Glen Preservation Group: Jean Baric
Authors: Derek Doefinger, Scott Ensminger, Dan Shea
Canandaigua Department of Parks: Dennis Brewer
Cayuga Trails Club: Kurt Seitz
Chittenango Falls State Park: Anne Marie Geiss
City of Rochester, Parks & Recreation: Jim Farr, Terri MacIntee
City of Rochester, Water & Lighting Bureau: Don Root
Cyclotour Guidebooks: Harvey Botzman
County of Erie, Department of Parks, Recreation & Forestry: Daniel Glowski, Lawrence Jasinski
DEC, Region 8: Gretchen Cicora, Ron Schroeder, Michael Allen
DEC, Region 9: Victor Anderson
Emery Park: Daniel Lewalski
Fillmore Glen State Park: Rick Banker
Finger Lakes Land Trust: Betsy Darlington
Finger Lakes Trail Conference: Howard Beye, Bob Emerson, Alex Gonzalez, Mark Hittle, Helen Jordan, Glenna Potts, Kurt Seitz, Ed Sidote, Irene Szabo, Fred Yahn, Ed Zemanick
Forest Lawn Cemetery: Janice Burnett
Finger Lakes National Forest: Al Wruck
Ithaca DPW: Andy Hillman
Manlius Historian: Barbara Rivette
Monroe County Parks: Eric Johnson
Niagara County Parks: Peter Miano
New Hope Mills: Dale Weed
Office of Parks, Recreation & Historic Preservation: Christian Nielsen, Doris Hampton
Onondaga County Department of Parks: Brent MacPherson
Ontario Pathways: Kyle Gage

Pack, Paddle, Ski Corp.: Randy French, Rick French
Penfield Parks and Recreation: Michael Cooper, Jim Britt
Proofreader: Sue Domina
Robert Treman State Park: William Brown
Sherburne Town Supervisor: Harry Conley
Spafford Town Historian: Barbara Shoemaker
Taughannock Falls State Park: Don Oliver
Town of Brighton, Parks & Recreation: Jerry LaVigne
Town of Naples: Donald Leysath
Town of Springport: Robert Bower
Village of Honeoye Falls: Jean Batte
Village of Manlius: Cheri Haskins, Linda Robinson
Village of Montour Falls: S. Casselberry, Deborah Riley
Village of Phelps: Dave Nieskes
Wayne County Parks: Kevin Scott
Westfield Water Department: Wayne Cardy
Zoar Valley Canoe & Rafting Company: Jim Redline

For updates we also extend our sincere thanks to Chris Babcock, Irene
Szabo, Mark Johnson and Java Joe (Joe Dabes) for their input in leading us
to changes and corrections. Thanks for taking the time to assist us.

Introduction

"There are more waterfalls in upstate New York than in any place in the east," says Robert Dineen, a glacial geologist for the New York State Geological Survey. "We've certainly got more than our share here."

He's right. We're loaded. You've probably heard of (and maybe even visited) the big ones like Niagara, Taughannock, Buttermilk, and Ithaca Falls. This book will lead you to those and to a wealth of others. It's a guide to waterfalls you can visit, either from your car at roadside, by taking a hike, or by walking up a creekbed. It is not an inventory of all the waterfalls that exist in central and western New York. Unfortunately many gorgeous waterfalls are on private property and we're not invited. But, don't let that get you down. This guide identifies locations where you can see over 250 waterfalls. It's enough to keep you busy exploring waterfalls for a long time, and guessing why so many have multiple names.

We made every attempt to include only publicly accessible waterfalls in this guide. But, property ownership changes so if you see a posted sign, please obey it. Some of the waterfalls are on private property. The waterfalls may be accessible from a public trail such as the Finger Lakes Trail or just by the benevolence of the landowner. Ownerships and permissible usage changes over time.

Please respect all lands, public and private. Leave no trace of your visit and if you see litter from less respectful visitors, please pick it up.

In these days of high stress and hectic lives, a visit to a waterfall can be a rejuvenating experience. Sit in the sanctuary of a cooling mist on a hot summer day or take in the sound of drumming waters when the leaves are ablaze in color. It doesn't matter when you go, but that you go. Getting there can be as much a part of the adventure as the waterfall itself. Many of the waterfalls are tucked in out-of-the-way locales that require a drive through small towns on back country roads. Enjoy the journey.

We've provided statistics on each waterfall. But, take them as broad estimates. Widths and heights of waterfalls change with the level of water flow and the forces of erosion. Published estimates for waterfalls vary significantly. We made no attempt to accurately measure waterfall heights or widths. This is not a quantitative guide. It is a guide that leads you along a path to personal discovery. Waterfalls are things of ever-changing beauty to be savored, not merely physical entities to be studied and quantified. Go on your waterfall quest with an open mind. It will be what it is when you get there. Just go.

Legend

At the beginning of each waterfall listing, you will find a description with the following information:

Location: The town and county where the waterfall is located.

Waterway: The name of the creek, river, or gully where the waterfall is found.

Directions: How to find the trailhead or creekbed parking area from a major road or town.

Alternative Parking: Directions to another parking area if one is available.

Best Viewing Locations: Where to go for the best views of the waterfall.

Waterfall Height: How far the water drops from crest to base. This figure is often a guess based on visual estimation. Even published heights of a specific waterfall vary widely. This figure is meant only as a rough estimation of how high you can expect the waterfall to be.

Best Season to Visit: The season for best viewing based on a compromise between having sufficient water to be aesthetically pleasing and the level of safety.

Access: Mode of transportation required to view the falls:

Bushwhack: To view the falls you have to cross fields or woods where no trails exist.

Creekwalk: The waterfall is viewable only by walking in a creekbed. You'll get wet feet.

Hike: A trail greater than 0.5-mile long leads to the falls.

Roadside: The waterfall is viewable from a road or parking lot.

Short walk: A trail less than 0.5-mile long leads to the falls.

Waterway: You'll need a boat to view this waterfall.

Wheelchair: The route to the falls is wheelchair accessible.

Hiking or Creekwalk Time: The estimated time it will take to get from the parking area to the farthest waterfall and back again.

Trail or Creekwalk Length: The estimated distance in miles, from the parking area to the farthest waterfall and back again.

Difficulty: A rating of the level of difficulty of the waterfalling experience.

> **1 Boot** – Very Easy – A waterfall that can be seen from roadside or a parking lot, or one that requires a very short walk on a level trail.

> **2 Boots** – Easy – A waterfall that requires a short walk on a rolling trail or a longer walk on an easy trail.

> **3 Boots** – Moderate – A waterfall that requires a creekwalk or a hike on a trail with hills.

> **4 Boots** – Strenuous – A waterfall that requires a more difficult creekwalk or a hike on a trail with significant hills.

Trail or Creekbed Surface: A description of the material you will find underfoot.

Trail Markings: Markings used to designate the trails in this book vary widely. Some trails are not marked at all but can be easily followed. Other trails are well marked with either signs, blazes, or markers, and sometimes a combination of all three. Blazing is done by the official group that maintains the trail.

> **Signs** – Wooden or metal signs with instructions in words or pictures.

> **Blazes** – Painted markings on trees showing where the trail goes. Many blazes are rectangular and placed at eye level. Colors may be used to denote different trails. If a tree has twin blazes beside one another, you should proceed cautiously because the trail either turns or another trail intersects.

> Sometimes you'll see a section of trees with painted markings which aren't neat geometric shapes. These are probably boundary markers or trees marked for logging. Trail blazes are generally distinct geometric shapes and are placed at eye level.

Markers – Small plastic or metal geometric shapes (square, round, triangular) nailed to trees at eye level to show where the trail goes. They also may be colored to denote different trails.

It is likely that at some point you will lose the blazes or markers while following a trail. The first thing to do is stop and look around. See if you can spot a blaze or marker by looking in all directions, including behind you. If not, back track until you see a blaze or marker, then proceed forward again, carefully following the markings.

Uses: The activity or activities allowed near this waterfall.

Dogs: Tells if dogs are or are not allowed.

Admission: The entrance fee, if there is one, to use the area.

Contact: The address and phone number of the organization to contact if you would like additional information or if you have questions not answered in this book.

Map Legend

Symbol	Description	Symbol	Description
▬▬▬	Major Road	★	Trail Location
───	Secondary Road	💧	Water
+++++++++	Railroad	～	River or Creek
············	Power Lines	▨	Park Boundary
▥	Boardwalk	☐	Marsh
⩬	Waterfalls	**P**	Parking
≈	Barrier	(104)	Route
⤝	Bridge	🛡90	Interstate Route
⌂	Lean-to or Shelter	▪▪▪▪▪	Trail
■	Building	▪▪▪▪▪	Other Trail
⑰	Trail Post Number		
✈	Airport		

Trail Blaze Colors:

Blue -	Ⓑ	Orange -	Ⓞ	White -	Ⓦ
Brown -	Ⓑᴿ	Purple -	Ⓟ	Yellow -	Ⓨ
Green -	Ⓖ	Red -	Ⓡ		
Grey -	Ⓖʸ	Violet -	Ⓥ		

Not OSHA Approved

Caution: You are about to enter a world that is not OSHA approved. You will rarely find guardrails, roped off areas, or signs warning of the dangers that lurk in every direction. But therein lies the adventure. You're about to leave our sanitized and protected *civilized* world and enter the domain of natural bliss. This is an environment where all animals, human and otherwise, need to exhibit caution, safe procedures, and that uncommon trait called common sense. Those who fail to do so will suffer the consequences.

The very nature of waterfalls means you'll be heading into terrain where there are steep cliffs, fast moving water and wet, slippery rocks.

- Stay on the trail where possible.
- Keep back from edges.
- Don't go alone.
- Obey all posted signs and structures. Never climb over fences. They're placed where they are for your protection. Stay behind them.

For diligence, your reward will be an awe inspiring beauty and the thrill of wondering what is around the next bend on a trail or in a creekbed. It's the anticipation of not knowing the height or composition of the next waterfall. The scene will unfold as you explore the areas described in this book. What you see will be different from what anyone else sees because waterfalls change rapidly with the seasons, with fluctuating water levels, and with the forces of erosion.

The price of your ticket for entrance into this natural wonderland is caution. Step carefully. The trails may be narrow, the rocks may be slippery or may move as you step on them. The gorge edge you approach may be an overhang with no support underneath. Rocks may fall from ledges above. Your goal is to watch the process of erosion as it reshapes our world, not to be personally involved in it on a physical level.

Be prepared. That's the scout motto, but you don't have to be a boy or girl scout to see its sense. We were walking a creekbed when I watched Rich slip on a wet, slimy rock and fall hard. He claims I pushed him, but I contend that's hard to do from a distance of 15 feet. Anyway, blood gushed from a gash in his elbow, but fortunately, nothing seemed to be broken. I immediately pulled a small first aid kit from my day pack and applied antibiotic cream and a bandage with compression to stop the bleeding. It sufficed until we got home and properly cleaned and bandaged his wound. Rich survived and I promised not to push him again.

The first area to focus your preparation is on your feet. Wear sturdy, high traction footwear. This includes day hiking boots or water sandals with a good tread. Low slip footwear is a must. Keep dry footwear and socks in the car—you never know when a dry set will come in handy. Same with clothes. In summer you may get wet on purpose, other times getting wet may not be on your original agenda. Sometimes it just happens. A dry set of clothes a short hike away (or in your day pack) can help stave off hypothermia.

Always take a day pack with you. Inside should be a standard set of safety gear including:

- small first aid kit
- water bottle (with water)
- bandanna
- flashlight
- map (this book)
- sun lotion
- compass
- waterproof matches
- whistle
- emergency space blanket
- insect repellent

For added enjoyment consider taking a camera, binoculars, snacks, a bag to pick up litter (yes, doing your part to clean up our environment can be fun).

Take A Hike Up A Creek

Rich Freeman strolls up Grimes Glen on a warm summer day.

This is not a punishment for bad behavior. We're inviting you into the magical world of creek-walking. It's where you step off the manicured trail into the bed of a creek and follow it—usually upstream—to see what delights hide around each bend. And yes, you will get wet—at least your feet will get wet.

Not all creeks are good for creekwalking. Muddy and weedy bottomed creeks are not fun. Neither are ones where the water is deep or rushing with a forceful current. They're too dangerous. What we look for are creekbeds where the forces of water have scoured them clean of dirt and vegetation to leave bare rock. The best are scoured down to flat slabs of limestone or sandstone.

Creekwalking is a summer activity. The torrents of water produced in spring runoff are far too powerful to make creekwalking safe in spring. By fall, most creeks have dried to a bare trickle, leaving them less scenic. Winter can be fun to creekwalk, wearing instep crampons, but it has the added risk of falling through a snow bridge to a water pocket and ending up with a cold soaker.

So, summer wins the "creekwalking time of the year" award. You can wear Teva® type sandals and splash in the inches-deep water, stop to sunbathe on sun-exposed rocks, sit in the spray of waterfalls, and lay in the narrow rock trenches as water surges past. Creekwalking is what we want to be doing on the hottest day of summer.

If you're new to creekwalking, try the ones rated three boots first. The walking and waterfall climbing will be easier. Or, join a creekwalking adventure led by Pack, Paddle, Ski Corp. (www.PackPaddleSki.com or call 585-346-5597) for a guided outing, until your creekwalking confidence is boosted.

Winter Waterfalls

Instep crampons attach easily to boots and aid in traction when walking up winter creekbeds and small waterfalls.

Ice and snow add sparkle to our world of glens and waterfalls. You can snowshoe on a trail to see many of the waterfalls in winter, or strap on instep crampons to walk up a creek and up minor waterfalls. Just be careful where you step, it's easy to fall through an ice or snow bridge and get soaked. For a safe winter adventure, join a guided Pack, Paddle, Ski Corp. (call 585-346-5597 or www.PackPaddleSki.com) outing—they even provide the instep crampons.

Extreme winter outdoors people get into the sport of ice climbing by climbing up frozen waterfalls. This is a very dangerous sport, so you should take lessons and only go with experienced individuals. Pack, Paddle, Ski Corp. (www.packpaddleski.com) and Adirondack Mountain Club (www.adk.org) offer lessons. Or, contact the Rochester Rock, Ice & Snow Climbing Club (www.frontiernet.net/~lilgamin/rriscc.htm).

Get Creative

Waterfalls are wonders of nature no matter what their size. Each has characteristics that make it unique and special. As you explore the waterfalls listed in this book, get creative and see how many different adventures you can devise. Here are a few suggestions to get the creative juices flowing:

- Load your day pack with a blanket, wine and cheese. Spread the blanket in view of the falls and enjoy a leisurely snack. Don't forget to take a knife and bottle opener.
- Take your camera and record views from various angles.
- In summer, splash up the creekbed to the falls (where allowed).
- As you visit each waterfall, find a comfortable place to sit. Close your eyes and listen to the sound of the waterfall. Record a description of the sounds. How different does one waterfall sound from another?

Standing behind Tinkers Falls, William Nitsche recites Henry Wadsworth Longfellow's poem *The Courtship of Miles Standish* as he proposes marriage to Laurie Magee. She said yes!

- Take along a full picnic to enjoy by your favorite waterfall.
- In winter, wear instep crampons and climb a small waterfall. Always take a friend with you.
- Propose marriage behind Tinkers Falls.
- Hunt for New York State's official fossil —the Eurypterid (pronounced you-RIP-ter-id), a scorpion-like animal that's related to today's Horseshoe Crab.

Then, there are crazy activities. If you've ever been to the Banff Film Festival (which travels through our area each year) you've seen people go over waterfalls in kayaks. We don't recommend it.

Dogs Welcome

Exploring outdoors with dogs can be fun because of their keen sense of smell and different perspective on the world. Many times they find things that we would have passed by. They're inquisitive about everything and make excellent companions. But to ensure that your companion enjoys the time outside, you must control your dog. Dogs are required to be leashed on most maintained public trails. The reasons are numerous, but the top ones are to protect dogs, to protect other hikers, and to ensure your pet doesn't chase wildlife. Good dog manners go a long way toward creating goodwill and improving tolerance toward their presence.

There are a great many areas listed in this book that welcome dogs. Please respect the requirement that dogs be leashed where noted.

Maps

This book is loaded with sketch maps to give you an idea of where to find each trail and creekbed and how to navigate once you get there. We've found the *New York State Atlas & Gazetteer* by DeLorme to be a valuable asset when trying to find a trailhead in unknown territory. Also, the many internet-based mapping services are very useful.

On the trail it's sometimes best to have a topographical map with you. You can order topographical maps from the United States Geological Survey or pick them up at area outdoor stores, generally for $4 apiece. Another option is to visit www.topozone.com on the internet to print a topo map of the the area you plan to cover.

Once Upon A Time, Long, Long Ago...

It's common knowledge that glaciers scoured the central and western New York area. The evidence is everywhere we look. It's in the kames, kettles, and eskers preserved in Mendon Ponds Park and Green Lakes State Park. It's in the glacial erratics we find near hiking trails throughout the region. It's in the terminal moraines, which are seen as east/west hills at the south ends of the Finger Lakes, especially near Dansville, and between Nunda and Portageville.

But, the history of our waterfalls begins before the glaciers ever arrived. 300-400 million years ago the land we call home was covered by a large shallow tropical sea. As the sea evolved it deposited undisturbed horizontal layers of shale, limestone, sandstone and dolomite. The limestone and dolomite formed from the carcasses of millions of tiny shelled creatures accumulating in layers. Over time the sea receded and our area was left with 24 parallel river valleys running north/south.

Then came the ice age. The glaciers (a series of them) headed south slowly where they ran into the Allegany Plateau and were funneled into the river valleys. They scraped deeply through the underlying layers of hard and soft rocks forming miniature U-shaped canyons. The hardest rocks they encountered were the dolomite rock layers that resisted erosion and formed escarpments or rock cliffs. Western New York has three major escarpments. They are roughly parallel, north-facing ledges. The best known is the Niagara Escarpment, which forms Niagara Falls. Sixteen miles south, the Onondaga Escarpment ranges from 30 to 70-feet high as it crosses western New York from Buffalo. The southernmost escarpment is the Portage or Lake Erie Escarpment, which forms the northern border of the Allegany Plateau.

In the Finger Lakes region, the eastern group of lakes was formed when the glacier met the Portage Escarpment at the southern end and continued to scour the earth deeper which was easier than pushing through the

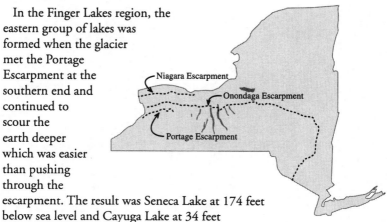

Niagara Escarpment

Onondaga Escarpment

Portage Escarpment

escarpment. The result was Seneca Lake at 174 feet below sea level and Cayuga Lake at 34 feet below sea level. The western group of lakes wasn't constricted at the south end so they didn't get scoured as deeply.

We started with 24 river valleys and ended with 11 Finger Lakes. The lakes formed only when water was trapped by glacial debris at the south end and rising ground to the north. The ground rose as it sprung back after release from the weight of the glacier. (Estimates say the Rochester area has risen 250 feet since the weight of the ice was removed, and is still rising.)

Presumably, the other valleys were blocked in the same way. Silver Lake, the only lake west of the Genesee River, is not normally thought of as a Finger Lake, but it was formed by this same process.

The ice sheet, which advanced and retreated several times, was 5,000 to 7,000-feet thick. It bid its final farewell and retreated about 8 to 10 thousand years ago. As it did, it produced great volumes of water. Hanging valleys were formed as east/west tributary streams, that originally joined the north/south river valleys, found their river valleys had been scoured deeply, leaving the tributaries hanging about 600 feet above the new valley floors. The water plummeted down as the glacier retreated forming our many waterfalls and gorges including Taughannock, Silver Thread, Buttermilk, Montour, Hector, Stony Brook, and Watkins Glen, among others.

All three escarpments interrupted the flow of water in our region and resulted in the creation of waterfalls. The Onondaga Escarpment is responsible for Akron Falls and Serenity Falls, among others. The Niagara Escarpment is responsible for Niagara Falls and the Upper Falls of the Genesee River in Rochester which is now obscured by a dam.

According to Robert Dineen, a glacial geologist for the NYS Geological Survey, "waterfalls are, by definition, very short-lived features. Eventually they commit geological suicide and eat away at themselves until they cease to exist."

The only constant in a waterfall's life is change. The hanging valley waterfalls have eroded back to a series of smaller waterfalls. Only Taughannock remains as a true hanging valley.

Rock slides at the American Falls at Niagara have left piles of boulders at the base. Heavy flooding, potentially including the flood caused by Hurricane Agnes in 1972, dramatically altered Lower Falls at Letchworth. As waterfalls erode, they creep upstream. Niagara Falls moves upstream 3 to 4 feet per year. Taughannock moves less than 1 foot per year.

Man also exerts his energies toward changing waterfalls. Try to find the waterfall at Seneca Falls. It's impossible. The falls were eradicated when the Seneca River was channelized to form the Seneca-Cayuga Canal as part of the New York State Canal System.

Deep in the gorges, near waterfalls, the rock layers of ancient millennia are exposed. Explore to your heart's content. In Onondaga limestone you can find corals from the ancient marine environment. In the dark shales and thin silty limestones of the Hamilton group you'll find a wealth of fossils including brachiopods, crinoids, corals, bryozoa, trilobites, mullosks, and ostracodes.

Sue Freeman sits on a concretion, one of many found while creekwalking.

One of the great joys we found while creekwalking was the discovery of concretions, commonly called turtle rocks. Concretions are solid, rounded masses of mineral matter that occur in sedimentary rock. They have a different composition from the rock in which they are found, such as a limestone concretion found in a bed of shale. Concretions form around a nucleus that commonly is a fragment of fossil shell, bone or plant material. We found them easily visible in many of central and western New York's creekbeds.

To better understand the geological history of this region, we recommend reading *Roadside Geology of New York* by Bradford B. Van Diver.

Terminology Quandary

What to call this rushing, tumbling, falling mass of water? The terminology associated with falling water isn't clear-cut. It overlaps and often the edges are fuzzy. When does a rapid become a cascade? Or should it be called a chute? How can massive rapids and a massive waterfall both be called a cataract? Welcome to the wonderful world of English. We snicker at the Eskimos for having 32 words to describe snow. At least their words are distinctive. We can't even agree on the definition of a waterfall. To USGS field surveyors who generate topographical maps, a tumbling of waters only gets designated a waterfall if it has value as a landmark and stands out in relation to the rest of the stream course. Falzguy (Scott A. Ensminger) who catalogs waterfalls in western NY on web site www.falzguy.com requires a drop of 5 feet to classify as a waterfall. Any definition is arbitrary.

Cascade:
1. A waterfall having small water volume
2. A waterfall that is part of a series of falls

Cataract:
1. A series of large river rapids
2. A large volume or high waterfall

Chute:
1. A waterfall or rapid
2. The quick descent of a river
3. A narrow, powerful section of a waterfall often squeezed by large rocks or cliff walls

Rapids:
1. An extremely fast-moving part of a river, caused by a steep descent in the riverbed where the surface is broken by obstructions (usually rocks)

Shoot:
1. A narrow, swift, or turbulent section of a stream
2. A place where a stream runs or descends swiftly

Waterfall:
1. Sudden sheer descent of a stream or river over a steep drop in its bed, sometimes in a free fall

Classifications of Waterfalls

Just as the definition of what constitutes a waterfall is a murky proposition, the subdivision of falls into classes and types is likewise a rather subjective and elusive venture. The nature of waterfalls is that they come in infinite variety and blur our feeble attempts to put them into neat categories. Plus, they are evolving entities; ever-changing as the forces of nature wear them down or move them upstream. If the caprock of a plunge falls takes the plunge after being undermined, it becomes an entirely different looking waterfall. Even water level can dramatically change the classification of a waterfall. So, take these classifications as general categories. They're basic terminology for discussing waterfalls but by no means definitive or permanent. Many waterfalls are a combination of types.

Types of Waterfalls (generally referring to steepness and directness of the water drop)

Plunge or Ledge: Water free-falls from the caprock to the base without touching the rock behind the falls.

Horsetail or Slide: Water runs rapidly down a nearly vertical wall, maintaining contact with the rock behind the falls.

Fan: A type of horsetail falls where the lower portion of water fans out or widens before reaching the base.

Segmented: A falls that divides into two or more channels as the water descends.

Parallel: Two waterfalls falling side-by-side.

Punchbowl: The water descends from a constricted opening to a pool at the base rather than hitting piles of rocks.

Staircase: A single stream waterfall that falls over many small ledges creating the image of a staircase.

Tiered: Water that descends through stages of distinctly different falls, all visible from a single vantage point. Each stage may be a different type of falls.

Serial: A section where the stages of falls are not all visible from a single vantage point, are separated by a distance of stream, or where there are many sections.

Cascade: Water that follows a sloped descent across a rock face with many breaks, leaps, and segments.

Classes of Waterfalls (comparison of height versus width)

Ribbon: A waterfall whose height is much greater than its width.

Classical: A waterfall whose height and width are roughly equal.

Curtain: A waterfall whose height is smaller than its width.

Now let's go find some waterfalls…

Waterfalls in Niagara, Erie, Orleans, Genesee and Wyoming Counties

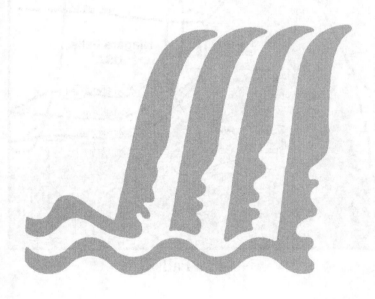

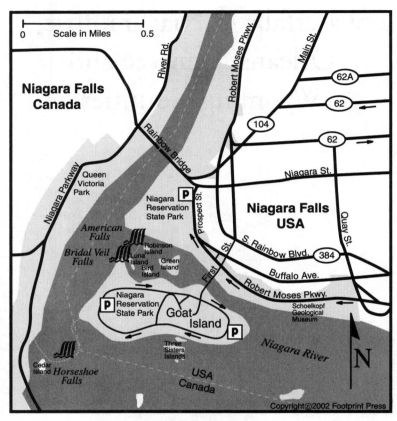

Niagara Falls

1.

Niagara Falls

Horseshoe Falls (or Canadian), American Falls and Bridal Veil Falls

Location: Niagara Falls, Niagara County

Waterway: Niagara River

Directions: In Niagara Falls:
From the north, exit the Robert Moses Parkway to S. Rainbow Boulevard (Route 384). Turn south onto First Street and cross the bridge onto Goat Island.
From the south, follow signs to the Niagara Reservation State Park entrance directly from the Robert Moses Parkway.

Parking: Pay parking lots are available on Goat Island (N43 4.856 W79 4.260) and on Prospect Street (N43 5.243 W79 3.967) in Niagara Reservation State Park.

Best Viewing Locations: By boat (Maid of the Mist), tunnel behind the falls (Table Rock Scenic Tunnel on the Canadian side), walkway on Goat Island (Cave of the Winds), shorelines on the US and Canadian sides, or the observation tower and elevator in Niagara Reservation State Park.

Waterfall Height: Horseshoe Falls: 170-feet high, 2,500-feet wide
American Falls: 180-feet high, 1,100-feet wide
Bridal Veil Falls: 181-feet high

Best Season to Visit: Year-round; the falls are even lit at night

Access: Short walk, Wheelchair

Difficulty: 1 boot

Trail Surface: Paved

Uses: Hike, Boat tour

Dogs: Not recommended, this is a very congested area
A 6-foot leash is required

Admission: Free for viewing (boat rides, tunnels, etc. charge a fee)

Contact: Niagara Reservation State Park, Prospect Park
Niagara Falls, NY 14303
(716) 278-17896
Niagara County
1-800-338-7890

Slowly I turn ... step by step ... inch by inch ....

Sorry, I couldn't resist. I grew up watching the *Three Stooges* and whenever I hear Niagara Falls, this skit is the first thing to pop into my mind. Pretty sad isn't it that one of the 7 Natural Wonders of the World evokes a *Three Stooges* skit from my memory banks. (Actually, there is no definitive list of the 7 Natural Wonders of the World. Niagara Falls shows up on some lists and not others.)

Niagara Falls isn't the highest waterfall—not even within New York State. But, for sheer size and volume of water, it can't be beat. Four Great Lakes drain through the Niagara River and spill over Niagara Falls. The volume of water varies depending on the season and how much water is being diverted through power plants, but 700,000 gallons per second is not unusual for summer. That's a lot of water.

There are actually three waterfalls at Niagara Falls, forming a giant arc across the Niagara gorge. The widest, at 2,200 feet, is Horseshoe Falls, forming the border between Canada and the US. Its plunge basin is deeper than the height of the waterfall you can view. In Niagara Reservation State Park, between Goat Island and Luna Island sits a narrow strand of falls called Bridal Veil Falls. Between Luna Island and mainland US is the 1,060-feet wide American Falls.

Today, millions of people from around the globe visit Niagara Falls each year. In the mid 1800s Niagara Falls was a tourist trap. Visitors had to pay to see the falls through peepholes. In the mid 1880s, a group called the Free Niagara Movement rallied to rid the area of factories, shacks, and mills. The US's first state park was designed for this area by famed landscape architect Frederick Law Olmsted. It opened in 1885, preserving 435 acres surrounding the American Falls. The New York State legislature used the right of eminent domain to buy private property and return it to a more natural state. Canadians quickly followed suit and began preserving their waterfront property.

Dare devils have always been attracted to Niagara Falls. Plunges in boats, rubber balls, and barrels began in the early 1800s. The first to survive going over the falls in a barrel was school teacher Annie Taylor in 1901. In 1859 a tightrope walker named Blondin walked across the Niagara Gorge. Stunts are illegal today.

The falls have fallen silent twice in recorded history. On March 29, 1848 ice dammed the Niagara River. Water flow was stopped for two days until the ice dam broke. Then, on June 12, 1969 water was rerouted to the Horseshoe Falls, leaving the American Falls dry so engineers could study erosion prevention. The falls resumed their natural flow in December 1969 after the engineers concluded that little could be done to control the erosive forces.

Niagara Falls was created some 12,000 years ago with retreat of the Wisconsin ice sheet, which was the last glacier. Originally it plunged over the Niagara Escarpment at present-day Lewiston. Since that time it has been constantly eroding upstream and has moved 7 miles south. It is a caprock falls, formed by horizontal or slightly tilted rock layers. A resistant rock layer (Lockport Dolomite) on top protects the underlying, less resistant rock. Eventually the water force undermines the caprock and it collapses. As the falls eroded back toward Lake Erie, it reached a bend about 700 years ago. An offshoot of the current took a short cut across the angle and formed Goat Island and the American Falls. Since that time the Horseshoe Falls has eroded 3,000 feet (a rate of 2 to 5 feet per year) and the American Falls has retreated less than 200 feet (a rate of <1 foot per year). According to geologists, it will be only 75,000 years until the falls cuts back, gradually forming a series of rapids from Lake Erie.

For a better understanding of the forces that created these waterfalls, visit the Schoelkopf Geological Museum on the Robert Moses Parkway, across from the Niagara Aquarium. This New York State Parks exhibit and show, relating the 435 million year geologic history of the Niagara gorge and 12,000 years of the Falls recession, is open April through October. Admission is charged.

Goat Island acquired its name from a pioneer farmer who pastured sheep and goats on the island one winter to protect them from wolves and bears. When the farmer returned in spring, all the animals had perished except for a lone goat.

Trail Directions:
- For the full effect, see how many vantage points you can rack up. The falls can be seen from a multitude of angles using a vast array of transportation modes. Then return at different times of year (when the water volume shifts) and day versus night viewing. Don't miss Niagara Falls in winter, it's truly magnificent.

Date visited:

Notes:

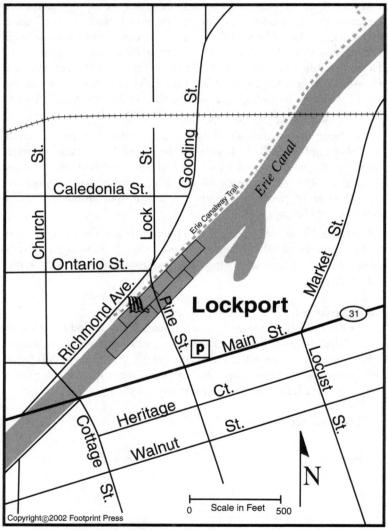

Lockport Canal Falls

2.
Lockport Canal Falls

Location:	Lockport, Niagara County
Waterway:	Erie Canal
Directions:	Park in the municipal parking ramp (N43 10.159 W78 41.479)at the corner of Main Street (Route 31) and Pine Street.

Best Viewing Locations: From the Pine Street bridge, Richmond Avenue, or from the Erie Canalway Trail

Waterfall Height: 56 feet through a series of 5 drops

Best Season to Visit: Spring, summer, or fall (the canal is drained in the winter)

Access:	Roadside or short walk
Hiking Time:	10 minutes round trip
Trail Length:	<0.1 mile round trip
Difficulty:	1 boot from bridge or street; 2 boots due to a long flight of stairs down to the Erie Canalway Trail
Trail Surface:	Paved
Trail Markings:	Erie Canalway Trail signs
Uses:	Hike, Bike, Ski, Snowshoe, Boat tours (the Erie Canalway Trail is 85 miles long, from Lockport to Palmyra)
Dogs:	OK on leash
Admission:	Free
Contact:	New York State Canal Corporation 1-800-4CANAL4 www.canals.state.ny.us

The series of waterfalls you can view today beside canal locks 34 and 35 have a long and important history. In 1825 when *Clinton's Ditch* was opened for business as the Erie Canal, its final challenge in reaching the western terminus was to climb the Niagara Escarpment in Lockport. A double flight of five locks was built to climb this mountain and allow boats to head simultaneously up and down stream. In 1840 these five flight locks were upgraded and one set remains today as the waterfall channel. The lock gates are gone, of course. They were massive hand operated wooden structures that cost $12,000 back in the early 1800s.

The five flights were replaced through two major expansions (the most recent in 1918) by locks 34 and 35, leaving one set of the original locks as a relic of history for us to enjoy. These long-gone days are commemorated in the Erie Canal Museum which is at the base of lock 34. It used to be the hydraulic power house that supplied electricity to operate the locks and lift bridges in Lockport.

You can view the Lockport Canal Falls from the Pine Street bridge, from Richmond Avenue, or head down the stairs to water level along the Erie Canalway Trail.

Trail Directions:
- From the parking lot, head right (N) on Pine Street. You'll have a view of the falls below as you cross the Pine Street Bridge over the canal.
- After the bridge, turn left (SW) on Richmond Avenue until you see a stairway leading down to the canal.
- Take the stairs downhill and walk beside the old locks.
- You can keep going for 85 miles (you're on the Erie Canalway Trail) but we recommend stopping at the Canal Museum then returning the way you came.

Date visited:

Notes:

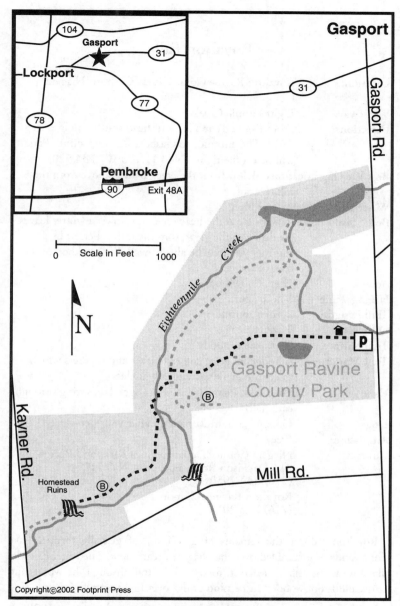

Royalton Falls

3.

Royalton Falls

Location: Royalton Ravine County Park, Gasport, Niagara County

Waterway: Eighteenmile Creek

Directions: From Route 31 in Gasport, head south on Gasport Road. The entrance to Gasport Ravine County Park will be on the right. (N43 11.178 W78 34.520)

Best Viewing Locations: Below from the creek bed or above from the hiking trail

Waterfall Height: 25-feet high

Best Season to Visit: Spring has the heaviest water flow; in winter leaves are down so the view from the trail is better; in summer you may be able to walk the creekbed to the base of the falls

Access: Hike, Snowshoe

Hiking Time: 1 hour round trip

Trail Length: 2 miles round trip

Difficulty: 3 boots

Trail Surface: Dirt, often muddy

Trail Markings: A hodgepodge of colored blazes and markers which make the markings virtually useless

Uses: Hike, Ski, Picnic (rest rooms open late spring through early fall)

Dogs: OK on leash, must pick up after your pet

Admission: Free

Contact: Niagara County Department of Parks and Recreation 314 Davidson Road, Lockport, NY 14094 (716) 439-7950

Royalton Ravine, Gasport Road (716) 772-2016

Royalton Falls is the remains of a spillway of glacially formed Lake Tonawanda as it tumbled over the Niagara Escarpment. The water cascades like a wedding veil. To reach it, follow a hilly trail through the woods and cross an 80-foot wooden suspension bridge over Eighteenmile Creek.

Just before the waterfall are the ruins of a homestead from the 1800s. It appears like any other country farm homestead but in fact, the roots of historic events began here. This is where Belva Ann Lockwood grew up. She went on to become a leader in the women's suffrage movement along side Susan B. Anthony, Elizabeth Cady Stanton and Lucretia Mott. Mrs. Lockwood fought for equal pay and physical education for women during an era when women still wore corsets. She became a lawyer, overcoming immense odds, and fought to be the first woman to try a case before the US Supreme Court—and won. In 1884 and 1888 she ran for president (another women's first), knowing she wouldn't win but so people would know a woman could run. She died at age 87, only three years before women gained the right to vote. As you gaze at Royalton Falls, think of how Belva must have sat by these falls pondering the inequalities of her time and developing the grit and determination which would take her far and change the course of history for us all.

The second waterfall shown on the map can be seen from Mill Road. It is on private property so it's off limits for exploration.

Trail Directions:
- From the parking lot, head west. Pass a pond on your left and an amphitheater on the right.
- In 0.3 mile enter the woods.
- Reach a "T" at 0.4 mile, turn right (W).
- At 0.5 mile reach another "T" at the ravine. Turn left (S).
- Pass a blue blazed trail on the left. Continue straight on the multi-colored trail and head downhill.
- Walk (S) parallel to the creek.
- Reach the swing bridge at 0.6 mile and cross the creek. (Or, head upstream in the creekbed from here if you want to do a creekwalk.)
- After the bridge the trail bends left and parallels the creek on the opposite bank.
- Climb a hill. The trail is now blue blazed.
- At 1 mile, pass the homestead ruins. The falls are on your left. A short trail to the left leads to the crest of the falls at the site of an old bridge or mill.
- After enjoying the falls, turn around and retrace your path back to the parking lot. (The trail does continue west for 0.1 mile to Kayner Road but this entrance to the park is posted as "no trespassing.")

Date visited:

Notes:

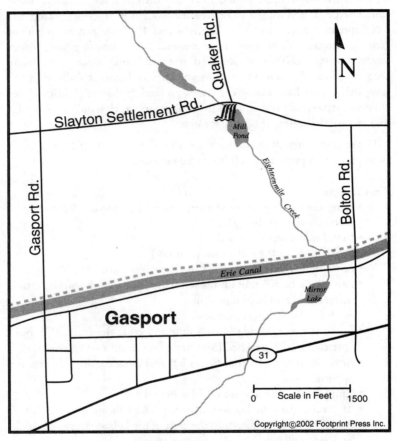

Mill Pond Falls

4.

Mill Pond Falls

Location: Gasport, Niagara County
Waterway: East Branch of Eighteenmile Creek
Directions: Head north through Gasport on Gasport Road. Cross
                       the Erie Canal. Turn right on Slayton Settlement Road.
                       Park along the road, near the junction with Quaker
                       Road. (N43 12.508 W78 33.916)
Best Viewing Locations: From shoulder of Slayton Settlement Road
Waterfall Height: Estimated at 20-feet high
Best Season to Visit: Year-round
Access: Roadside
Difficulty: 1 boot
Uses: View only
Dogs: OK
Admission: Free
Contact: Town of Royalton
                       5316 Royalton Center Road, Middleport, NY 14105

This was once an active mill district. From 1812 through 1965 there were flour, grist and saw mills. The Gottlieb Otto Mill lasted from 1895 to the 1960s. The dam which forms the waterfall was built before 1849 and was restored in 1990.

Look across the street on Quaker Road for the remains of the Mabee Mills gristmill. This large stone structure was built in 1872 and was destroyed by a fire in 1880. This is one of the stops on the Niagara Historic Trail—a car route of historic sites in the Niagara region.

Date visited:

Notes:

Medina Falls in winter

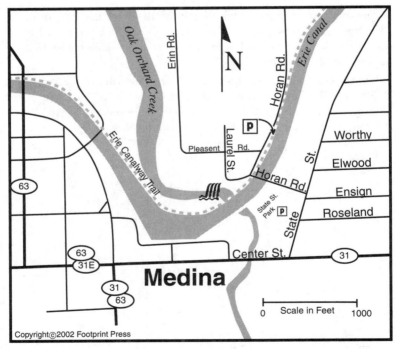

Medina Falls

5.
Medina Falls

Location: Medina, Orleans County
Waterway: Oak Orchard Creek
Directions: From Route 31, turn north on State Street in Medina. Turn left (W) on Horan Road. Cross the canal and bear right to a parking area on the right. (N43 13.531 W78 22.822)
Alternative Parking: Park in State Street Park (N43 13.305 W78 22.851), walk across the Horan Street bridge. Turn left on Laurel Street then left on a trail to the canal. At the canal turn right and follow the Erie Canalway Trail to the waterfall.
Best Viewing Locations: From the Erie Canalway Trail
Waterfall Height: 40-feet high
Best Season to Visit: Year-round (best views are in winter when leaves are off the trees)
Access: Short walk
Hiking Time: 20 minutes round trip
Trail Length: 0.5 mile round trip
Difficulty: 1 boot
Trail Surface: Paved
Trail Markings: Erie Canalway Trail signs
Uses: Hike, Bike, Ski, Snowshoe (the Erie Canalway Trail is 85 miles long, from Lockport to Palmyra)
Dogs: OK on leash
Admission: Free
Contact: New York State Canal Corporation
                       1-800-4CANAL4
                       www.canals.state.ny.us

The Erie Canal crosses Oak Orchard Creek on a large aqueduct. Cement walls are your only indication of it, until you peer over the edges to see a creek flowing below. Just north of the canal, this creek cascades over a precipice forming Medina Falls.

Trail Directions:

- From the Horan Road parking area, head right (W) on the Erie Canalway Trail for 0.25 mile. You'll pass under the Horan Road bridge before reaching the aqueduct and waterfall.

Date visited:

Notes:

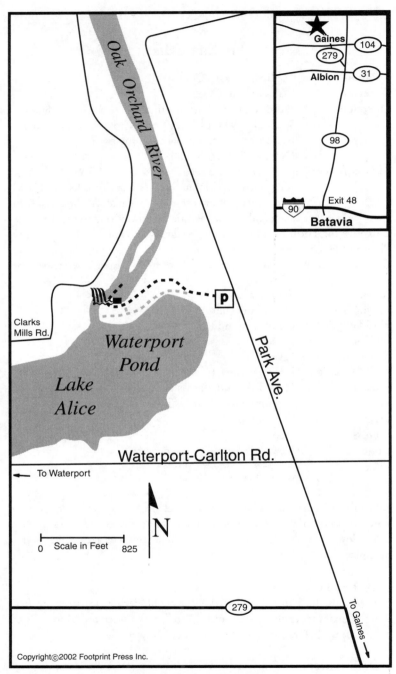

Oak Orchard Falls

6.

Oak Orchard Falls (or Waterport Falls)

Location:	Waterport, Orleans County
Waterway:	Oak Orchard River
Directions:	From Route 104, head north on Route 279 (north of Albion). When Route 279 curves left to enter Waterport, continue north on Park Avenue. Cross Waterport-Carlton Road then watch for a gravel parking area on the left (W) side of the road marked with a white and black sign "Niagara Mohawk Power Corp. Property." Park here but do not block the metal gates. (N43 19.641 W78 14.076)

Best Viewing Locations: From a cement pier at the base of the waterfall
Waterfall Height: Estimated at 40-feet high
Best Season to Visit: Year-round

Access:	Hike
Hiking Time:	30 minutes round trip
Trail Length:	0.6 mile round trip
Difficulty:	2 boots
Trail Surface:	Gravel road
Trail Markings:	None
Uses:	Hike, Snowshoe, Fish
Dogs:	OK
Admission:	Free
Contact:	Niagara Mohawk
	300 Erie Boulevard West, Syracuse, NY 13202-4205
	1-800-642-4272

Albert L. Swett of Medina harnessed the waters of Oak Orchard River by building a dam and power plant in 1919. This dam caused the widening of the waters in the vicinity of Waterport that is known locally as Lake Alice. On many maps it's labeled Waterport Pond. In earlier times, this wide-water was called Lake Carlton of the Waterport Pond. Today the Orin hydro plant is operated by Niagara Mohawk Power Corporation. They allow visitors to use their access road (on foot only) to reach the water for fishing and waterfall viewing.

Oak Orchard Falls is found below the overflow dam, beside the Niagara Mohawk Power Plant. It's a 40-foot gradual cascade over red rock. You can view it from an upper road or take the lower road, walk behind the power plant and view the falls from its base while standing on a cement pier.

Trail Directions:

- From the parking area, head west on the gravel road, past the metal gates.
- At the "Y," go right and head downhill for the best view from the base of the falls. (Left leads to the top of the dam with an upper view of the falls along the way.)
- Walk behind the power plant and onto the cement pier.

Date visited:

Notes:

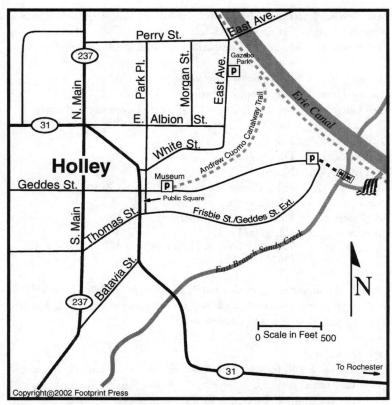

Holley Canal Falls

7.

Holley Canal Falls (or Glen Falls)

Location:	Holley, Orleans County
Waterway:	Erie Canal spilling into East Branch Sandy Creek
Directions:	Take Route 31 into Holley. At the south end of the public square turn east on Frisbie Street. Pass the village DPW and Pollution Control Facility. The road dead ends at the parking area. (N43 13.529 W78 1.162)
Alternative parking:	Gazebo Park (N43 13.677 W78 1.315) on East Avenue (from here, follow the Andrew Cuomo Canalway Trail for 1 mile to the base of the falls.)

Best Viewing Locations: Short path from parking lot at the base of the falls
Waterfall Height: Estimated at 35-feet high
Best Season to Visit: Spring, summer, or fall (the canal is drained in the winter)

Access:	Roadside or short walk
Hiking Time:	1 minute round trip
Trail Length:	You can follow a 100-foot trail from the parking lot to the base of the falls
Difficulty:	1 boot
Trail Surface:	Dirt & gravel
Trail Markings:	None
Uses:	Hike, Picnic (restrooms in Gazebo Park)
Dogs:	OK on leash
Admission:	Free (closes at 10 PM)
Contact:	Village of Holley
	72 Public Square, Holley, NY 14470
	(585) 638-6367

Follow the map closely, Holley is an easy town to get lost in, even if it is small. The waterfall is a man-made waste weir from the Erie Canal but certainly a pretty one, and well worth a visit.

Trail Directions:

• Follow a 100-foot trail from the Frisbie Street parking lot to the base of the falls. For a longer walk, follow the trail from the back of the parking lot for 1 mile to the canal at Gazebo Park. This park offers rest room and shower facilities, picnic tables, a drinking fountain, grills, and dockage with electric power for boaters.

Date visited:

Notes:

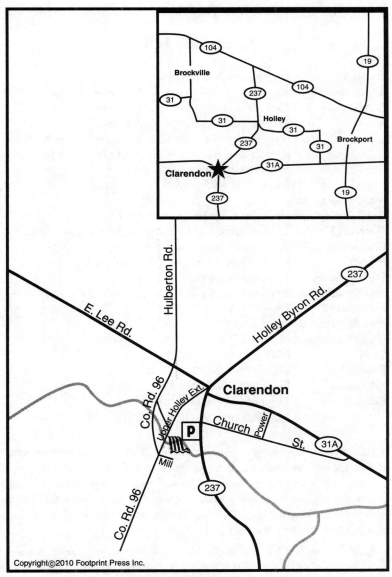

Clarendon Falls

8.

Clarendon Falls

Location: Clarendon, Orleans County
Waterway: A tributary to the East Branch of Sandy Creek
Directions: Take Route 104 to Route 237 (Morganville Road) south for three miles through Holley. Continue on 237 (now Holley Byron Road) south another three miles to the village of Clarendon. Just past the intersection with 31A will be a small park to the west.
(N43 11.516 W78 3.911)

Alternative parking: None
Best Viewing Locations: From the base of the waterfall
Waterfall Height: 25 foot cascade, lit by a single light at night
Best Season to Visit: Spring or after heavy rain
Access: Visible from the parking lot or via a short walk
Hiking Time: 2 minute round trip
Trail Length: 200 feet west of parking lot to base of falls
Difficulty: 1 boot
Trail Surface: Grass
Trail Markings: None
Uses: Hike
Dogs: OK on leash
Admission: Free
Contact: Town of Clarendon
16385 Church St, Clarendon, NY 14429

Unless you like looking at moss and mud, be sure to visit this waterfall during spring snow melt, or after a heavy rain. With water it's pretty wisps of water, set in a wooded hillside. The town park has a pavillion, a bench and a porta-potty. It offers a bridge across the creek that leads into a wooded area along the cliff. You can't see the waterfall from this area but you will find remains of an old mill.

According to the Orleans County Historical Association, the town has it roots in the story of a lost horse. In 1810, Eldridge Farwell tracked a lost horse south from Ridge Road and came upon Clarendon Falls. Realizing the potential of the falls for power generation, he relocated there the following year and soon built a cabin, saw and grist mills; essentially founding Farwell's Mills, NY. When Orleans County was formed in the 1820's, the Farwells renamed the settlement to Clarendon after their home town in Vermont. In 1937 Morris Bracket donated land for a community park at the falls. The now-defunct Clarendon Grange worked to develop the area below the falls. Mr. Brackett's dream became a reality in 1965.

The waterfall exists because of the Clarendon-Linden fault system (i.e. the limestone cliff) which is named in part for Clarendon.

Trail Directions:
- From the parking area, cross the grass to the base of the falls.

Date visited:

Notes:

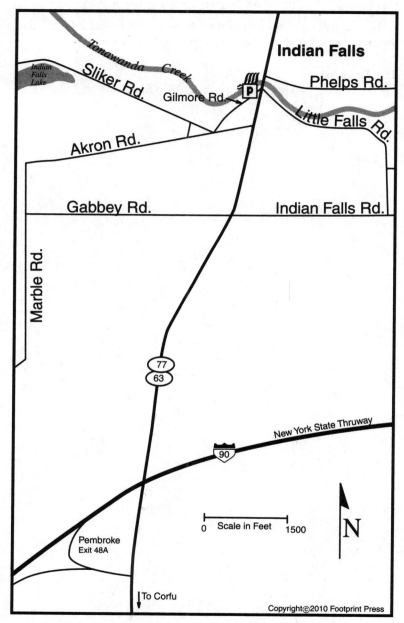

Indian Falls

9.

Indian Falls

Location: Indian Falls, Genesee County
Waterway: Tonawanda Creek
Directions: From the Pembroke exit 48A off the Thruway (I-90), head north on Route 63. Just before crossing Tonawanda Creek in Indian Falls, turn left on Gilmore Road and park on the right in the Log Cabin Restaurant parking lot. (N43 1.583 W78 23.938)

Best Viewing Locations: From behind the Log Cabin Restaurant
Waterfall Height: 20-feet high
Best Season to Visit: Year-round
Access: Short walk
Hiking Time: 1 minute round trip
Trail Length: <0.1 mile round trip
Difficulty: 2 boots (a few stairs)
Uses: View only
Dogs: OK on leash
Admission: Free
Contact: Log Cabin Restaurant
1185 Sliker Road, Corfu, NY 14036
(585) 762-8422

Indian Falls, as its name implies, has a special Indian history. Tonawanda is Iroquois for "swift water." On the swift water banks at Indian Falls, a Seneca baby named Hasanoanda was born in 1828 in a log cabin. He took on the English name of Ely Samuel Parker and eventually became President Ulysses S. Grant's military secretary. Parker drafted the terms of the Confederacy's surrender at Appomattox in 1865 and later became the first Commissioner of Indian Affairs.

Today, Indian Falls sits behind the Log Cabin Restaurant. Why not plan a visit for lunch or dinner? The Log Cabin is open 7 days/week and serves family favorites such as steak, chicken wings, and Friday fish fries. The waterfall is a 100-feet wide, 20-feet high curtain cascade that shrinks to twin channels in summer.

Trail Directions:
- From the parking area, view the waterfall from the picnic platform or head down a few steps to the back of the restaurant.

Date visited:

Notes:

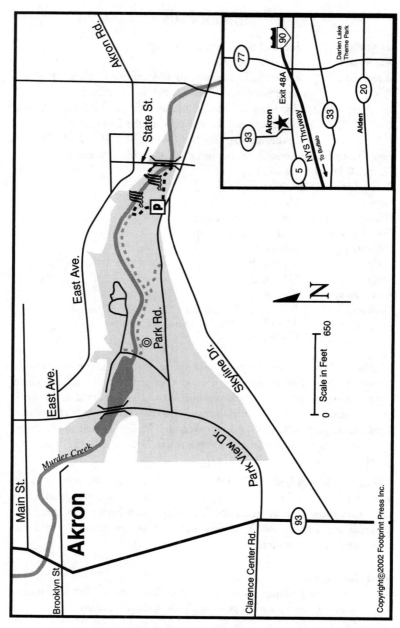

Lower & Upper Akron Falls

10.

Lower & Upper Akron Falls

Location:	Akron Falls Park, Akron, Erie County
Waterway:	Murder Creek
Directions:	From Route 5, head north on Route 93. Turn right onto Skyline Drive. At the end, turn left onto Park Road. Pass stone buildings on the right and park at the next parking area on the right or at any of the other lots in the park. (N43 0.904 W78 29.087)

Best Viewing Locations: From the trails
Waterfall Height: Lower Akron Falls: 50-feet high
Upper Akron Falls: 20-feet high
Best Season to Visit: Spring; creek dries in summer

Access:	Hike
Hiking Time:	30 minutes round trip to both falls
Trail Length:	1 mile round trip to see both waterfalls
Difficulty:	2 boots
Trail Surface:	Dirt, grass and stone trails
Trail Markings:	None
Uses:	Hike, Snowshoe, Picnic
Dogs:	OK on leash
Admission:	Free, open from 7:00 AM until 9:00 PM daily
Contact:	Akron Falls Park
(716) 542-2330

Erie County Parks
95 Franklin Street, Buffalo, NY 14202
(716) 858-8352 |

The northern portion of this park is a picnickers haven. It's loaded with tables, grills, swings, jungle gyms, the gurgle of a flowing creek, and the shade of large trees. Who'd suspect that the docile waterway that winds through this park is called Murder Creek? It was named for a murder that occurred near it long ago. Akron Falls Park is a 284-acre county park with a trail that climbs through the woods to 2 waterfalls, where the waters of Murder Creek slip though the rocks and plummet over the Onondaga Escarpment.

Western New York has three major escarpments or rock ledges. They are roughly parallel, north-facing ledges. The best known is the Niagara Escarpment, which forms Niagara Falls. Sixteen miles south, the Onondaga Escarpment ranges from 30 to 70-feet high as it crosses western New York from Buffalo. The southernmost escarpment is the Portage or

Lake Erie Escarpment, which forms the northern border of the Allegany Plateau (see page 22).

The water in Lower Akron Falls is channeled at the crest. Depending on water level it may form a curtain or several narrow wisps as the water free-falls to the gorge below. Upper Akron Falls, found 600 feet upstream, is also a free fall from an overhung caprock but it fills the width of the creek channel. In summer you can walk the creekbed to the base of the falls, but it is a dangerous place to walk. The rocks are unsupported and loose. Erosion is an ongoing event here as the waterfall slowly walks upstream. There is a cave below the main part of the upper waterfall. It used to be blocked by a metal grate but the forces of nature have damaged the grating, so it's now open. Do not attempt to enter the cave.

Trail Directions to Lower Akron Falls:

- From the parking area, head northwest to where stone steps lead downhill toward Murder Creek.
- Bear right to reach an observation landing with a view of Lower Akron Falls.
- Retrace your steps back to the parking area.

Trail Directions to Upper Akron Falls:

- From the parking area, head east (upstream) on the grass parallel to Murder Creek, passing a stone building and picnic area.
- Continue on the grass with a fence and the creek to your left.
- Turn left and cross the State Street bridge.
- Immediately turn left and head down a wide, grassy trail.
- In a few hundred feet, at the end of the grassy trail, take a narrow path on the left that leads to the Upper Akron Falls crest.
- Retrace your steps back to the parking area.

Date visited:

Notes:

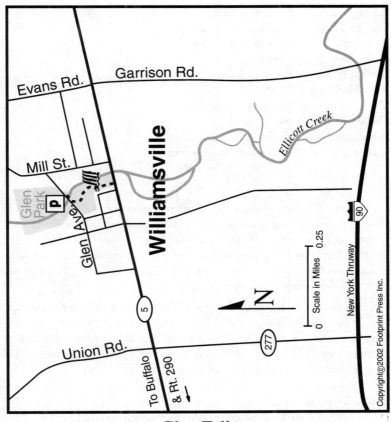

Glen Falls

11.

Glen Falls

Location: Glen Park, Williamsville, Erie County
Waterway: Ellicott Creek
Directions: From Main Street (Route 5), Williamsville, turn north on Mill Street (the first street east of where Ellicott Creek crosses Main Street). Take the first left onto Glen Avenue and park in the Glen Park parking lot on the right. (N42 57.938 W78 44.670)

Best Viewing Locations: From the trails in Glen Park
Waterfall Height: 27-feet high
Best Season to Visit: Year-round

Access:	Hike, wheelchair
Hiking Time:	30 minutes round trip
Trail Length:	0.7 mile round trip
Difficulty:	2 boots
Trail Surface:	Paved paths
Trail Markings:	None
Uses:	Hike, Snowshoe, Picnic
Dogs:	Not allowed.
Admission:	Free
Contact:	Amherst Parks Department
	450 Maple Road, Amherst, NY 14221
	(716) 631-7113

Glen Falls is a wide, multi-tiered combination waterfall that cascades in some sections and free-falls in others as the water plunges down the Onondaga Escarpment. It has a good water flow year-round, even during a dry summer. It sits in a pretty little park of winding paths, ponds, and trees which was created in the late 1970s as the result of a citizen's campaign to overcome opposition by the town board.

Notice the red buildings to the west of the waterway. In front of one (as seen from Glen Park) is part of an old wooden sluiceway which used to carry water to the mill. The other red building is a gristmill which has operated since 1811. Today it operates as a cider mill and gift shop. An original millstone sits on the building's front porch.

Trail Directions:
- From the parking lot, cross Glen Avenue and turn right.
- Cross the bridge over Ellicott Creek on the pedestrian walkway. Notice the 3-foot drop in the creek near the bridge.
- Follow the trail to the left, through the park, passing ponds full of ducks.
- The trail will lead in 0.2 mile, to the base of Glen Falls.
- Continue on the trail uphill, past the crest of Glen Falls.
- The trail ends on Main Street at 0.35 mile.

Date visited:

Notes:

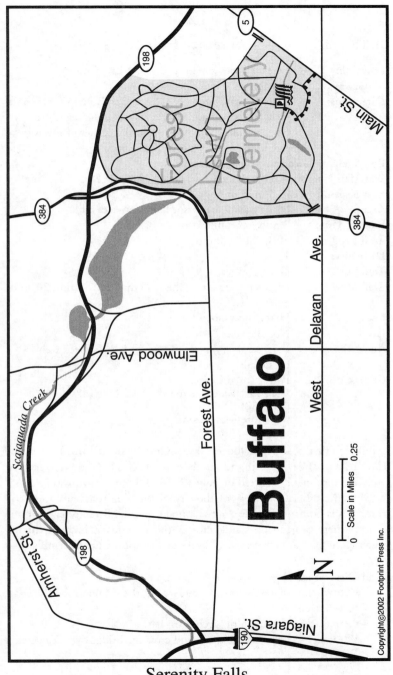

Serenity Falls

12.

Serenity Falls

Location: Forest Lawn Cemetery, Buffalo, Erie County
Waterway: Scajaquada Creek
Directions: Forest Lawn Cemetery is located in Buffalo near Route 5 (Main Street) and Route 198. Use the main gate entrance off Main Street, near the corner of Delavan Avenue. (N42 55.458 W78 51.565)

Best Viewing Locations: From creekside
Waterfall Height: A series of step cascades, the largest about 5-feet high
Best Season to Visit: Spring through Fall

Access: Short walk; park is not handicap-accessible
Hiking Time: 2 minutes round trip
Trail Length: <0.1 mile round trip
Difficulty: 1 boot
Trail Surface: Grass graveyard
Trail Markings: Wooden signs along the road marking Section 20 and Serenity Falls
Uses: Hike, Snowshoe
Dogs: Not allowed
Admission: Free, cemetery usually closes at 5 PM; check website for details.
Contact: Forest Lawn Cemetery
1411 Delaware Avenue, Buffalo, NY 14209
(716) 885-1600
www.forest-lawn.com

Buffalo's first postmaster Judge Erastus Granger owned this land in the early 1800s. After his death, his family sold 80 acres for use as a cemetery. The first interment occurred on July 12, 1850. Forest Lawn was incorporated as the official cemetery of the city of Buffalo. Today it covers 267 acres and is home to Buffalo's only natural waterfall. Serenity Falls can be found where Scajaquada Creek crosses the Onondaga Escarpment. As waterfalls go, it's a small cascade, but it's perfect for serene contemplation.

Trail Directions:
- Drive into Forest Lawn Cemetery at the Main Street/Delavan Avenue entrance.
- After driving through the arch, turn left.
- Bear right at the next junction and cross the bridge over Scajaquada Creek.

- Park along the road immediately after the bridge. (This area is marked by wooden signs for "Section 20" and "Serenity Falls."
- Walk upstream along the south bank of Scajaquada Creek through the grassy graveyard.
- In a few hundred feet you'll see a dirt area on the right that leads to a cement abutment with a good view of the waterfall.

Date visited:

Notes:

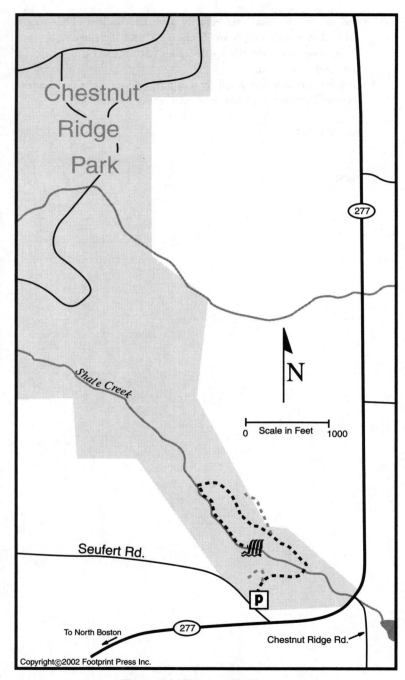

Eternal Flame Falls

13.

Eternal Flame Falls

Location: Chestnut Ridge Park, Shale Creek Preserve, Orchard Park, Erie County

Waterway: Shale Creek, a tributary to Eighteenmile Creek

Directions: From Buffalo, head south on Route 219. Exit at Hamburg/Boston to Route 391 south. In North Boston take Route 277 north. Take a left onto Seyfert Road and park in the gravel pull-off area immediately to the right. (N42 42.005 W78 45.153)

Best Viewing Locations: From the creekbed

Waterfall Height: 30-feet high

Best Season to Visit: Year-round

Access: Hike and creekwalk

Hiking Time: 1.5 hours round trip

Trail Length: 2.0 miles round trip

Difficulty: 4 boots

Trail Surface: Dirt trail and stone creekbed

Trail Markings: None

Uses: Hike, Snowshoe

Dogs: OK on leash

Admission: Free—open 7 AM–9 PM

Contact: County of Erie, Department of Parks, Recreation and Forestry
Chestnut Ridge Park
6121 Chestnut Ridge Road, Oak Orchard, NY 14127
(716) 662-3290

Eternal Flame Falls cuts deep into a gorge through a layer of Hanover Shale of the Late Devonian Epoch that is 85 to 95-feet thick. This shale is greenish-gray to gray colored with some black bands. The water of Shale Creek slides over the rough shale in two distinct stages to form the waterfall. The walk to this waterfall begins through a pleasant forest of pine, maple and hemlock trees, then heads steeply into the gorge on a well-trodden dirt trail. The final 0.2 mile requires a walk in the creekbed.

Upon entering the gorge at the base of Eternal Flame Falls you'll notice a change in the ambient aroma. What you smell is the natural gas that leaks from between the shale layers. When we visited in late August, two flames were burning at eye level to the right of the waterfall, each in its own little indented area in the shale. We've heard there can be 3 flames visible, sometimes even behind a wall of water.

The flame heights vary from 3 to 8 inches depending on the pressure of the escaping gas. Occasionally the flame is extinguished but can easily be relit (unless there are high winds) using a cigarette lighter. You may want to take one in your pocket just in case. Try holding the lighter into the indented areas of rock. If you have trouble locating the gas emission, use your nose to locate the highest intensity smell or look for small bubbles when you splash water into the indents. (Don't worry, it won't explode, flare up, or pose a danger.)

Unfortunately, this is a popular location to visit and people leave litter in the creek area. Take a plastic bag with you to pick up litter before leaving this enchanted locale.

Trail Directions:

- From the parking area, pass metal gates supported by white brick pillars.
- Follow the wide gravel trail.
- Bear right at the "Y."
- Pass a large redwood log on your left at 0.1 mile. (A very strange log to find in a pine and hemlock forest.)
- Bear right to stay on the trail, passing some old foundations to the left.
- At 0.2 mile, cross a seasonal stream.
- At 0.3 mile, cross Shale Creek then head uphill.
- At 0.4 mile you'll be on the flat hilltop. Bear left at the "Y."
- Follow the trail along the edge of the ravine, passing the sound of falling water far below.
- Begin downhill, at first gradually, then more steeply as you descend into the ravine.
- At 0.7 mile, reach a "T" and turn left toward the water.
- The trail will bend left to backtrack along the creek at water level.
- Eventually you'll have to walk in the creekbed, heading upstream.
- Pass a tributary waterfall to your right (a 20-foot cascade) and continue upstream.
- At 1.0 mile, reach Eternal Flame Falls in a deep shale canyon.

Date visited:

Notes:

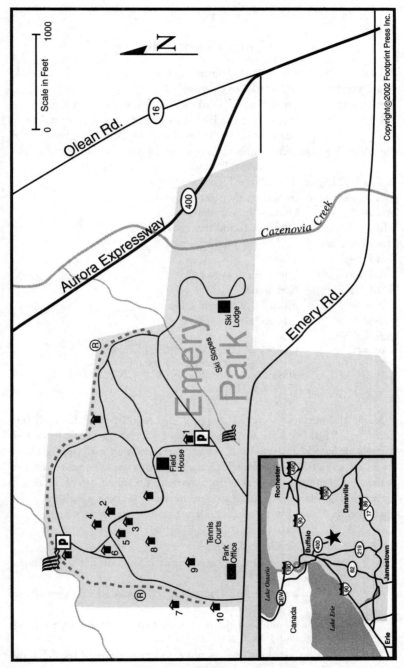

Emery Park Falls

14.

Emery Park Falls

Location:	Emery Park, South Wales, Erie County
Waterway:	Tributaries to Cazenovia Creek
Directions:	From Buffalo, head east on Route 400 until it turns into Route 16. Turn west onto Emery Road and drive one mile to the first park entrance on the right.

Best Viewing Locations: From the trail behind a pavilion for one waterfall; across a grass field for the second waterfall

Waterfall Height: Two 25-feet high waterfalls

Best Season to Visit: Spring; they dry in summer

Access:	Short walk, wheelchair
Hiking Time:	1 minute round trip each
Trail Length:	<0.1 mile round trip each
Difficulty:	1 boot
Trail Surface:	Dirt trail; mowed grass
Trail Markings:	Red blazes
Uses:	Hike, Snowshoe, Ski, Picnic
Dogs:	OK on leash
Admission:	Free
Contact:	County of Erie, Department of Parks, Recreation and Forestry 2084 Emery Road, South Wales, NY 14139 (716) 652-1380

Seeing the northern waterfall can be a challenge. It's easy to reach but access is blocked (for obvious safety reasons) by an orange plastic fence and visually impeded by trees. You'll have a better view in early spring when leaves are still off the trees. Reaching the southern waterfall requires a short walk across a mowed grass field. Time your visit for spring run-off or after a heavy rainfall. These waterfalls dry up in summer. The Emery Park waterfalls each cascade 25 feet from a concave, arched crest to their gorges below.

Trail Directions - Northern Waterfall:
- From the main entrance, bear left at each junction to pass pavilions 1, 2, 3, and 4.
- At pavilion 6 turn right to get to the most northern portion of the park.
- Park at the pavilion on the back loop that is marked with a hand painted #6. (N42 43.176 W78 35.874)
- Walk directly behind this pavilion to cross the red-blazed hiking trail. Beyond the orange plastic fence you'll see the waterfall.

Trail Directions - Southern Waterfall:

- From the main entrance, park at pavilion 1. (N42 42.901 W78 35.553)
- Cross the park road and continue across the mowed field, heading south toward the tributary creek.

Date visited:

Notes:

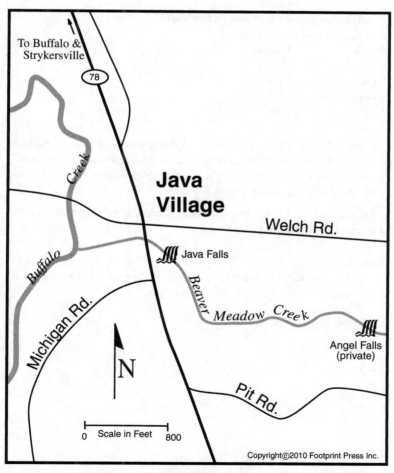

Java Falls

15.

Java Falls (or Turtle Falls)

Location: Java Village, Wyoming County
Waterway: Beaver Meadow Creek
Directions: From Buffalo, head east on Route 78. Java Village is the second town over the Wyoming County line (the first is Strykersville). Park in the parking spots along Route 78 near the creek crossing in Java Village. (N42 40.328 W78 26.149)
Best Viewing Locations: From the Route 78 bridge over Beaver Meadow Creek
Waterfall Height: 21-feet high in two stages
Best Season to Visit: Year-round
Access: Roadside
Difficulty: 1 boot
Uses: View only
Dogs: OK on leash
Admission: Free

Located behind the Java Insurance Agency, this waterfall can easily be seen from the Route 78 bridge over Beaver Meadow Creek. It's a multi-staged drop over large slabs of rock. The first drop is approximately 15-feet high, followed by a 6-foot drop.

Roughly 0.5 mile upstream on Beaver Meadow Creek is Angel Falls, but it sits on heavily posted private property.

Trail Directions:
- You can see this waterfall as a drive-by but for a better view, park and walk to the bridge, looking upstream.

Date visited:

Notes:

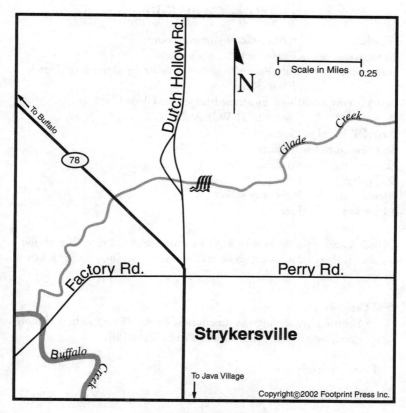

Glade Creek Falls

16.
Glade Creek Falls

Location: Strykersville, Wyoming County
Waterway: Glade Creek
Directions: From Route 78 in Strykersville, head north on Dutch
                         Hollow Road.
Best Viewing Locations: From the bridge over Glade Creek
                         (N42 42.521 W78 26.887)
Waterfall Height: 15-feet high
Best Season to Visit: Spring
Access: Roadside
Difficulty: 1 boot
Uses: View only
Admission: Free

Glade Creek Falls starts with a 3-foot drop and finishes with a 15-foot cascade. It dries in summer, so be sure to visit in spring or after a heavy rain.

Trail Directions:
- Shortly after leaving the junction of Route 78 and Dutch Hollow Road, watch to the right (E) for Glade Creek Falls.

Date visited:

Notes:

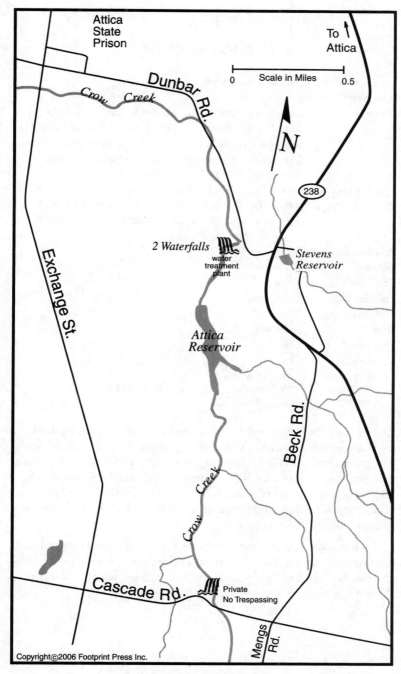

Cascades of Attica

17.

Cascades of Attica

Location:	Attica, Wyoming County
Waterway:	Crow Creek
Directions:	Head south from Attica on Route 238. Turn right (S) onto Dunbar Road. To the left, at the base of the hill, will be an access road to a water treatment plant. From Dunbar Road, look up the access road to see 2 waterfalls. (N42 50.225 W78 15.443)

Best Viewing Locations: From Dunbar Road

Waterfall Height: 2 falls. The upper one is a dam with a 10-foot free fall. The lower one, closest to Dunbar Road, is a natural waterfall about 4-feet high.

Best Season to Visit: Spring

Access:	Roadside
Difficulty:	1 boot
Trail Surface:	Paved road
Trail Markings:	None
Uses:	View only
Dogs:	OK
Admission:	Free
Contact:	Town of Attica 285 Main Street, Attica, NY 14011 (585) 591-0252

Crow Creek flows into and out of the Attica Reservoir, creating drinking water for the Attica area. The water continues to flow into Tonawanda Creek, then into the Niagara River at Tonawanda. The 3 official waterfalls that comprise the Cascades of Attica are near Cascade Road. But, they're on private property and off-limits to visitors. These waterfalls are estimated to be 6-feet-high, 60-feet-high, and a 6-foot-high gradual cascade spreading downhill for 24 feet.

The waterfalls you can view in Crow Creek are near Dunbar Road, downstream from the Attica Reservoir. The upper one is a dam with a 10-foot free fall. The lower one, closest to Dunbar Road, is a natural waterfall about 4-feet high.

Cascades of Attica

Date visited:

Notes:

18.

Letchworth State Park - West Side

Location: Mt. Morris to Portageville, Livingston & Wyoming Counties

Directions: From Mt. Morris, head north on Route 36. The park entrance will be on the left shortly after crossing the Genesee River.
From Portageville, head north on Route 436 and 19A. The Portageville entrance will be on the right.

Best Season to Visit: The Upper, Middle and Lower Falls and some of the smaller falls are spectacular to view year-round. Many of the smaller falls only have water during spring (April/May) or after a heavy rainfall. The challenge though is that in spring the level of the river gets backed up by Mt. Morris Dam so some of the trails to waterfalls and many bottom sections of the waterfalls themselves are hidden underwater. Another water surge occurs in October when we begin to get fall rains.

Dogs: OK on leash no longer than 6 feet.

Admission: $10/vehicle May through October

Contact: Letchworth State Park
NYS Office of Parks, Recreation & Historic Preservation
1 Letchworth State Park
Castile, NY 14427
(585) 493-3600

The Indian name for the Genesee River was Cas-con-sha-gon, meaning "river with falls upon it," an apt name. In Letchworth State Park alone you'll find 3 major waterfalls and over 25 smaller cascades.

The falls described below assume traveling from north (Mt. Morris) to south (Portageville) with stops at falls that are best viewed from the west side of the Genesee River. See page 86 for descriptions of the waterfalls best viewed from the east side of the river.

A great way to see many of the falls is to take a raft trip with Adventure Calls Outfitters (1-888-270-2410, email: acorafting@gmail.com, website: www.adventure-calls.com). On a 6-mile trip from the Lower Falls area, you can see Denton Brook Cascade, the Three Sisters Cascades, Stepmother Cascade, and the lower section of Wolf Creek Cascade.

The lands of Letchworth State Park were preserved by the vision of William Pryor Letchworth. In 1859 he purchased the Glen Iris Inn building and 1,000 acres of land. Over the next 50 years he developed his picturesque estate. In the early 20th century, industriali~ Gorge as an ideal spot for generating hydroelectri~ foiled their attempts by deeding the property to Ne~ with the provision that it be used as a park. In 2015, New York's "Best State Park."

Mr. Letchworth's home, overlooking Middle Falls, has ~~ the Glen Iris Inn, offering fine dining, overnight accommodations in tne style of an old-fashioned country inn, and a gift shop. The word *iris* is greek for rainbow—a common occurrence at Middle Falls.

The formation of Letchworth Gorge dates back to the ice age. As the glaciers melted, a great lake was formed, dammed by the moraines left in its wake. Water was forced to flow northward over a series of alternatively hard and soft rock layers of the Upper Devonian strata. The mighty volume of water cut the largest, deepest canyon east of the Mississippi River. The harder, more resistant rock layers (sandstone) resulted in the waterfalls we enjoy today as the shales were carved and washed away.

Letchworth State Park is actually comprised of three gorges separated by two valleys. The southernmost gorge is Portage Gorge or Portage Canyon. This is where you'll find all three of the major waterfalls (Upper, Middle, and Lower Falls). It is 3 miles long, averages 1,000-feet wide and 200-feet deep. To the Senecas this was Seh-ga-hun-da or "vale of the three falls."

The first valley is called Lee's Landing. It's 1.5 miles long and 3,500-feet wide. Continuing north, comes Great Bend Gorge, which is 3.75 miles long, averages 1,600-feet wide, and is 550-feet deep in one section. The second valley is Gardeau Valley which measures 6.5 miles in length, 4,500-feet wide and 250-feet deep. Finally, there's Mt. Morris Canyon or Mt. Morris High Banks stretching 7.5 miles and averaging 2,000-feet wide and 300-feet deep. This is where Mt. Morris Dam can be found today.

Letchworth State Park is an active place. A wide variety of programs and guided outings are offered year-round. For a schedule of events, get a copy of the *Genesee Naturalist* at the visitors center. Also available at the visitors center are trail and road guides to Letchworth, produced by the Friends Group.

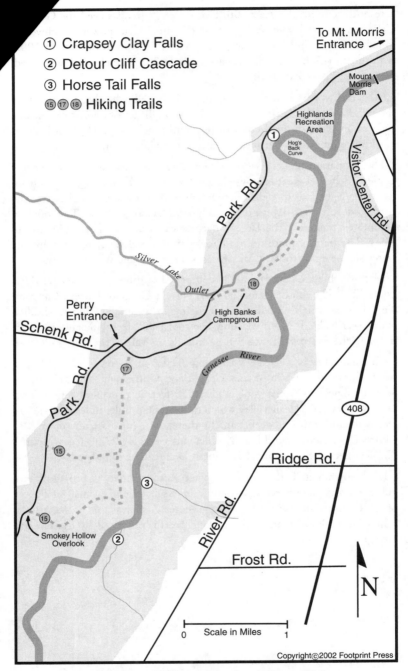

① Crapsey Clay Falls
② Detour Cliff Cascade
③ Horse Tail Falls
⑮⑰⑱ Hiking Trails

To Mt. Morris Entrance →

Mount Morris Dam

Highlands Recreation Area

Hog's Back Curve

Visitor Center Rd.

Park Rd.

Silver Lake Outlet

⑱

High Banks Campground

Perry Entrance

Schenk Rd.

Park Rd.

⑰

Genesee River

408

Ridge Rd.

⑮

③

River Rd.

⑮

Smokey Hollow Overlook

②

Frost Rd.

N

0 Scale in Miles 1

Copyright©2002 Footprint Press

Letchworth State Park - West Side
North End

Crapsey Clay Falls

Waterway: A tributary into the Genesee River

Directions: From the Mt. Morris entrance, head south on Park Road for 1.6 miles. Turn left into the Highlands Recreation Area.

Best Viewing Locations: Straight back from the parking area, along the river gorge (Highbanks Trail 20)

Waterfall Height: Estimated at 200-feet high

Best Season to Visit: After heavy rain. This waterfall dries up after spring and during spring the bottom portion is under water.

Access: Short walk, wheelchair

Hiking Time: 2 minutes round trip

Trail Length: <0.1 mile round trip

Difficulty: 1 boot

Trail Surface: Gravel and dirt trails

Trail Markings: Yellow blazes on Trail 20

Uses: Hike, Snowshoe, Picnic

Crapsey Clay Falls is a tall ribbon waterfall. With high water it's 6-feet wide as it plunges 200 feet to the river. The upper half is overhung and the lower half forms a steep cascade. However, in spring with the river backed up from Mt. Morris Dam, the lower portion of the falls will be under water.

Trail Directions:

- From the Highlands Recreation Area parking lot, pass the police station and picnic pavilion. Walk through the picnic table area, heading straight back toward the Genesee River gorge.
- At the chain link fence you're on Highbanks Trail 20. Bear left along the fence. Look right (W) across the Hogs Back curve to see Crapsey Clay Falls.

Date visited:

Notes:

Detour Cliff Cascade and Horse Tail Falls

Waterway: Tributaries into the Genesee River
Directions: From the Mt. Morris entrance, head south on Park Road for 7.2 miles, passing the Perry entrance. Park at the Smokey Hollow Overlook. There isn't a sign, just pull-off at the first viewing loop after the Trail 15 sign.
Best Viewing Locations: From Trail 15
Waterfall Height: Detour Cliff Cascade is estimated at 100-feet high Horse Tail Fall is estimated at 130-feet high
Best Season to Visit: After a heavy rain
Access: Hike
Hiking Time: 1 hour round trip
Trail Length: 1.5 miles round trip
Difficulty: 4 boots
Trail Surface: Dirt trail
Trail Markings: Yellow blazes on Trail 15
Uses: Hike

Trail 15 isn't particularly steep but it is a constant downhill to the falls viewing and a constant uphill to return to Smokey Hollow Overlook. The trail is a 10-foot wide dirt swath through woods. You have to time a visit here to occur after a heavy rain but not too early in spring. When water is backed up behind Mt. Morris Dam, the lower portion of the trail is flooded and you can't reach the best vantage point.

We've heard you can see these falls from the Smokey Hollow Overlook but we weren't able to find them on the day we visited. Binoculars and a heavy rain run-off would probably help. Detour Cliff Cascade is a 6-foot wide ribbon cascade. Horse Tail Falls in a 10-foot wide ribbon falls.

Trail Directions:
- From the Smokey Hollow Overlook walk south along Park Road to the Trail 15 sign. (Trail 15 is a crescent shaped trail which comes out to Park Road at each end.)
- Turn left onto the trail and head downhill.
- At the low point on the trail look across the gorge to find the falls. Horse Tail is the one on the left, Detour Cliff is on the right.
- Turn around to head back up the trail.

Date visited:

Notes:

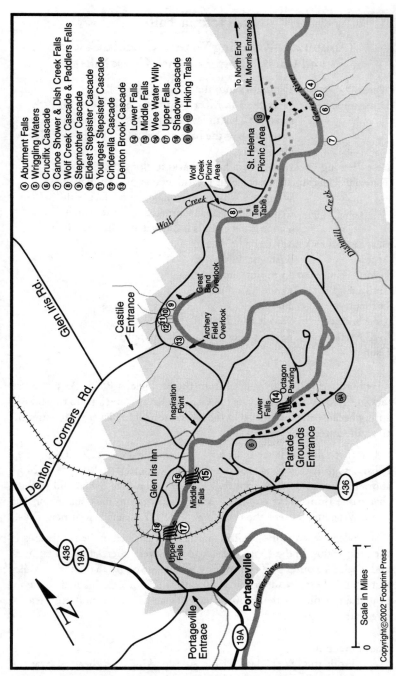

Letchworth State Park - West Side
South End

Copyright©2002 Footprint Press

④ Abutment Falls
⑤ Wriggling Waters
⑥ Crucifix Cascade
⑦ Canoe Shower & Dish Creek Falls
⑧ Wolf Creek Cascade & Paddlers Falls
⑨ Stepmother Cascade
⑩ Eldest Stepsister Cascade
⑪ Youngest Stepsister Cascade
⑫ Cinderella Cascade
⑬ Denton Brook Cascade
⑭ Lower Falls
⑮ Middle Falls
⑯ Wee Water Willy
⑰ Upper Falls
⑱ Shadow Cascade
⑥ ⑭ ⑱ Hiking Trails

Scale in Miles
0   1

St. Helena Falls

(Abutment, Wriggling Waters, Crucifix Cascade, and Canoe Shower or Dish Creek Falls)

Waterway: Tributaries into the Genesee River

Directions: From the Mt. Morris entrance, head south on Park Road for 11.2 miles, passing the Perry entrance. Park in the loop at the base of the hill in the first St. Helena Picnic Area.

Best Viewing Locations: From bushwhacking along the river edge

Waterfall Height: Abutment Falls is estimated at 50-feet high
Wriggling Waters is estimated at 60-feet high
Crucifix Cascade is estimated at 70-feet high
Canoe Shower Falls is estimated at 40-feet high

Best Season to Visit: After a heavy rain

Access: Bushwhack

Hiking Time: 45 minutes round trip

Trail Length: 1 mile round trip

Difficulty: 3 boots

Trail Surface: Woods and dirt trail

Trail Markings: Yellow blazes on St. Helena Trail 13

Uses: Hike

By hiking down to river level from the St. Helena Picnic Area you can view 4 ribbon waterfalls across the Genesee River. You can't do this hike in spring because the water level in the river is too high. Never try to enter the river, the currents are strong.

The first falls you'll see is Canoe Shower Falls (also called Dish Creek Falls), a slightly overhung, 16-foot wide ribbon waterfall. Imagine getting a shower as you glide under this falls in your canoe. Gee, where did they get that name? Next comes Crucifix Cascade. In quick succession will come Wriggling Waters, then the final ribbon falls called Abutment Falls.

St. Helena was a pioneer village on the river flat below the picnic area in the early 1800s. In the 1850s the village had several merchants, 25 families, and a school house. The community was bypassed by the Genesee Valley Canal and the railroads so by 1920 only 12 families remained. It disappeared altogether in the 1940s. Today it's active as the pull-out area for river rafting trips.

Trail Directions:
- From the St. Helena Picnic Area parking area, head east on St. Helena Trail 13 (marked by a large sign).

- At the bottom of the hill turn right (S) on an unmarked side trail. (Before turning, look right (SE) through the trees to see if you can glimpse Crucifix Cascade.)
- Continue 0.4 mile to the bank of the river.
- Turn left (SE) and head down river along the bank, keeping the river to your right. (Look 1,000 feet northwest to see if you can spot Crucifix Cascade.)
- In 0.2 mile, look across the river to see Canoe Shower Falls.
- Continue down river along the bank until you're opposite Crucifix Cascade.
- Continue down river (NE) another 400 feet past Crucifix to see if you're lucky enough to spot the strands of Wriggling Waters.
- In another 900 feet downstream, just before what used to be the western abutment of the St. Helena bridge (removed in 1950) is Abutment Falls. Here too, you'll find St. Helena Trail 13.
- Turn left (W) away from the river and follow the trail 0.5 mile to the parking area.

Date visited:

Notes:

Wolf Creek Cascade and Paddlers Falls

Waterway: Wolf Creek
Directions: From the Mt. Morris entrance, head south on Park
                   Road for 12 miles to the Tea Table parking area.
Best Viewing Locations: From Gorge Trail 1
Waterfall Height: 4 steep cascades for a total drop of about 225 feet
Best Season to Visit: Year-round; but most water flow is in spring
Access: Short walk
Hiking Time: 30 minutes round trip
Trail Length: 0.8 mile round trip
Difficulty: 2 boots
Trail Surface: Dirt trail with stairs
Trail Markings: Yellow blazes on Trail 1
Uses: Hike

Wolf Creek Cascade is a series of 25-feet wide cascades in a narrow, curving ravine. It's hard to see the entire length, so we have to settle for viewing segments at a time. The best view is via a raft trip, but we land lubbers can hike a short segment of the Gorge Trail, which originated as an old Seneca Indian footpath. For less of a hike, park at Tea Table and walk to the gorge edge to see the lower cascade, then drive to Wolf Creek parking area to see another segment.

The bottom segment of this waterfall is called Paddlers Falls at Wolf Creek. It can only be seen by taking an Adventure Calls raft trip (see page 72) and walking up Wolf Creek from the Genesee River.

Trail Directions:
- From Tea Table parking area, cross Park Road and head toward the gorge. At the edge turn right to follow Gorge Trail 1. At an outcropping you'll get a good view of the lowest cascade.
- Continue on the trail, down a flight of stairs to the Wolf Creek picnic area for a close-up view of the upper cascade.
- For an even better view, continue on the trail, crossing Wolf Creek and climbing a flight of steps. At the top is the best view of upper Wolf Creek Cascade.

Date visited:

Notes:

The Three Sisters Area

(Stepmother Cascade, Eldest Stepsister Cascade, Youngest Stepsister Cascade, Cinderella Cascade, and Denton Brook Cascade)

Waterway: Unnamed streams and Denton Brook

Directions: From the Mt. Morris entrance, head south on Park Road to the Great Bend Overlook (just before the Castile entrance).

Best Viewing Locations: From Great Bend Overlook and Archery Field Overlook (both are marked with signs)

Waterfall Height: Stepmother Cascade is estimated at 470-feet high
Eldest Stepsister Cascade is estimated at 500-feet high
Youngest Stepsister Cascade is estimated at 500-feet high
Cinderella Cascade is estimated at 500-feet high
Denton Brook Cascade is estimated at 500-feet high

Best Season to Visit: Spring or after a heavy rain; these falls dry in summer

Access: Short walk

Hiking Time: 1 minute round trip

Trail Length: < 0.1 mile round trip

Difficulty: 1 boot

Trail Surface: Paved walks

Trail Markings: None

Uses: View only

Each of these high cascades originates from a different stream but they're clustered together near the Castile entrance. These are seasonal streams which run from late March to mid-May and after heavy rain. Try walking the Gorge Trail from the Great Bend Overlook to the Archery Field Overlook to get the best vantage points.

The northernmost cascade is Stepmother. It has the largest water volume and is a 3-foot wide ribbon cascade. It is steeply sloped with some vertical sections. Halfway down the cliff face is a vertical part called "The Vulture's Nose." You'll have to take a raft trip to see the nose profile however. In the early 1980s turkey vultures were seen flying in and out of the nostrils, hence the name. The next cascade heading south is Eldest Stepsister. It's another ribbon cascade, about 3-feet wide with a steep slope and one overhung area halfway down the cliff.

Continuing south we reach Youngest Stepsister, very much like her siblings. Next is Cinderella Cascade, the southernmost of the official Three

Sisters. She suffers from low water volume and is often hidden by tree cover. Otherwise, she does resemble her sisters.

Finally there's Denton Brook Cascade south of Castile entrance. It's helpful to have binoculars to spot this 2-foot wide ribbon cascade, 0.5 mile north of Archery Field Overlook.

Two explanations exist for the origin of the name Three Sisters. One is an obvious reference to the characters in the Cinderella fairy tale. The other predates Cinderella and refers to an Iroquois Indian reference to corn, beans, and squash as the three sisters, when grown together.

Trail Directions:
- From the Great Bend Overlook, look right (SW) to view the falls.
- Drive south on Park Road to the Archery Field Overlook, just south of the Castile Entrance. Look left (N) to view the falls.

Date visited:

Notes:

Lower Falls

Waterway: Genesee River

Directions: From the Mt. Morris entrance, head south on Park Road to the southern end of Letchworth State Park. Follow signs to the Lower Falls and Octagon parking area.

Best Viewing Locations: From a side trail off Footbridge Trail 6A

Waterfall Height: 3 drops for a total of 70 feet

Best Season to Visit: Year-round

Access: Short walk

Hiking Time: 15 minutes round trip

Trail Length: 0.6 mile round trip

Difficulty: 3 boots (127 steps)

Trail Surface: Dirt trail with stone steps

Trail Markings: Yellow, brown and white signs, well marked

Uses: Hike

Lower Falls, the least picturesque of the 3 major falls, was once a mightier waterfall. Since the 1950s, large sections have eroded and dropped off leaving Lower Falls a misnomer. It is now three waterfalls with deeper water between the upper two. The first fall drops approximately 55 feet. Then there's 250 feet of deep water, followed by the second drop and a slight run to the third fall. The second and third falls together drop about 15 feet. Downstream from Lower Falls is a section of shales and sandstones known collec-

Lower Falls in Letchworth State Park

tively as the Rhinestreet. It was classified in the 1840s by James Hall, from top to bottom as Gardeau sandstone, Grimes sandstone, Hatch shale and Rhinestreet shale.

A footbridge spans the flume (a narrow channel in the gorge that is 65-feet deep). Continuing across the bridge to the east side of Letchworth State Park on Trail 6A, leads to Paul Rock Cascade (see page 88).

The large, flat, ripple-marked sandstone surface at the flume is called Table Rock. It was once the crest of Lower Falls and the bed of the Genesee River and shows how the river has moved over time. The Lower Falls is visible from its western end, now hugging the southern wall of the gorge through the flume.

Ahead of Table Rock, look for a conical pillar with a flat top, called Cathedral Rock. There are two theories concerning its origin. One says the current through the flume acted as a drill, boring through a rectangular projection of the right sidewall to form a high archway. Eventually, the arch collapsed, leaving just its outer support. The more probable theory says the pillar was an island between two waterfalls, much like Goat Island at Niagara Falls.

Trail Directions:
- From the Octagon parking area, head west on Gorge Trail 1.
- In 0.1 mile, take Footbridge Trail 6A and descend into the gorge via 127 steps.
- Shortly after the steps end, take a side trail to the right (W) to reach the best view in another 0.1 mile.

Date visited:

Notes:

Middle Falls & Wee Water Willy

Waterway: Genesee River

Directions: From the Mt. Morris entrance, head south on Park Road to the southern end of Letchworth State Park. Follow signs to the Glen Iris Inn parking area or continue downhill, bearing left to the Falls parking area. (N42 35.281 W78 2.386)

Best Viewing Locations: From behind Glen Iris Inn and on the lower trail from the Falls parking area.

Waterfall Height: 107-feet high

Best Season to Visit: Year-round

Access: Short walk, wheelchair

Hiking Time: 1 minute round trip

Difficulty: 1 boot

Trail Surface: Paved trails

Trail Markings: None

Uses: Hike

The Middle Falls is the most scenic of Letchworth's falls. The Seneca Indians called it Ska-ga-dee. We look at it and say "wow!" The day we visited in April, a brilliant rainbow arched across the falls.

The westernmost crest of Middle Falls is overhung but most of it is steeply terraced. It is illuminated at night from May through October.

Middle Falls in Letchworth State Park

Another good view of Middle Falls (as well as Upper Falls) can be had from Inspiration Point. This is a lookout area off Park Road, northeast of the falls. It is also the crest of Inspiration Falls which is better seen from the east bank (see page 89).

Trail Directions:
- From the Glen Iris parking area, simply head toward the gorge on a short, paved path to the high overlook area. The waterfall will be obvious.
- From the Falls parking area, head left (NE) on the paved trail. It's a short walk to the falls overlook where in spring, you'll be sprayed with mist.

Wee Water Willy

Waterway: A tributary into the Genesee River
Best Viewing Locations: On the lower trail from the Falls parking area
Waterfall Height: 117-feet high
Best Season to Visit: Spring or after heavy rainfall
Access: Short walk, wheelchair
Hiking Time: 1 minute round trip
Difficulty: 1 boot
Trail Surface: Paved trail
Trail Markings: None
Uses: Hike

While you're enjoying the awesome beauty of the Middle Falls, don't forget to look for Wee Water Willy. This ribbon waterfall, barely 2-feet wide, is best viewed from the crest of Middle Falls or 100 feet northeast of the overlook area. Its upper half is nearly vertical and its lower half is overhung. Count yourself lucky if you find it flowing.

Date visited:

Notes:

Upper Falls & Shadow Cascade

Waterway: Genesee River
Directions: From the Mt. Morris entrance, head south on Park Road to the southern end of Letchworth State Park. Follow signs to the Falls parking area. (N42 34.901 W78 2.733)
Best Viewing Locations: From the Gorge Trail 1
Waterfall Height: 71-feet high
Best Season to Visit: Year-round
Access: Short walk
Hiking Time: 15 minutes round trip
Trail Length: 0.3 mile round trip
Difficulty: 2 boots
Trail Surface: Gravel trail
Trail Markings: None
Uses: Hike

Portage High Bridge over Upper Falls in Letchworth State Park, which had to be replaced in 2015 to accommodate modern rail traffic.

The Upper Falls has a horseshoe shaped crest more than 300-feet wide. Its caprock is comprised of Nunda Sandstone. The crest is overhung so the water crashes over the lip for its free-fall. In the late 1870s the curve of the horseshoe was shored up with concrete in an attempt to slow erosion.

From the falls area, look upstream and toward the sky to see the Portage High Bridge 400 feet away. In 1852 when this bridge opened, it was the world's largest and highest wooden railroad bridge. The Erie Railroad ran across it, linking Buffalo and

Hornell. It sits 234 feet above the waterfall and spans the gorge for 850 feet. The original wooden bridge burned down on May 6, 1875 under suspicious circumstances. The Erie Railroad built this iron bridge using the same specifications. In 2015, the old bridge was replaced with a new bridge that could withstand the weight and speed of modern rail traffic.

Trail Directions:
- From the Falls parking area, bear right (upstream) on Gorge Trail 1.
- It's a gradual uphill for <0.1 mile to the falls.

Shadow Cascade

Waterway: Deh-ge-wa-nus Creek
Best Viewing Locations: From Gorge Trail 1
Waterfall Height: 14-feet high
Best Season to Visit: Spring or after heavy rainfall
Access: Short walk
Hiking Time: 15 minutes round trip
Difficulty: 2 boots

Just past the crest of Upper Falls, Deh-ge-wa-nus Creek crosses the Gorge Trail. Look to the right (NW) to see if Shadow Cascade is flowing, 30 feet away. Shadow Cascade is a 6-feet wide ribbon cascade.

Date visited:

Notes:

Waterfalls in Monroe, Livingston and Ontario Counties

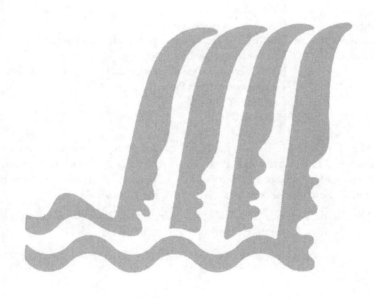

19.

Letchworth State Park - East Side

Location: Portageville, Livingston County

Directions: From Portageville, head south on Route 436 (from Nunda head west on Route 436). Turn north into the Parade Grounds area of Letchworth State Park.

Best Season to Visit: The Upper, Middle and Lower Falls and some of the smaller falls are spectacular to view year-round. Many of the smaller falls only have water during spring or after a heavy rainfall. The challenge though is that in spring the level of the river gets backed up by Mt. Morris Dam, so some of the trails to waterfalls and many bottom sections of the waterfalls themselves are hidden underwater.

Dogs: OK on leash no longer than 6 feet.

Admission: Free (on the east side); entrance closed in winter.

Contact: Letchworth State Park
NYS Office of Parks, Recreation & Historic Preservation
1 Letchworth State Park
Castile, NY 14427
(585) 493-3600

The falls described below can all be reached from the Parade Grounds entrance to Letchworth State Park. They are arranged from north to south but can easily be visited in reverse order. See page 68 for descriptions of the waterfalls best viewed from the west side of the Genesee River.

The Parade Grounds is a picnic and playground area today. During the Civil War, it was an actual infantry parade grounds.

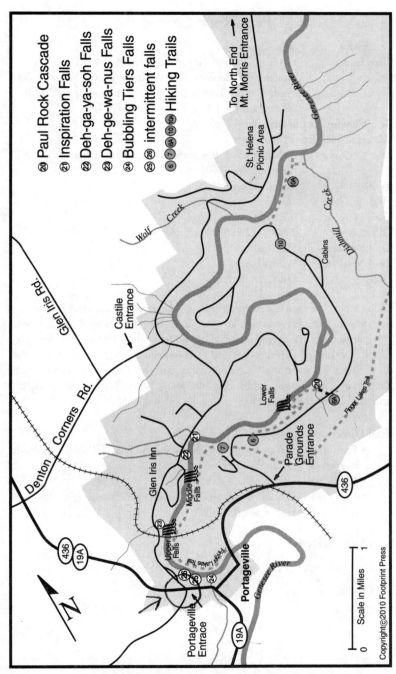

Letchworth State Park - East Side
South End

Paul Rock Cascade

Waterway:	Bogs Brook
Directions:	From the Parade Grounds entrance, drive 1.5 miles past the Parade Grounds parking area, the Finger Lakes Trail, and the Trail 6 entrance. Park in the gravel pull-off area on the left at the start of Trail 6A.

Best Viewing Locations: From Trail 6A
Waterfall Height: 35-feet high
Best Season to Visit: Year-round; this waterfall has water when many of the other small falls don't

Access:	Short walk
Hiking Time:	10 minutes round trip
Trail Length:	0.2 mile round trip
Difficulty:	2 boots (25 steps)
Trail Surface:	Dirt trail
Trail Markings:	Yellow blazes
Uses:	Hike, Snowshoe

Paul Rock Cascade is a steeply sloping, 12-feet wide cascade. Only a partial view is available because its crest is traversed by a chain-link fence. Farther down in the same creek bed are additional 10 feet and a 6 feet cascades, but they are unaccessible and can't be seen from the trail. Please stay on the trail. This waterfall is named after the large rock at the crest which has "Paul" and some other illegible words carved into the rock by unknown graffiti artists.

Trail Directions:
- From the gravel parking area, follow yellow-blazed Trail 6A through the woods and down 25 steps.
- Cross the creek on a slate slab.
- Peer down through the chain-link fence (which crosses at the crest of the waterfall) to see the falls.

Date visited:

Notes:

Inspiration Falls

Waterway:	Trout Pond Outlet
Directions:	From the Parade Grounds entrance, park at the Parade Grounds parking area.

Best Viewing Locations: From Trail 7 (Finger Lakes Trail)
Waterfall Height: 350-feet high
Best Season to Visit: Spring or after heavy rainfall

Access:	Short walk
Hiking Time:	12 minutes round trip
Trail Length:	0.4 mile round trip
Difficulty:	1 boot
Trail Surface:	Dirt trail
Trail Markings:	Yellow blazes
Uses:	Hike, Bike, Snowshoe, Ski

This is the grandmother of Central and Western New York's waterfalls—higher than Niagara Falls (184 feet) and higher than Taughannock Falls (215 feet), both of which often get top billing. Of course, the water volume pales in comparison. But, in height, this waterfall is top on the chart. Inspiration Falls is a ribbon waterfall, only one foot wide. For its 350 foot drop, the first 65 feet are vertical, the middle section drops from an overhang for 145 feet, followed by another 140 feet of vertical, making an impressive fall when the water volume is high. In high wind conditions, the middle section gets blown by the wind adding a wispy effect to the falls.

Inspiration Falls plummets into the Genesee River from Inspiration Point on the west side of Letchworth State Park. You can view the crest of the falls from there (plus get a great view of Middle Falls) but by far the better view is from Trail 7 on the east side.

Trail Directions:
- From the Parade Grounds parking area, head left (W) on Trail 7.
- After about 0.2 mile, look across the gorge to see Inspiration Falls on the opposite bank.
- Continue on Trail 7 for additional waterfalls (see pages 90–92).

Date visited:

Notes:

Deh-ga-ya-soh Falls

Waterway: Deh-ga-ya-soh Creek

Directions: From the Parade Grounds entrance, park at the Parade Grounds parking area.

Best Viewing Locations: From Trail 7 (Finger Lakes Trail)

Waterfall Height: 150-feet high

Best Season to Visit: Spring or after heavy rain

Access: Hike

Hiking Time: 30 minutes round trip

Trail Length: 1.0 mile round trip

Difficulty: 1 boot

Trail Surface: Dirt trail

Trail Markings: Yellow blazes

Uses: Hike, Bike, Snowshoe

As you walk southwest from Parade Grounds parking area, past Inspiration Falls, the next falls you may see across the gorge is Deh-ga-ya-soh Falls as it bursts from under a stone bridge. The view of this 10-feet wide ribbon falls with three closely spaced drops, is impeded by trees. Deh-ga-ya-soh is Seneca for "nameless spirits."

Trail Directions:

- From the Parade Grounds parking area, head left (W) on Trail 7.
- After Inspiration Falls, continue to look across the gorge to see Deh-ga-ya-soh Falls on the opposite bank. If you reach Middle Falls, you've gone 0.2 mile too far.

Date visited:

Notes:

Deh-ge-wa-nus Falls (and Upper Falls)

Waterway: Deh-ge-wa-nus Creek
Directions: From the Parade Grounds entrance, park at the Parade Grounds parking area.
Best Viewing Locations: From Trail 7 (Finger Lakes Trail)
Waterfall Height: 14-feet high
Best Season to Visit: Spring or after heavy rain
Access: Hike
Hiking Time: 1 hour round trip
Trail Length: 2 miles round trip
Difficulty: 1 boot
Trail Surface: Dirt trail
Trail Markings: Yellow blazes
Uses: Hike, Bike, Snowshoe

Slightly west of the crest of Upper Falls, Deh-ge-wa-nus Creek rushes to meet the Genesee River, forming the 10-feet wide Deh-ge-wa-nus Falls. The name is Seneca for "two falling voices."

Trail Directions:
- From the Parade Grounds parking area, head left (W) on Trail 7 for 1 mile.
- Shortly before passing under Portage High Bridge you'll reach Upper Falls in the Genesee River and Deh-ge-wa-nus Falls on the bank across the gorge.

Date visited:

Notes:

Bubbling Tiers Falls (and 2 intermittent falls)

Waterway: Unnamed

Directions: From the Parade Grounds entrance, park at the Parade Grounds parking area.

Best Viewing Locations: From Trail 7 (Finger Lakes Trail)

Waterfall Height: 38-feet high

Best Season to Visit: Spring or after heavy rain

Access: Hike

Hiking Time: 2 hours round trip

Trail Length: 3.6 miles round trip

Difficulty: 2 boots

Trail Surface: Dirt trail

Trail Markings: Yellow blazes

Uses: Hike, Bike, Snowshoe

At the southern end of Trail 7, across the Genesee River lies Portageville. Remnants of an old stone aqueduct still can be spotted in the river bed. It's hard to get a good view of Bubbling Tiers Waterfall through the trees. It's a 10-feet wide ribbon falls with three closely spaced drops. If you've visiting in spring run-off or after a heavy rain, you may see 2 intermittent waterfalls. The first is 300 yards downstream from Bubbling Tiers (on the same bank). It's a 20-foot cascade partially obscured by trees. Another 100 yards downstream is a 50-foot cascade spilling almost directly into the river.

Trail Directions:
- From the Parade Grounds parking area, head left (W) on Trail 7 for 1.8 miles.
- When the trail reaches a "Y," bear right to go to a vantage point across the Genesee River from Portageville.
- From the end of the trail, Bubbling Tiers Falls is across the river and 0.1 mile south. The view is impeded by trees.

Date visited:

Notes:

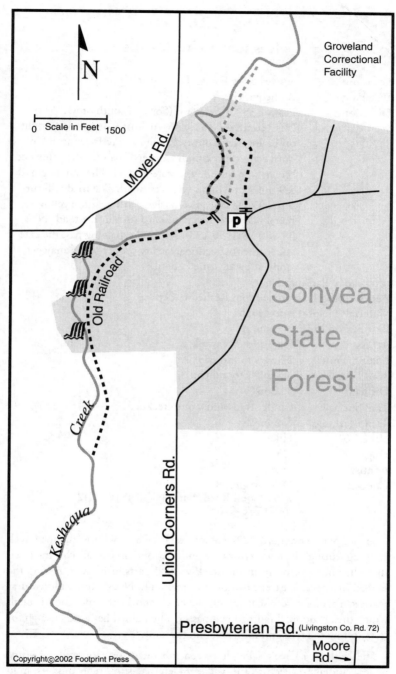

Groveland
Correctional
Facility

N

0 Scale in Feet 1500

Moyer Rd.

Old Railroad

Sonyea
State
Forest

P

Creek

Union Corners Rd.

Keshequa

Copyright©2002 Footprint Press

Presbyterian Rd. (Livingston Co. Rd. 72)

Moore
Rd. →

Keshequa Creek Falls

20.
Keshequa Creek Falls

Location:	Sonyea State Forest, Livingston County
Waterway:	Keshequa Creek
Directions:	From I-390, take exit 6 (Sonyea) south of Mt. Morris. Head south on Route 36. At Ross Corners, turn right on Livingston County Route 72 (Presbyterian Road). Turn right onto Union Corners Road (at the yellow & brown sign for Sonyea State Forest). The trail begins 2.9 miles up Union Corners Road. The road will turn into a single lane gravel drive. Park near the yellow metal barricade before a sharp turn in the road (N42 39.980 W77 50.198). (If you keep going past the gate you'll enter correctional facility property and may get stopped by an armed guard.)

Alternative Parking: None
Best Viewing Locations: From Keshequa Creek
Waterfall Height: 4-feet high
Best Season to Visit: Summer

Access:	Hike and creekwalk
Hiking Time:	2 hours round trip
Trail Length:	4.6 miles round trip
Difficulty:	3 boots
Trail Surface:	Cinder trails and stone creekbed
Trail Markings:	None
Uses:	Hike
Dogs:	OK
Admission:	Free
Contact:	DEC Region 8
	7291 Coon Road, Bath, NY 14810-7742
	(607) 776-2165

Sonyea State Forest is a 922-acre reforestation area with Keshequa Creek running through it in a picturesque gully. At one time a railroad traversed the valley but erosion from the creek washed parts of it away making the railbed inaccessible except by doing a creekwalk. Nature has sculpted dramatic cliffs in the soft shale along the creek and in the rockcuts through which the abandoned railroad bed passes. The railbed has aged enough for trees to hug the trail and form a cooling canopy.

The Keshequa Creek valley has been inhabited for thousands of years. Seneca Indians called it "the valley of eternal sun" reflecting its mild weather, outside the reach of lake-effect storms. From the 1830s through the 1890s the area was home to a community of the United Society of Christian Believers, commonly called Shakers because of their whirling and twitching in religious frenzy. The Shakers ran into financial problems and saw their numbers dwindle, so in 1894 the state of New York bought their land, promising to use it for charitable purposes.

At the time epileptics were confined to insane asylums due to mistreatment and ostracism. William Pryor Letchworth (of Letchworth State Park fame) along with Dr. Fred Peterson worked to establish a European styled treatment center for epileptics in New York. Oscar Craig who headed the State Board of Charities, was appointed to find a site and selected the Shaker community in Sonyea. Mr. Craig died before the epileptic colony was opened, and it was named the Craig Colony in his honor. Buildings in the complex were named after Letchworth and Peterson. The first patients arrived in 1896. As medication was developed to control epileptic seizures, the Craig Colony's population dwindled. The facility was shifted to the care of mental health patients.

The Craig Colony was gradually phased into the Groveland Correctional Facility as inmates began moving in, in 1982. The last mental health patient left in 1989. Today, Groveland Correctional Facility houses male inmates.

The waterfalls in Keshequa Creek consist of small cascades, a 4 foot ledge, and a long gradual slide of water over flat rock. The route suggested is a hike down to the creek, a creekwalk past the railbed washout, then a hike following the railbed trail to the waterfalls. You can creekwalk the entire way, but the first 1.1 miles consists of walking on loose rock. It's much easier to walk the trail, then walk the creekbed once the rock becomes flat sheets in the waterfall areas.

Trail and Creekwalk Directions
- Head down the trail, behind the yellow metal barrier.
- The wide dirt path will lead you down into the creek gully.
- The trail "Ts" near water level at 0.5 mile. Continue straight on a small path to the water. (To the right are steep, weathered shale banks. To the left is a short walk to a barricade. This was once the railroad bed, but you can see how the powerful water washed it away.)
- Put on your water shoes and walk into Keshequa Creek, heading left (upstream).
- Cross the creek two times to get past the washed out area (marked by yellow metal barriers at each end).

- Then head left, into the woods, on a double track. It will lead to an abandoned cinder railroad bed.
- Turn right and continue upstream on the railroad bed.
- At 1.8 miles you'll pass the first series of cascades in a bend in the creek. You can take a side trail to the right to explore the cascades then continue upstream either in the streambed or by returning to the railroad bed trail.
- At 2.0 miles find a 4 foot ledge waterfall that covers the full width of the creek. It's easy to hear the sound of falling water from the trail.
- At 2.3 miles you'll again hear the sound of rippling water. In the creek is a long, gradual cascade over flat rock. It's the type of spot that beckons you to go play in the water.
- You can turn around here to head back or continue on the trail. It ends at 1.8 miles where a trestle used to carry trains over Keshequa Creek. The trestle is long gone and the trail to the left leads onto private property.

Date visited:

Notes:

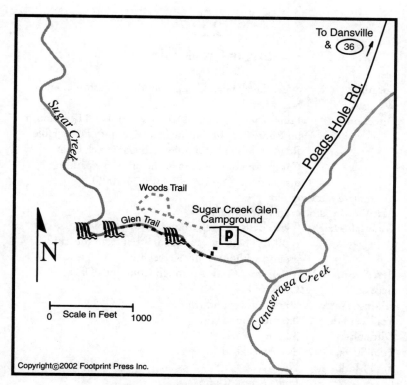

Sugar Creek Glen

21.
Sugar Creek Glen

Location:	Sugar Creek Glen Campground, Livingston County
Waterway:	Sugar Creek
Directions:	From Route 390 take Dansville exit 4 and head south on Route 36. Turn at the first right onto Poags Hole Road and follow it 5 miles to Sugar Creek Glen Campground. Check in at the office for parking instructions. (N42 29.177 W77 44.005)

Alternative Parking: None

Best Viewing Locations: Creekwalk

Waterfall Height: 9 waterfalls ranging from 2 to 50-feet high
A 30-feet high cascade can be seen from the camp ground without doing a creekwalk

Best Season to Visit: Summer (May 1 through Columbus Day)

Access:	Creekwalk
Hiking Time:	40 minutes round trip
Trail Length:	0.6 mile round trip
Difficulty:	3 boots
Trail Surface:	Stone creekbed
Trail Markings:	None
Uses:	Hike, Swim, Camp
Dogs:	OK on leash in campground, clean up after pets. No aggressive dogs; leash length cannot exceed 6 feet. No digging. No pets in waterway or on trails.
Admission:	Day visit: $5 per person
	Camping: $21 for 2 adults, $2/child
	We have heard reports of some people being turned away by the campground, so please phone ahead and verify that Sugar Creek Glen Campground is currently accepting visitors.
Contact:	Sugar Creek Glen Campground
	PO Box 143, Dansville, NY 14437
	(585) 335-6294

This campground, nestled in the woods, sits at the confluence of Canaseraga Creek and Sugar Creek. Stop in for a day to walk the creek and play in the water, or plan to camp awhile. Sugar Creek drops 300 feet over 1.7 miles before it feeds into Canaseraga Creek in Poags Hole. A short walk up Sugar Creek is a waterfaller's delight with another cascade every

100 feet. The culmination is a 50-foot cascade in a stone amphitheater. The water cascades straight down on the left side but fans wider at the bottom on the right side. Look closely and you can glimpse another 30-foot waterfall high above this beauty.

Creekwalk Directions:
- From the campground area, head west past sites 15 through 18 to the Memory Garden, a small perennial garden with benches, set next to Sugar Creek. The first waterfall, a 30-feet high, 15-feet wide cascade in two stages, is visible from here. It is illuminated at night.
- Continue west on the trail from the Memory Garden until it ends at the creek.
- Begin the creekwalk, heading upstream.
- Pick your way carefully over the rocks and up one cascade after another.
- In 0.3 mile you'll reach the 50-foot cascade where you'll have to turn around.

Date visited:

Notes:

22.
Paper Mill Falls

Location:	South of Avon, Livingston County
Waterway:	Conesus Creek
Directions:	From Avon, head south on Route 39. Turn east onto Paper Mill Road. Park in 0.5 mile before a stone bridge in a small park. (N42 52.276 W77 45.686)

Alternative Parking: Another parking area for the park on the far side of the bridge.

Best Viewing Locations: From the west bank near the parking area or from a trail that runs along the east bank.

Waterfall Height: Estimated at 20-feet high

Best Season to Visit: Year-round; although it dries to a trickle in summer

Access:	Short walk
Hiking Time:	4 minutes round trip
Trail Length:	0.1 mile round trip
Difficulty:	1 boot
Trail Surface:	Dirt trail
Trail Markings:	None
Uses:	Hike, Picnic (park closed from Sunset–7 AM)
Dogs:	OK on leash
Admission:	Free
Contact:	Town of Avon 27 Genesee Street, Avon, NY 14414 (585) 226-2425

This former mill site is now a community park. The waterfall has a jagged edge and free-falls from the caprock then rumbles through a multi-level cascade. There are two bridges here. The current road passes over a stone bridge with arched supports. Notice the old millstone in the center. Closer to the falls crest is an old road bridge, now a pedestrian walkway. Cross this bridge to walk the east bank for some great views of the falls.

Trail Directions:
- From the west bank parking area walk toward the water to see the falls.
- Continue east across the pedestrian bridge.
- Shortly after the bridge, turn left to follow a dirt path along the east bank.
- In less than 0.1 mile you'll be rewarded with a clear view of the falls.

Date visited:

Notes:

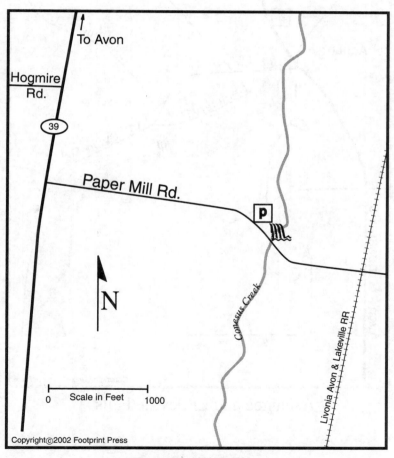

Paper Mill Falls

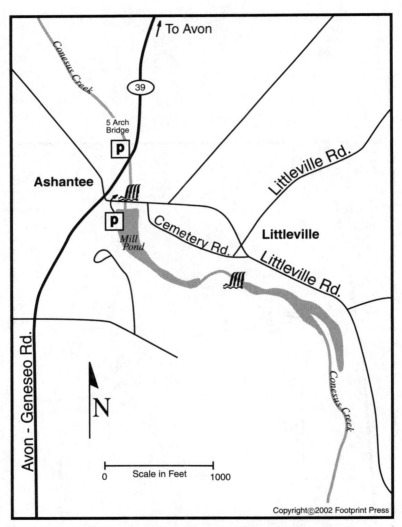

Ashantee and Littleville Falls

23.
Ashantee and Littleville Falls

Location: Ashantee and Littleville, Livingston County
Waterway: Conesus Creek

Ashantee Falls

Directions: From Routes 5 & 20 in Avon, head south 1.5 miles on
Route 39. Park at the Ashantee Antique
Shop.

(N42 53.813 W77 45.858)

Alternative Parking: Across Route 39 at the 5 Arch Bridge
Best Viewing Locations: From the windows inside the antique shop
Waterfall Height: Estimated at 10-feet high
Best Season to Visit: Year-round; although it dries to a trickle in summer
Access: Short walk into the antique shop
Difficulty: 1 boot
Uses: View only (and antique shopping of course)
Dogs: NOT allowed in the shop
Admission: Free

Ashantee Falls is an old dam tucked under the Littleville Road bridge. It's hard to see, except from the antique shop windows. Directly across the creek you'll see a red building with a water wheel. It's currently a private residence.

The Ashantee 5 Arch Bridge

Conesus Creek leaves the mill pond above Littleville bridge, free-falls over the dam then winds its way over a series of stone slabs and small falls on its way to the 5 arch bridge. This bridge was built in 1856-57 by the Genesee Valley Railroad to span Conesus Creek. It's 200-feet long and 12-feet wide and made of limestone. In its heyday, the trains crossing this bridge made 13 runs per day between Rochester and Mount Morris. The line was electrified in 1907 and was abandoned in 1941.

Littleville Falls

Directions: From Ashantee Antique Shop, turn east onto Littleville Road then take the first right onto Cemetery Road. Pass a cemetery then look right, before a house, you may be able to catch a glimpse of Littleville Falls.

Alternative Parking: None

Best Viewing Locations: From Cemetery Road, the falls is on private property

Waterfall Height: Estimated at 20-feet high

Best Season to Visit: Early spring, fall, or winter (your only chance for a glimpse of this falls is when there are no leaves on the trees)

Access: Roadside

Difficulty: 1 boot

Uses: View only from the road

Littleville Falls was once the site of Light's Grist Mill. Today a private home sits beside this majestic, wide cascade. The best we can do is steal a glimpse of it through trees when the leaves are off.

Date visited:

Notes:

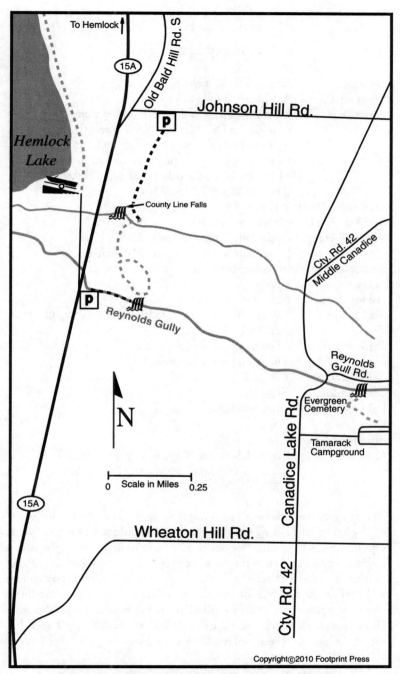

Reynolds Gully & County Line Falls

24.

County Line Falls

Location: Hemlock Lake, Livingston County

Waterway: A tributary into Hemlock Lake

Directions: From Route 15A at the south end of Hemlock Lake, turn east on Old Bald Hill Road South then quickly turn right on Johnson Hill Road. In 0.1 mile turn right into a grassy parking area marked by a green and white "Hemlock-Canadice Watershed" hiker sign. (N42 40.583 W77 35.283)

Alternative Parking: None

Best Viewing Locations: From the trail

Waterfall Height: Upper falls is approximately 50-feet high
Lower falls is approximately 25-feet high

Best Season to Visit: Spring; becomes a trickle in summer

Access: Hike

Hiking Time: 30 minutes round trip

Trail Length: 1.0 mile round trip (Or follow the trail along its entire loop for 1.5 miles.)

Difficulty: 2 boots to see the upper waterfall
4 boots to see the lower waterfall

Trail Surface: Tall grass

Trail Markings: None

Uses: Hike, Snowshoe

Dogs: OK

Admission: Free

Contact: City of Rochester, Water & Lighting Bureau
7412 Rix Hill Road, Hemlock, NY 14466
(585) 346-2617

Long ago, Hemlock Lake had cottages along its shore. In 1872, the city of Rochester decided to use Canadice and Hemlock Lakes as a water supply. The first conduit for water was completed in 1876. By 1947, Rochester purchased all of the shoreline property and removed the cottages so that it could protect the water supply for its growing population. Although it was difficult for the cottage residents to leave their land, this area is now free of the commercialization that is so rampant on the other Finger Lakes. Hemlock and Canadice Lakes are small Finger Lakes, but they sit at high elevation, making them a good water supply for the city.

To protect Rochester property and the supply of drinking water, the city requires all visitors to obtain a Watershed Visitor Permit, one of the easiest permits to obtain. Just stop at the visitor's self-serve, permit station located at the north end of Hemlock Lake on Rix Hill Road off Route 15A or go online to www.ci.rochester.ny.us/watershedpermit.htm. There are no fees or forms to fill out, but the permit document details the do's and don'ts to help keep the area pristine, so it's important to read it.

County Line Falls is actually two waterfalls, an upper and a lower, in a drainage tributary to Hemlock Lake. The upper fall is a 50-foot steep cascade over a rock ledge to a deep gorge with a sharp bend at the base of the waterfall. To get to the lower waterfall requires a walk down a steep bank. This waterfall is a 25-foot free-fall. The trail to the waterfalls is generally unmowed, tall grass. It was developed in 1995 as part of a small timber harvest. In winter this trail would make a nice snowshoe route to view the upper (but not the lower) waterfall. You can hike to the waterfalls and directly back for 1.0 mile or take the loop trail for 1.5 miles. At the far end of the loop you're at the top of Reynolds Gully, but too high up to see any of its waterfalls.

Trail Directions:
- From the parking area, hike past the metal gate on the wide, grass trail.
- The trail heads downhill gradually.
- Reach the creek at 0.4 mile.
- Turn right along the creek to immediately see the upper waterfall.
- Follow the edge of the north bank of the gorge steeply downhill for 0.1 mile to find the lower waterfall.
- Retrace your steps back to the parking area.

Date visited:

Notes:

25.

Reynolds Gully (Reynolds Gull) - Access #1

Location: Hemlock Lake, Livingston County
Waterway: The watershed into Hemlock Lake
Directions: From Route 15A at the south end of Hemlock Lake,
                     look for an orange sign "Public Water Supply." Directly
                     across the street on the east side of Route 15A is a
small   dirt parking area. (N42 40.093 W77 35.507)
                     (See map on page 109)
Alternative Parking: None
Best Viewing Locations: From creekbed
Waterfall Height: Two falls 15 and 20-feet high on public property
                     Two falls 12 and 70-feet high on private property
Best Season to Visit: Summer
Access: Creekwalk
Hiking Time: 30 minute round trip
Trail Length: 0.3 mile round trip on public land
Difficulty: 4+ boots
Trail Surface: Stone
Trail Markings: None
Uses: Hike
Dogs: Not allowed
Admission: Free
Contact: City of Rochester, Water & Lighting Bureau
                     7412 Rix Hill Road, Hemlock, NY 14466
                     (585) 346-2617

As described for County Line Falls (see page 110) this is part of the watershed to Rochester's drinking water.

Walking this gully is a challenge. There are lots of downed trees to scramble over, and steep, slippery cliffs to scale. The rocks here are particularly slippery. Take extra care with your footing. To top it off, the water is cold—colder than most creekwalks. But the scenery is well worth the effort and you can count on the gully being cool, even on the warmest days of summer.

You'll find two waterfalls, 15 and 20-feet high respectively. If you could finish the creekwalk, you'd pass a 12-foot overhung waterfall that sits sideways in the channel, then reach the 70-foot dual ribbon cascade waterfall. It would be a 0.6 mile round trip, taking a full hour to go up and back. However, the final leg is on private property, and is heavily posted.

One of the Reynolds Gully Waterfalls

Creekwalk Directions:
- From the parking area, hike on the trail (E) toward the gully.
- The trail quickly peters out and you begin the creekwalk, upstream.
- Pass a one-foot slab drop then a 2-foot cascade.
- Continuing upstream, pass a 15-foot waterfall with a free-fall top that drops to a long, gradual cascade.
- At 0.15 mile reach a 20-foot waterfall. The first 5 feet free-falls to a 15-foot steep cascade.
- This is as far as you can go on public land. Trespassing on private property is strictly prohibited.

Date visited:

Notes:

Reynolds Gully (Reynolds Gull) - Access #2

Location:	Hemlock Lake, Livingston County
Waterway:	The watershed into Hemlock Lake
Directions:	Follow Canadice Lake Road south (along the east side of Canadice Lake). Pass Johnson Hill Road, County Road 37, and Reynolds Gull Road. Turn left into Evergreen Cemetery and drive to the back (E). (N42 39.768 W77 34.707)

Alternative Parking: None
Best Viewing Locations: From trail
Waterfall Height: A 15-foot waterfall
Best Season to Visit: Spring or after rain

Access:	Hike
Hiking Time:	3nd trip
Trail Length:	0.25 mile round trip
Difficulty:	2 boots
Trail Surface:	Mowed grass and woods paths
Trail Markings:	None
Uses:	Hike
Dogs:	OK
Admission:	Free
Contact:	Evergreen Cemetery Association (also known as Covered Bridge Cemetery) Springwater Town Hall 8022 S. Main Street, Springwater, NY 14560 (585) 669-2545

Reynolds Gully is also know as Reynolds Gull as evidenced by the name of the road that parallels part of this gully: Reynolds Gull Road. Much of the land along Reynolds Gully is private and off bounds. Besides access #1 off Route 15A, you can access the gully and a small waterfall via Evergreen Cemetery off Canadice Lake Road.

Another access is via a gated old logging road along the south side of Reynolds Gull Road. This property is now owned by The Nature Conservancy. You can follow this unmaintained trail into the gully for approximately 0.5 mile, but you won't find any major waterfalls. If you venture onto The Nature Conservancy land, keep in mind that camping, fires, fishing, and swimming are prohibited.

Trail Directions:

- Follow the mowed trail at the back, left corner (NE) of the cemetery.
- In 50 yards, bear left and follow the graded path gently into the gully. (You can take the right fork for a 0.5-mile hike, but no waterfalls. It turns into a rougher trail, passes an old cabin and follows the upper rim of the gully. This trail ends at the back of Tamarack Campground.)
- Part way down you'll pass a 10 to 15 foot waterfall.
- Return back up the trail. (If you continue downhill, you'll find a 3-foot drop into the gully)

Date visited:

Notes:

26.
The Ledges of Honeoye Creek

Location:	North Bloomfield, Livingston County
Waterway:	Honeoye Creek
Directions:	From Honeoye Falls, take Route 65 (East Street then Ontario Street) south for 1 mile. Turn right (W) on Martin Road. Park along the road before the bridge. (N42 56.314 W77 34.514)

Alternative Parking: For second set of falls, continue west on Martin Road. Turn right on Ideson Road and park along the road before Route 65. (N42 56.477 W77 34.694) Walk around the corner to the Route 65 bridge.

Best Viewing Locations: From Martin Road bridge and the Route 65 bridge

Waterfall Height: A series of 2-foot drops (5 ledges visible from Martin Road and 6 ledges visible from Route 65)

Best Season to Visit: Spring has largest water flow, but ledges are visible year-round

Access:	Short walk or roadside
Difficulty:	1 boot
Uses:	View only
Dogs:	OK
Admission:	Free

Honeoye Creek drops down a series of small ledges on its northward journey to Honeoye Falls. These pretty little falls are easily viewable from the bridges that span the creek. At the Martin Road ledges, the creek drops 15 to 20 feet in 1,000 feet. At the Route 65 ledges the creek drops another 15 to 20 feet over 500 feet.

Directions:
- From Honeoye Falls, head south on Route 65 (East Street then Ontario Street).
- After crossing Honeoye Creek three times, turn right onto Martin Road.
- Park along the road before the bridge and walk to the bridge to see the 5 small drops south of the bridge.
- Continue west on Martin Road in your car. Take the first right onto Ideson Road.
- Park along the road before it meets Route 65.

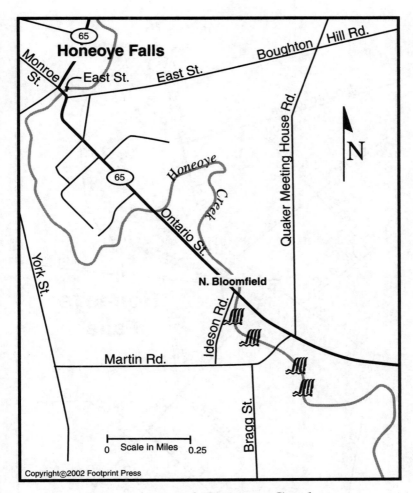

The Ledges of Honeoye Creek

• Walk around the corner to the right where Route 65 crosses Honeoye Creek to view 6 small drops upstream.

Date visited:

Notes:

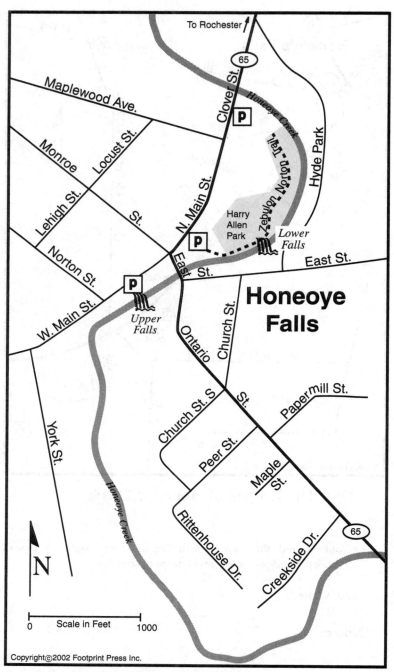

Honeoye Falls

27.

Honeoye Falls

Location: Honeoye Falls, Monroe County
Waterway: Honeoye Creek

Two falls can be found in the village of Honeoye Falls. Honeoye (pronounced honey-oy) is an Iroquois word for "finger-lying." It relates to an incident where an Indian was bitten by a snake and cut his finger off to save his life. In the 17th century this was the site of a Seneca Indian village known as Totiakton. The village of Honeoye Falls grew as a thriving mill district beginning in 1791.

Upper Falls

Directions: The upper falls can be seen from the East Street bridge (Route 65) in the center of Honeoye Falls (N42 57.157 W77 35.447)

Alternative Parking: The Mendon Town Hall parking lot at 16 W. Main Street, Honeoye Falls (N42 57.125 W77 35.516)

Best Viewing Locations: Both locations offer splendid views

Waterfall Height: Estimated at 30-feet high

Best Season to Visit: Year-round; although it dries to a trickle in summer

Access: Roadside

Difficulty: 1 boot

Uses: View only

Dogs: OK on leash

Admission: Free

Contact: Village of Honeoye Falls
5 East Street, Honeoye Falls, NY 14472
(585) 624-1711

Zebulon Norton built the first grist and sawmill on each bank at the upper falls, called "Norton's Mills" in 1791. It was destroyed by fire in 1824. From 1827 to 1837 Henry Culver operated a gristmill. In 1951 the Beam Milling Company ground buckwheat flour. From 1972 through 1983 the building was used for a restaurant called "The Mill." In 1985 this cut limestone building became the Mendon Town Hall.

There is a viewing platform at the southwest corner of the town hall building, near the parking area. From it, you look at the crest of the falls. Across Honeoye Creek sits a red building on a stone foundation right at water's edge. This was the "red sawmill" which burned in the great fire of 1885. The building you see was built to replace it and is currently a private residence. Upstream, to the right you can see a concrete abutment in the creek. This is all that remains of an old rail line. A train first steamed across a covered bridge at this location in 1853. The bridge was replaced with an iron structure in 1893.

The caprock of the upper falls is Onondaga limestone. Onondaga limestone was used as a building stone in structures such as the Mendon Town Hall building, the NY Central Railroad viaduct along Central Avenue in Rochester, and the Court Street bridge in Rochester.

Lower Falls

Directions: For the lower falls, park at Harry Allen Park on N. Main Street (Route 65). Look for the white gazebo. (N42 57.145 W77 35.479)

Alternative Parking: None
Best Viewing Locations: From the Zebulon Norton Trail
Waterfall Height: Estimated at 6-feet high
Best Season to Visit: Year-round; although it dries to a trickle in summer

Access: Short walk
Hiking Time: 15 minutes round trip
Trail Length: 0.5 mile round trip
Difficulty: 2 boots
Trail Surface: Dirt trail
Trail Markings: None
Uses: Hike, Snowshoe, Picnic, Basketball
Dogs: OK on leash
Admission: Free
Contact: Village of Honeoye Falls
5 East Street, Honeoye Falls, NY 14472
(585) 624-1711

Named for the founder of Honeoye Falls' first mill, the Zebulon Norton Trail is a short stroll through woods along the edge of Honeoye Creek.

Trail Directions:
- From the Harry Allen Park parking area, bear left passing the basketball court.
- Head toward the wooden "Zebulon Norton Trail" sign
- Follow the dirt trail parallel to Honeoye Creek. You'll pass the falls and end near the Lower Mill building.

Date visited:

Notes:

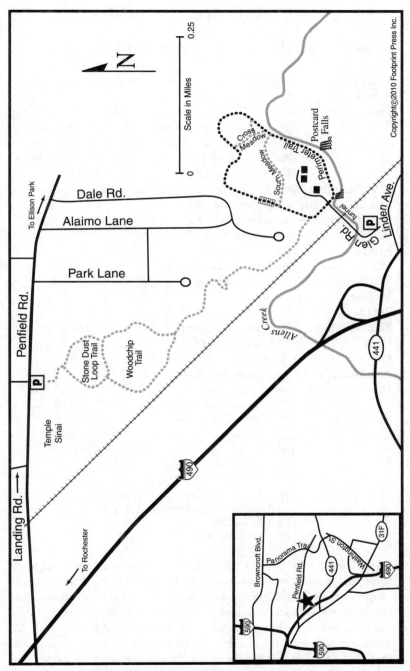

Corbett's Glen - Postcard Falls

121

28.

Corbett's Glen / Postcard Falls

Location: Brighton, Monroe County
Waterway: Allens Creek
Directions: From I-490 exit to Route 441 heading east. At the first light turn left on Linden Avenue then turn immediately left on Glen Road. Look for the green and gold signs on the left and right "Park Here to Curve for Corbett's Glen Nature Park." (N43 7.724 W77 31.314)

Alternative Parking: A parking area along Penfield Road
Best Viewing Locations: From the trail
Waterfall Height: Estimated at 6 and 8-feet high
Best Season to Visit: Year-round

Access: Hike
Hiking Time: 15 minutes round trip
Trail Length: 0.3 mile round trip
Difficulty: 2 boots
Trail Surface: Paved road, gravel and dirt trails
Trail Markings: Green and gold signs and blue and white signs
Uses: Hike, Snowshoe, Picnic
Dogs: OK on leash
Admission: Free. Park open 7 AM–10 PM
Contact: Town of Brighton
                   2300 Elmwood Avenue, Rochester, NY 14618
                   (585) 784-5250

                   Genesee Land Trust
                   10 Tobey Village Office Park, Pittsford, NY 14534
                   (585) 381-7310
                   www.geneseelandtrust.org

                   Allens Creek/Corbett's Glen Preservation Group
                   PO Box 25711, Rochester, NY 14625-0711
                   (585) 385-2293
                   www.corbettsglen.org

The Allens Creek valley is a natural oasis in the middle of a suburban landscape. It was saved from development by the efforts of many caring people and officially became a nature park in 1999. Native Americans had one of their major footpaths through this valley and a sacred burial ground was documented in the 1800s. European traders established ties with the Indians at nearby Indian Landing. With the coming of more Europeans, the valley was turned into farmland and mills were built to harness the power of Allens Creek.

The first wooden railroad trestle was built over Allens Creek in 1851 for the Rochester and Syracuse Railway. Pre Civil War, a powder mill, owned by John Tyron, operated in the glen to produce blasting powder. In 1889 Patrick Corbett bought the land that today is called Corbett's Glen. He built a large farm and irrigated his crops with water from Allens Creek using a unique system. For decades he operated the glen as a privately-run picnic ground. He built dancing pavilions, picnic tables, baseball diamonds, and beer halls.

The Waterfall in Allens Creek Near the Railroad Tunnel.

In 1956, part of the glen was purchased by Howard Meath who operated Camp Hideaway for children. He staged small concerts in the 1970s. Between the 1930s and 1970s the area was a target of vandalism and Allens Creek became polluted from a nearby waste disposal plant, creating an environmental disaster. It wasn't until the 1980s that a Pure Waters Project helped clean up the land and water.

In the 1990s we came very close to losing Corbett's Glen to make way for industrial parks and expensive housing. The Meath and Corbett families were looking to sell their land and developers salivated. But residents of the area banded together to form the Allens Creek/Corbett's Glen Preservation Group and eventually the Town of Brighton and Genesee Land Trust joined forces in the first ever public-private collaboration in the Greater Rochester area to acquire a 17.7 acre parcel of land in Corbett's Glen. That parcel has grown into a 52-acre park. Their work is far from done, so if you'd like to contribute funds or volunteer time, contact either the Genesee Land Trust or the Allens Creek/Corbett's Glen Preservation Group.

Corbett's Glen owes its existence to the glaciers that once covered this area. As the glacier melted it formed a large lake called Iroquois Lake. It was bigger than Lake Ontario is today. Streams drained into this lake and widened their valleys. As the land sprung back, released from the weight of the ice, the streams cut deeper causing a series of terraces. 20 or more of these terraces have been mapped in Corbett's Glen.

On your way into Corbett's Glen you'll walk through a railroad tunnel with Allens Creek bubbling beside you. This tunnel was built in 1882 to replace the original trestle. Limestone was quarried from bedrock at the edge of the glen. At the end of the tunnel is the first waterfall, a cascade over jagged dolomite outcroppings. A short walk on an easy trail takes you to the second waterfall, called Postcard Falls. Keep an eye out for wildlife. Foxes, owls, birds, mink, opossum, turkey, and deer are all prevalent. Beyond the waterfall you can continue on several loop trails within the park: Perimeter Trail Loop: 0.65 mile
Glen Road to the Penfield Road Parking Area: 0.75 mile
Stone Dust Trail Loop: 0.35 mile

Trail Directions
- Walk downhill on Glen Road and continue through the tunnel.
- You'll find the first waterfall at the far end of the tunnel. It's a jagged edged, 6-foot cascade.
- Follow the signs, straight on the gravel road, then bear right just before the Corbett house.
- Pass blue & white signs saying "To Corbett's Glen Nature Park."
- At 0.4 mile you'll reach a wide grassy area. Follow your ears to the right to find an 8-foot high jagged, multi-level cascade filling the full width of Allens Creek.
- Reverse your route back to your car, or continue walking and enjoy the loop trails within this park.

Date visited:

Notes:

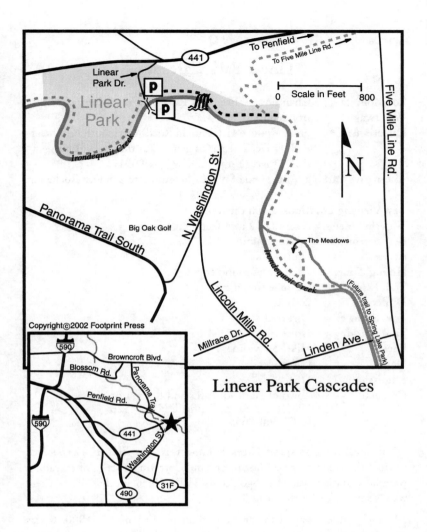

Linear Park Cascades

125

29.
Linear Park Cascades

Location:	Channing H. Philbrick Park, Penfield, Monroe County
Waterway:	Irondequoit Creek
Directions:	From Route 441 (Penfield Road) turn south on Linear Park Drive. The parking area is at the end of Linear Park Drive. (N43 7.638 W77 29.091)
Alternative Parking:	At the end of N. Washington Street in East Rochester (N43 7.624 W77 29.038)
Best Viewing Locations:	From the trail
Waterfall Height:	A series of 2 to 3-feet high cascades
Best Season to Visit:	Year-round
Access:	Short walk
Hiking Time:	25 minutes round trip
Trail Length:	0.6 mile round trip
Difficulty:	2 boots
Trail Surface:	Dirt trail
Trail Markings:	None
Uses:	Hike, Snowshoe
Dogs:	OK on leash
Admission:	Free
Contact:	Town of Penfield, Parks and Recreation 1985 Baird Road, Penfield, NY 14526 (585) 340-8655

This area of Irondequoit Creek is known as *The Falls* or *The Hollow* because the creek drops 90 feet in one mile, creating a series of cascading waterfalls. Indians called it Sgoh-Sa-Is-Thah which means "place where waters smash against the rocks."

Daniel Penfield settled the area and built the first mill in 1800. It was soon followed by many mills. If you look closely along the creek banks, you'll see some raceway foundations that still remain. The years 1800 through 1840 were a time of rapid settlement and growth, encouraged by Mr. Penfield's policy of accepting wheat and other farm products for his mills in lieu of mortgage payments, until a farmer had enough time to become established.

The businesses built along this section of Irondequoit Creek included flour mills, sawmills, an ashery, an oil mill and soap factory, distilleries, wool and clothing mills, grist mills, a tannery, a blacksmith shop, and a slaughter house. Produce from the mills was shipped via Tryon (a village that was near the intersection of N. Landing Road and Blossom Road, now part of Brighton) to Charlotte, then transported across Lake Ontario to Canada. When the Erie Canal was built, produce was hauled to the ports at Fairport and Pittsford for shipment to markets in the east.

To see the waterfalls you only need to hike a 0.3 mile section of the trails within Channing Philbrick Park. (This park used to be called Linear Park.)

Trail Directions
- From the parking area, head toward the creek to the pedestrian bridge. Waterfalls are visible from this bridge and from the observation platform on the south shore.
- Return to the parking area and head toward the red "Trail" sign. Walk upstream on the wide dirt path, keeping Irondequoit Creek to your right. Periodically check the overlooks on the right to see waterfalls.
- The waterfalls are mainly in the first 0.3 mile section of the trail so when you reach the first of four wooden bridges that span small ravines, turn around and head back.

Date visited:

Notes:

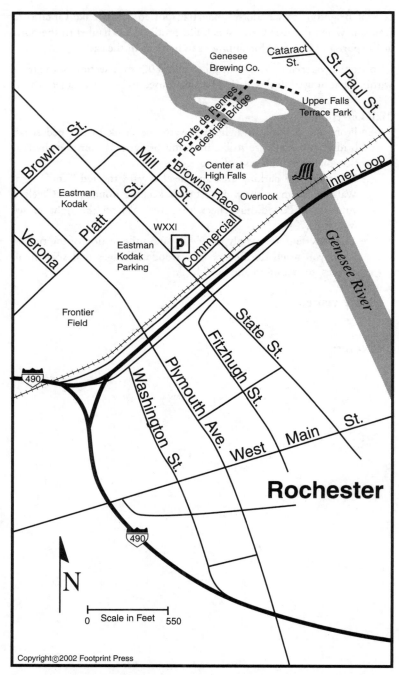

Genesee
Brewing Co.

Cataract
St.

St. Paul St.

Upper Falls
Terrace Park

Ponte de Rennes
Pedestrian Bridge

Brown St.

Mill St.

Browns Race

Center at
High Falls

Inner Loop

Eastman
Kodak

Platt St.

WXXI

P

Commercial

Overlook

Genesee River

Verona

Eastman
Kodak
Parking

Frontier
Field

State St.

Fitzhugh St.

490

Plymouth Ave.

Washington St.

West Main St.

Rochester

490

N

0   Scale in Feet   550

High Falls of the Genesee River

30.
High Falls of the Genesee River

Location: Rochester, Monroe County

Waterway: Genesee River

Directions: From I-490, exit north onto the Inner Loop. Exit at State Street and turn northwest, away from downtown. Park in the High Falls Garage (a bright blue super-structure) next to WXXI and across from a Kodak parking lot. (N43 9.503 W77 37.007)

Alternative Parking: Meters along the streets in the High Falls area

Best Viewing Locations: From Ponte de Rennes pedestrian bridge

Waterfall Height: 96-feet high

Best Season to Visit: Year-round

Access: Hike, wheelchair

Hiking Time: 30 minutes round trip

Trail Length: 0.8 mile round trip

Difficulty: 1 boot

Trail Surface: Sidewalks and paved bridge

Trail Markings: None

Uses: Hike

Dogs: OK on leash

Admission: Free (there is a fee for the parking garage)

Contact: City of Rochester, Parks & Recreation
City Hall, 30 Church Street, Rochester, NY 14614
(585) 428-7538

Currently called High Falls, this waterfall has also been referred to as Main Falls. Today the area surrounding this waterfall is the Brown's Race Historic District with bars, nightclubs, restaurants, shops, and a museum in a historic waterworks building. It also features Brown's Race Street with a replicated water raceway and the triphammer archeological site which reveals a restored waterwheel. In summer a laser light show is projected onto the cliff walls next to the waterfall. The show runs May through December, approximately one hour after sunset. Call (585) 292-8280 for current information.

High Falls is a 96-foot free-falling waterfall into a deep gorge. The rock it cuts through is Dolomitic Limestone (a rock containing considerable quantities of the magnesium-calcium carbonate mineral known as dolomite), part of the Lockport Formation. Below this lies the Williamson Shale Formation (7-feet thick), the Irondequoit Limestone Formation (22-feet thick) and the Rochester Shale Formation (95-feet thick).

High Falls is partially responsible for the existence of Rochester. Mills along the Genesee River made the area the largest wheat flour producing city in the world for a brief period in the 19th century, and earned it the nickname "Flour City." This was changed to "Flower City" years later as milling declined and the nursery and seed industries grew.

The first mill was built here in 1789 by Ebenezer "Indian" Allen to grind grain for the Indians. The waterfall produced the power needed to turn the millstone. Eventually 21 gristmills were built at the falls on the Genesee River in the Rochester area.

High Falls gained notoriety in 1829 when Sam Patch made his first leap off the upper ledge. Then he built a 25-foot tower over the falls and attempted a second dive. First he pushed his pet bear over the brink. This time Sam Patch (and his bear) drowned. He's buried in the old Charlotte cemetery.

The Genesee River is 163 miles long and is the only major stream that completely crosses New York state. It was named "Ge-ne-see" by the Seneca Indians, meaning pleasant banks. The river is born in a pasture spring in Potter County, Pennsylvania near the town of Gold. The trickle starts on the 2,500-foot high Allegany Plateau and reaches Lake Ontario at an elevation of 246 feet above sea level.

It is also the only major river that maintains its preglacial northward flow (although the outlet did shift from Irondequoit Bay to the Charlotte area). At Rochester, the glacially flooded Genesee River found its way blocked and had to cut through alternately hard and soft rock layers of Lower Silurian strata to form a canyon with 6 waterfalls. Three remain today: High Falls, Middle Falls and Lower Falls. The southernmost three falls (previously called Upper Falls) which were drops of 3 feet, 4 feet, and 7 feet respectively, were tamed by a dam and flood control gates near Court Street.

Trail Directions
- From the parking garage, head northwest on Mill Street.
- Turn right (NE) on Platt Street.
- Continue straight as the street becomes the Ponte de Rennes pedestrian bridge. (Rennes is Rochester's sister city in France.)
- Look upstream from the bridge to the High Falls.
- You can continue to the end of the bridge and turn right along a paved path in Upper Falls Terrace Park to get additional views of the falls if you wish.

Overlook Directions
- For another vantage point, visit the newly developed High Falls overlook at the end of Commercial Street.

Date visited:

Notes:

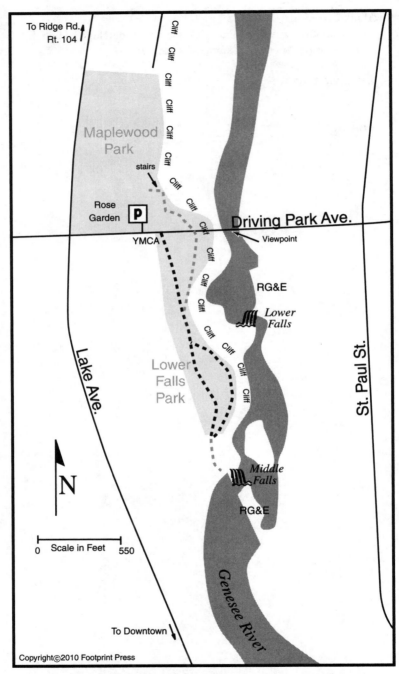

Lower & Middle Falls of the Genesee River

31.
Lower and Middle Falls of the Genesee River

Location: Rochester, Monroe County
Waterway: Genesee River
Directions: From Lake Avenue, turn east on Driving Park Boulevard. Park in the Maplewood Park parking area. (N43 10.910 W77 37.812)
Alternative Parking: None
Best Viewing Locations: From the trails in Lower Falls Park
Waterfall Height: Lower Falls: 78-feet high
Middle Falls: 20-feet high
Best Season to Visit: Year-round
Access: Hike, wheelchair
Hiking Time: 30 minutes round trip
Trail Length: 0.8 mile round trip
Difficulty: 2 boots
Trail Surface: Gravel and paved trails
Trail Markings: None
Uses: Hike
Dogs: OK on leash
Admission: Free
Contact: City of Rochester, Parks & Recreation
City Hall, 30 Church Street, Rochester, NY 14614
(585) 428-7538

Of the two waterfalls, Lower Falls is definitely the most spectacular with its 78-foot vertical plunge. Middle Falls is smaller and is dammed to provide water via a tunnel to the RG&E Substation #5 generators at the base of Lower Falls. Until 2001, Middle Falls was inaccessible. Now a path in Lower Falls Park leads to a viewing area below the dam and passes the crest of Lower Falls, providing easy viewing of both waterfalls. Lower Falls Park also features a sculpture by local artist Adriana Slutzky. It uses casts of the hands and faces of over 600 children and adults to celebrate the diversity of our community. A good view of Lower Falls can be had from the sidewalk of the Driving Park bridge.

Looking across the river gorge at the base of Lower Falls, you'll see RG&E Substation #5. To the left of this is a cliff bank that showcases the layers of rock in the gorge. They're all sedimentary rocks (shales and sandstones), set down in a shallow sea over 485 million years ago. At water level is the red Queenston Formation shale (45-50-feet thick). Above this is the Grimsby Formation sandstone (50-55-feet thick) followed by a thin layer

Lower Falls of the Genesee River

of Kodak Formation sandstone (3-5-feet thick). Because of its resistance to erosion, this forms the caprock of the Lower Falls. The caprock of the Middle Falls is Wallington Limestone.

In the fall Chinook Salmon gather at the base of Lower Falls so you're likely to see many fishermen in the gorge below the falls. Indians fished in this area for hundreds of years before white men appeared. In 1820 three McCracken brothers established McCrackenville at the Lower/Middle Falls area by building a sawmill and paper mill. Over the years, the manufacturing businesses built here included a furniture factory, a carpet mill, a trunk factory, and a flour mill, all deriving power from the river. Many of these factories moved away when hydroelectric power was established and decreased their need to be located near the river.

Below McCrackenville, on the west bank of the Genesee River a landing was built in the 1800s called Kelsey's Landing. Steamboat passengers regularly boarded here for passage to Canada and Detroit. It was also a major jumping off point for slaves escaping to freedom in Canada via the Underground Railroad.

In the 1800s there were several villages along the Genesee River in what is now the Rochester Area. These included Charlotte, Carthage, McCrackenville, Rochesterville, and Castletown. Each had mills and competed for the Canadian milling business. Rochesterville was the only one with a bridge over the Genesee gorge. So, in 1819 Elijah Strong built a wooden bridge over the gorge between Carthage and McCrackenville. At the time it was the largest bridge in the world and came with a one-year guarantee. It collapsed after 15 months and devastated Carthage and McCrackenville. In 1856 a suspension bridge was built. But, it closed after only one month because it swayed in the wind. After seven months, it collapsed under the weight of snow. A metal grating bridge was built in 1891. This lasted until 1986 when it was torn down and replaced with the current Driving Park Bridge.

If you visit in summer, be sure to leave time to enjoy the roses in Maplewood Park. This park, along with Seneca and Genesee Valley Parks, were the original Rochester parks designed by Frederick Law Olmsted. Maplewood Park has been used as a showcase for roses since 1916. Today the garden contains over 5,000 roses of 300 varieties. Many are rare, old garden varieties and most are labeled.

Trail Directions
- From the Maplewood Park parking area you have two choices:
  1. Follow the trail down 59 steps on a path that leads under Driving Park Bridge.
  2. Cross Driving Park Boulevard and take a sloped, paved path down to the falls. (This is the handicapped accessible route.)

Option 1 - Trail with Steps
- From the parking area head northeast to find the start of the trail at a break in the fence line.
- Follow the paved trail down 2 flights of steps.
- Pass under Driving Park Bridge.
- Pass Lower Falls.
- At a "T," turn left into Lower Falls Park. (Right leads to Driving Park Boulevard.)
- At the next junction, turn left to visit the crest of Lower Falls.
- Continue along the trail, enjoying 2 more views of this magnificent waterfall.
- At 0.3 mile you'll reach a view of the base of Middle Falls. Lean in toward the edge of the water (but stay behind the fence) to see a stone arch from an old sluiceway that used to carry water to RG&E.
- Continue on the paved trail as it bends sharply right. (A short gravel path to the left leads through gates, uphill for <0.1 mile to the top of the dam over Middle Falls. It does not offer a view of Middle Falls.)
- Continue straight on the paved path, uphill to Driving Park Boulevard.
- Cross Driving Park Boulevard to reach the Maplewood Park parking area.

Middle Falls of the Genesee River

Option 2 - Sloped Trail (handicapped accessible)
- From the parking area head south and cross Driving Park Boulevard.
- Bear left to find the paved trail between the YMCA and Driving Park Bridge.
- Head downhill on the paved path into Lower Falls Park.
- Continue straight, passing a trail to the left.
- At the next junction, turn left to visit the crest of Lower Falls.
- Continue along the trail, enjoying 2 more views of this magnificent waterfall.
- At 0.3 mile you'll reach a view of the base of Middle Falls. Lean in toward the edge of the water (but stay behind the fence) to see a stone arch from an old sluiceway that used to carry water to RG&E.
- Continue on the paved trail as it bends sharply right. (A short gravel path to the left leads through gates, uphill for <0.1 mile to the top of the dam over Middle Falls. It does not offer a view of Middle Falls.)
- Continue straight on the paved path, uphill to Driving Park Boulevard.
- Cross Driving Park Boulevard to reach the Maplewood Park parking area.

Date visited:

Notes:

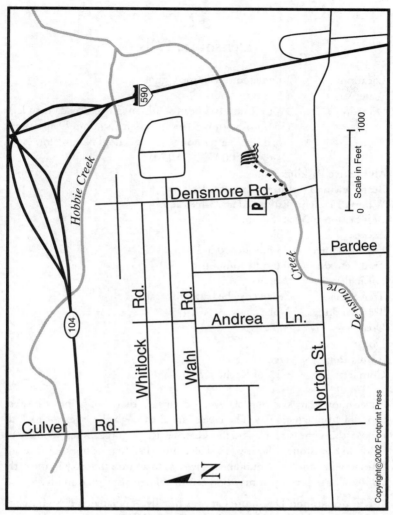

Densmore Falls

137

32.

Densmore Falls

Location:	Irondequoit, Monroe County
Waterway:	Densmore Creek
Directions:	From Route 104 head south on Culver Road. Turn left (E) onto Norton Street, then left (N) onto Densmore Road. Park, after hours, in the school parking lot. (N43 11.400 W77 33.124)

Alternative Parking: None
Best Viewing Locations: From the trail
Waterfall Height: Estimated at 25-feet high
Best Season to Visit: Summer

Access:	Hike
Hiking Time:	25 minutes round trip
Trail Length:	0.6 mile round trip
Difficulty:	2 boots
Trail Surface:	Stone creekbed and dirt trail
Trail Markings:	None
Uses:	Hike
Dogs:	OK
Admission:	Free
Contact:	City of Rochester

Densmore Creek is one of several drainages that dump into the west shore of Irondequoit Bay. The creek carved through the layers of rock to expose the same strata as in the Genesee River gorge. These consist of Thorold sandstone, Maplewood shale, and Medina sandstone. A layer of Furnaceville limestone found here gave rise to an iron industry in the early 1900s. The red rock you may find is mineral hematite, an iron ore.

The area around Densmore Creek is heavily populated and we humans have not been kind to this creekbed and waterfall. Trash is abundant along the banks and in the pool below the waterfall. Still, it's hard to spoil the beauty of any waterfall. Densmore Falls begins with a series of ledges with drops of 10 feet and flat sections between. Then the water rushes over a gradual cascade down the layers of shale for 15 feet.

There is a trail from Densmore Road to the waterfall, but it crosses private property. To stay on public property you need to do a very short creek-walk from the bridge. In summer you can do this creekwalk and keep your boots dry. Then it's an easy walk on a dirt trail to reach the waterfall.

Trail Directions:
- From the parking area, head back down (S) Densmore Road for 0.1 mile to the creek crossing.
- Take the small trail on the north side of the bridge down into the creek.
- Head downstream.
- Shortly, climb to a trail on the left bank. (This trail does wind up to Densmore Road but it crosses private property).
- Bear right to stay along the creek.
- Reach the falls in 0.3 mile.

Date visited:

Notes:

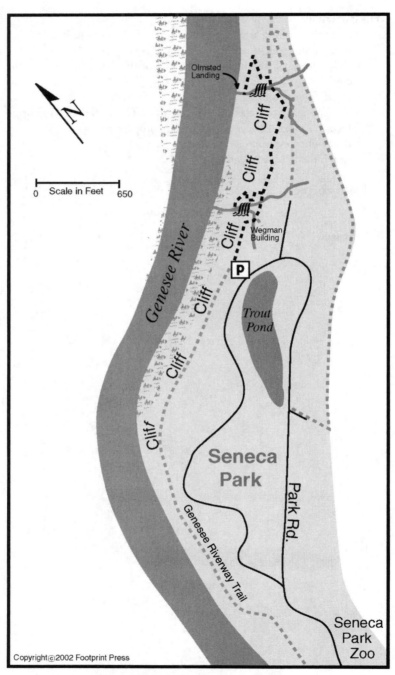

Zoo Cascade & Zoo Falls

33.
Zoo Cascade and Zoo Falls

Location:	Seneca Park, Rochester, Monroe County
Waterway:	Tributaries to Genesee River
Directions:	From Route 104, exit north onto St. Paul Boulevard. Turn left (W) onto Park Road toward Seneca Park Zoo. Pass the zoo and head downhill on Park Road. Round Trout Pond and park along the road at the northern edge of the pond. (N43 12.761 W77 37.235)

Alternative Parking: Near Wegman Building
Best Viewing Locations: From the Olmsted/Seneca Trail
Waterfall Height: Two 15-feet high waterfalls
Best Season to Visit: Year-round

Access:	Hike
Hiking Time:	1 hour round trip
Trail Length:	1.7 mile round trip
Difficulty:	4 boots
Trail Surface:	Woodchip and dirt trails with stairs
Trail Markings:	None (blazing planned in 2002)
Uses:	Hike, Picnic
Dogs:	OK on leash
Admission:	Free
Contact:	Monroe County Parks Department 171 Reservoir Avenue, Rochester, NY 14620 (585) 256-4950

The 297-acre Seneca Park was designed by Frederick Law Olmsted who is considered to be the founder of American landscape architecture. He was prolific in the Rochester area where he designed four major parks: Seneca, Genesee Valley, Highland, and Maplewood.

Olmsted's designs were revolutionary for the late 1800s. Instead of laying out precise squares and gardens, he planned clumps of woods, meandering trails, bridle paths and spectacular views. He planted trees carefully to effect a "forested" look. This natural, quiet look was half of Olmsted's design philosophy. The other half created spaces for more active use, such as the open areas for ball fields and ponds for swimming in summer and ice skating in winter. Pavilions and bridges were designed in a neo-classic style to separate activity areas.

"A park should be accessible to the poor as well as the rich. It should be the beauty of the fields, the meadows, the prairies of green pastures, and the still waters. What we want to gain is tranquility and rest to the mind."

Frederick Law Olmsted

In its days of grandeur, swan boats plied back and forth taking passengers for a ride on Trout Pond. The boats carried 15 to 20 passengers on bench seats while the driver sat on a cast iron seat between two 4-foot high swans and peddled the pontoon boat. Today a paved path and picnic tables encircle the lake. The park is also home to the Seneca Park Zoo.

The Genesee Riverway Trail runs parallel to the steep Genesee River gorge. The trail is well defined and up to 8-feet wide at times. Along the trail are dock access trails leading to the river's edge. Hiking down reveals the 400 million years of geologic history in the gorge walls. You'll hike to some of these on your way to Zoo Cascade and Zoo Falls.

We visited Zoo Cascade in July and were less than impressed. With little water flow the water basically dribbled through debris in a steep channel. I'm sure this waterfall is much prettier with more water. However, Zoo Falls was quite pretty. It begins as an overhung caprock with a 4-foot free-fall. Next comes a 10-foot cascade to a second caprock which produces a 2-foot free-fall. The water runs out at the base through rubble rock until it flows into the Genesee River.

Trail Directions
- From the parking area near Trout Pond head toward the gorge (and a chain link fence) and turn right onto the Genesee Riverway Trail.
- Pass a bench then quickly pass a rest area to the left with tables and benches.
- Bear right to cross a small stream then immediately bear left.
- At 0.3 mile, after the second boardwalk bridge, turn left and head down 77 steps.
- At the base of the stairs turn left and cross a muddy stretch to reach Zoo Cascade. (Straight leads to the Genesee River edge via a boardwalk through cattails.)
- Climb back up the stairs and turn left to continue along the Genesee Riverway Trail.
- Pass a bench.
- At 1.4 miles cross a boardwalk bridge over a creek. (The crest of Zoo Falls is to your left.)
- Continue straight on the Genesee Riverway Trail.
- At the "Y" bear left toward a split rail fence and head downhill.
- Turn left and continue down 46 steps.

- Pass steps to a dock on the right. Continue straight, parallel to the river.
- Reach the base of Zoo Falls at 1.1 miles.
- Head back up the stairs and turn right on the Olmsted/Seneca Trail to return to your car.

Date visited:

Notes:

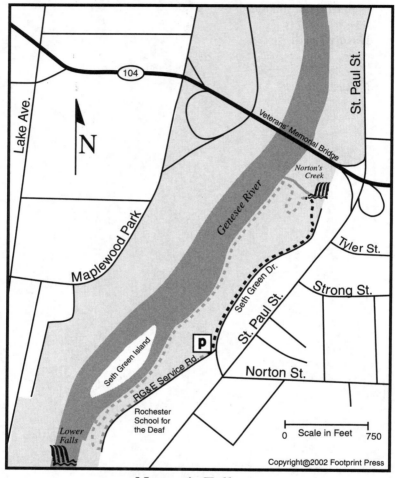

Norton's Falls

34.
Norton's Falls

Location:	Rochester, Monroe County
Waterway:	Norton's Creek
Directions:	From Route 104 head south on South Clinton (the zoo exit). Turn right (W) onto Norton Street. Continue straight as it turns into Seth Green Drive. Take the first left to find the parking area. (N43 11.239 W77 37.395)

Alternative Parking: None
Best Viewing Locations: From the Seth Green Trail
Waterfall Height: Estimated at 45-feet high
Best Season to Visit: Year-round

Access:	Short walk
Hiking Time:	25 minutes round trip
Trail Length:	0.6 mile round trip
Difficulty:	3 boots
Trail Surface:	Paved road and dirt trail
Trail Markings:	Wooden sign at trailhead
Uses:	Hike
Dogs:	OK on leash
Admission:	Free
Contact:	Monroe County Parks Department 171 Reservoir Avenue, Rochester, NY 14620 (585) 256-4950

To reach Norton's Falls, you'll walk a historic trail used by Native Americans for thousands of years. The trail terminates at the river's edge at a spot called Brewer's Landing where people portaged across the river. You only need to descend half way into the Genesee River gorge to see Norton's Falls. In the early 1800s this area was home to the village of Carthage. It thrived as a steamboat landing and active mill site but was absorbed into Rochester upon its incorporation in 1834. Today it's part of Seneca Park.

Norton's Falls has a very thick caprock which launches water on it's free-fall for the first 15 feet. Then the water cascades for 20 feet over sloped shale to a narrow trench. Exiting the trench, it finishes its fall toward the Genesee River with a 10-foot gradual cascade.

So, who was Norton? Well, we don't know, but we can tell you the history of Seth Green. Adonijah Green ran a tavern at the corner of St. Paul and Norton Streets. His son Seth, born in 1817, spent many hours as a boy fishing, hunting, and trapping along the river. He observed the habits of fish. After running a successful fish and chowder business, he started the Caledonia Fish Hatchery. Seth Green received national and international fame as a fish grower and conservationist. The salmon stocked in the Genesee River today comes from the Caledonia Fish Hatchery.

You can also follow the RG&E service road southwest from the parking area to the base of the Lower Falls.

Trail Directions
- From the parking area, walk northeast along Seth Green Drive.
- In 0.2 mile, find a sign on the left that reads "This historic trail was used by Native Americans for thousands of years. Pioneer settlers expanded the trail and founded Carthage here in 1817." Turn left (W) and head downhill on the dirt trail.
- Follow the trail downhill.
- Reach Norton's Falls at 0.3 mile.

Date visited:

Notes:

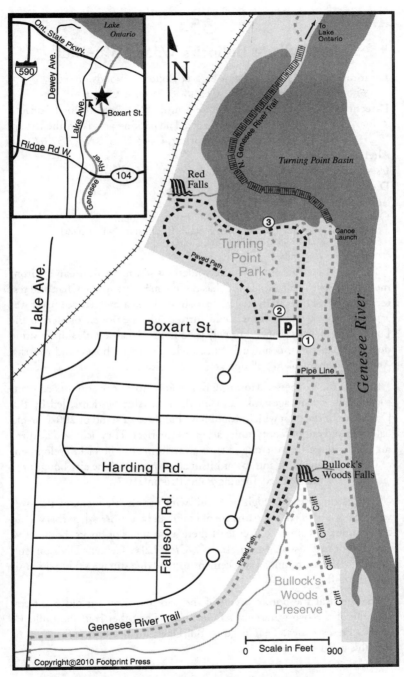

Red Falls & Bullock's Woods Falls

35.
Red Falls & Bullock's Woods Waterfall

Location:	Turning Point Park & Bullock's Woods Preserve, Boxart Street, Charlotte, Monroe County
Directions:	From Lake Avenue (south of Stonewood Road), turn east on Boxart Street. The parking area is on the left, at the end of Boxart Street. (N43 13.658 W77 37.077)

Alternative parking: None

Uses:	Hike, Bike, Snowshoe
Dogs:	OK on leash
Admission:	Free
Contact:	Monroe County Parks Department 171 Reservoir Avenue, Rochester, NY 14620 (585) 256-4950

Turning Point Park is a 112-acre wilderness setting in an urban environment. The term "Turning Point" has double meaning to the Charlotte residents nearby. Historically, the wide basin in the nearby Genesee River was a physical place where ships could turn around before encountering the Lower Falls. This was once a heavily used industrial area with ships visiting docks to load and unload coal, wheat, feldspar, paper boxes, and tourists. An active cement plant still operates on this site.

In 1972 the Rochester-Monroe County Port Authority announced plans to build an oil storage tank farm on the site. Area residents, led by Bill Davis fought the plan which would have bulldozed a stand of 200-year-old oak trees and cut off community access to the river. They achieved a "turning point" in getting the city to turn away from commercial development of the river waterfront and toward its recreational use. The city bought the land in 1976 and opened Turning Point Park in 1977.

The parking area sits high on a cliff with panoramic views of the river valley below. Some of the paths are old railroad beds from when this was an active industrial area. At river level there are a series of docks, both active and abandoned. Essroc Materials, Inc., Great Lakes Cement Division still uses these docks to unload dry cement to the large storage tanks which sit atop the cliff.

The forest at the northern end of the park has 200-year-old oak trees, and one of the two waterfalls is found here. The other is in the Bullock's Woods Preserve area. Thanks go to Bill Davis for having the foresight to save this urban treasure.

Red Falls

Waterway: Unnamed
Best Viewing Locations: From the trail at the north end of the park
Waterfall Height: Estimated at 60-feet high
Best Season to Visit: Year-round
Access: Short walk, wheelchair accessible if you go out and return on the paved path
Hiking Time: 25 minute loop
Trail Length: 0.7 mile loop
Difficulty: 1 boot
Trail Surface: Paved and dirt trails
Trail Markings: Brown posts with numbers and destinations in red

This waterfall is a gradual cascade with three major steps. It's roughly 60-feet long and 10-feet wide. Many small trails have been cut through the woods leading to this waterfall but stay on the wide dirt or paved trails.

Trail Directions
- Head out the northwest corner of the parking area, past post #2 (to Red Falls).
- Bear left at the first junction.
- Turn right onto the paved path.
- Stay on the paved path as it bends.
- At 0.3 mile, pass a paved path to the right. Bear left.
- In a very short distance the pavement ends. The waterfall is directly ahead. (You can turn right and climb down to the base of the falls but it's a very steep climb.)
- You can retrace your steps back (the handicapped accessible route) or continue on the loop described below.
- Head back on the paved path, but bear left at the first paved path junction.
- At 0.4 mile (total loop) the pavement ends. Continue straight.
- Pass a junction with post #3. Continue straight keeping the turning basin to your left.
- Continue straight past another junction.
- At 0.6 mile, reach a paved path and turn right, passing metal gates.
- Continue on this old road to the parking area.

Bullock's Woods Waterfall

Waterway: Unnamed
Best Viewing Locations: From an old railroad bed, looking into Bullock's Woods Preserve

Waterfall Height: Estimated at 33-feet high
Best Season to Visit: Year-round; best when leaves are off trees
Access: Hike
Hiking Time: 30 minute loop
Trail Length: 1.0 mile loop
Difficulty: 2 boots
Trail Surface: Paved and dirt trails
Trail Markings: Brown posts with numbers and destinations in red

This waterfall is hard to see through the leaves so your best view may be when leaves are off the trees. There used to be an observation platform jutting out from the hillside, but alas, it is gone. The best you can do is lean over from a cement footing that remains. The waterfall starts from a 3-foot fall then cascades down a gradual slope for 30 more feet. It's approximately 20-feet wide. You can get another view by hiking to the northernmost point on the trails inside Bullock's Woods Preserve.

Trail Directions
- From the parking area, head south on the paved path past post #1 (to Bullock's Woods).
- Pass under the green Essroc cement pipes.
- Pass 6 small cutoff trails on the left.
- At the 7th junction (0.4 mile), turn left and head downhill on a gravel trail.
- At the 6th small trail on the right you'll see a cement platform which used to support a viewing platform. The waterfall is through the trees to the right.
- Return to the parking area via the same route or explore the other trails in Turning Point Park and Bullock's Woods Preserve.

Date visited:

Notes:

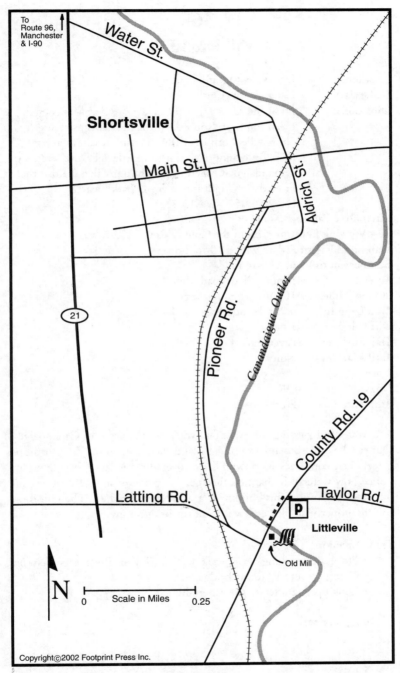

Mill Drop Falls

36.
Mill Drop Falls

Location:	Littleville, Ontario County
Waterway:	Canandaigua Outlet
Directions:	From the Thruway (I-90) take exit 43 at Manchester. Head south on Route 21 through Manchester and Shortsville. Turn left (E) on Latting Road, then left (NE) on County Route 19 to Littleville. After crossing Canandaigua Outlet, turn right onto Taylor Road then immediately right into a gravel parking area. (N42 56.657 W77 13.233)

Alternative Parking: None
Best Viewing Locations: From the County Route 19 bridge
Waterfall Height: A dam with a 10-foot drop
Best Season to Visit: Year-round

Access:	Short walk or roadside
Hiking Time:	10 minutes round trip
Trail Length:	0.2 mile round trip
Difficulty:	1 boot
Trail Surface:	Pavement
Trail Markings:	None
Uses:	View only
Dogs:	OK
Admission:	Free

As you stand viewing this waterfall, you'll see the water of Canandaigua Outlet take a sharp bend around an island then over an old dam. It drops 6 feet then continues its downhill run over three ledges. To your right, notice how water still channels through the remains of an old stone mill building. In front of this building is a wooden waterwheel. The mill is on private property, so please view it from the bridge only.

Trail Directions
- From the parking area, walk left on Taylor Road then left on County Route 19 to the bridge.
- Look upstream to see the waterfall.

Date visited:

Notes:

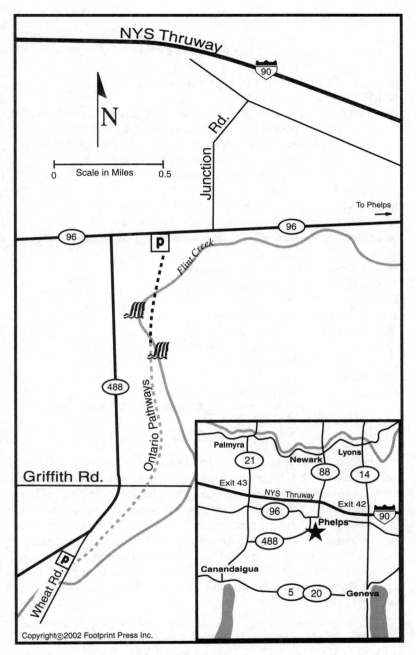

Double Drop

37.

Double Drop Falls

Location:	Ontario Pathways, Phelps, Ontario County
Waterway:	Flint Creek
Directions:	From the NYS Thruway (I-90) take exit 43 and head south on Route 21. Turn east on Route 96. Pass Route 488 then watch on the right for the Ontario Pathways parking area, just west of Phelps. (N42 57.705 W77 5.476)

Alternative Parking: None
Best Viewing Locations: From Ontario Pathways Trail
Waterfall Height: A series of ledges totalling 10 and 5-feet high
Best Season to Visit: Spring; although water flows year-round

Access:	Hike
Hiking Time:	45 minutes round trip
Trail Length:	1.2 miles round trip
Difficulty:	1 boot
Trail Surface:	Grass and dirt trail
Trail Markings:	Trailhead signs
Uses:	Hike, Bike, Ski, Snowshoe
Dogs:	OK on leash
Admission:	Free
Contact:	Ontario Pathways
	PO Box 996, Canandaigua, NY 14424
	(585) 394-7968
	www.ontariopathways.org

Ontario Pathways purchased the abandoned Sodus Point and Southern Railroad bed in 1994. Since then volunteers have worked tirelessly to clear the trail and build the beautiful bridges you're about to cross. This rail line began service in 1873 as the Sodus Point and Southern Railroad carrying coal from the Pennsylvania mines to the port at Sodus Bay. By 1911, five million tons of coal were transported each year. Passenger service ran until 1935. A steam engine last traveled these tracks in 1957 and the last coal shipment occurred in 1967. To read the full history and see pictures of the steam trains, stop at the kiosk in the Ontario Pathways parking area on Route 96.

White water kayakers named these waterfalls Double Drop. They're part of the Flint Creek run that these adventurers run in spring when the water is high (see web site www.americanwhitewater.org/rivers). Thanks to Ontario Pathways, you can stay dry and still visit these waterfalls.

Trail Directions

- From the parking area, head south on the grass trail.
- Cross the first bridge over Flint Creek.
- At 0.3 mile you'll reach a bench along the trail. The first set of waterfalls is in the creek to the right. It's a series of creek-wide ledges with a total drop of 10 feet.
- Return to the main trail and continue south.
- At 0.5 mile, pass old railroad bridge abutments the quickly reach the second bridge over Flint Creek.
- From this bridge you'll see the second set of creek-wide ledges. Here the creek drops 5 feet in three stages.

Date visited:

Notes:

Double Drop Falls

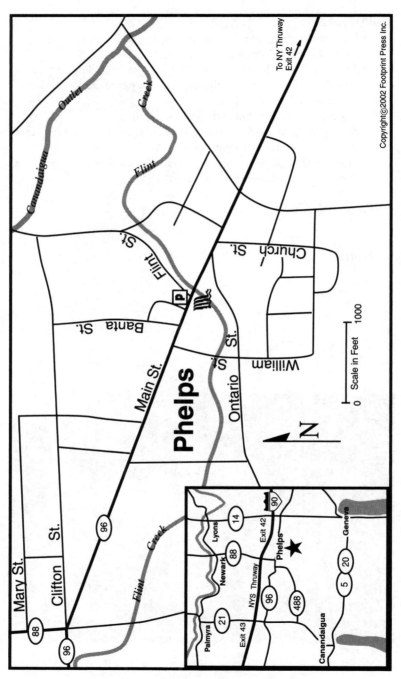

Old Mill Falls

38.
Old Mill Falls

Location:	Phelps, Ontario County
Waterway:	Flint Creek
Directions:	This waterfall is in the middle of Phelps on Route 96. Park in a small lot on the corner of Flint Street and Main Street (N42 57.524 W 77 3.633)

Alternative Parking: None
Best Viewing Locations: From the Route 96 bridge
Waterfall Height: A dam with a 11-foot drop followed by a natural 4-foot drop
Best Season to Visit: Spring; although water flows year-round

Access:	Short walk or roadside
Hiking Time:	2 minutes round trip
Trail Length:	<0.1 mile round trip
Difficulty:	1 boot
Trail Surface:	Pavement
Trail Markings:	None
Uses:	View only, Picnic
Dogs:	OK on leash
Admission:	Free
Contact:	Village of Phelps 7 Exchange Street, Phelps, NY 14532 (585) 548-8017

The Old Mill (125 Main Street) is now a wine bar and bistro. Quite an evolution from its gristmill beginnings. It was built in 1792 by early Phelps settlers Seth Dean and Oliver Phelps. Over the years the site was also used as a sawmill and plastermill.

The 11-foot high waterfall is formed by stone block built into a dam above a natural waterfall. On the east side of Flint Creek is a small park with a bench and picnic table. You can drive by slowly to observe this waterfall or for better viewing, park and walk onto the bridge. Just be mindful of passing traffic.

Trail Directions
- From the parking area, walk across Route 96 (Main Street) to the bridge.
- Look upstream to see the waterfall.

Date visited:

Notes:

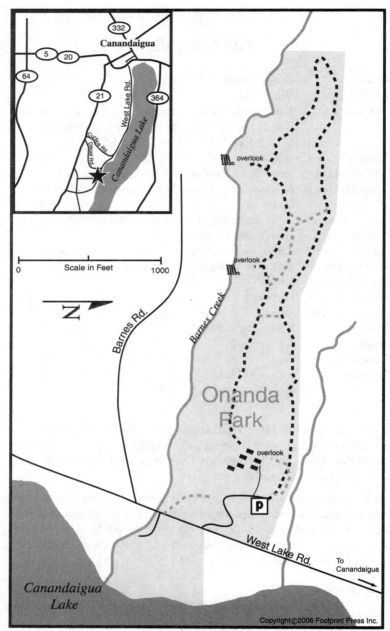

Barnes Creek Falls

39.
Barnes Creek Falls

Location:	Onanda Park, Canandaigua Lake, Ontario County
Waterway:	Barnes Creek
Directions:	From Canandaigua, head south for 7 miles on West Lake Road. The park is south of Deuel Road. Enter the park on the west side of the road, away from the lake. Follow the park road uphill to the parking lot. (N42 47.062 W77 18.943)

Alternative Parking: None
Best Viewing Locations: Lookouts along the hiking the trails
Waterfall Height: 3 waterfalls estimated at 35, 8, and 50-feet high
Best Season to Visit: Year-round

Access:	Hike
Hiking Time:	45 minutes round trip
Trail Length:	1.2 miles round trip
Difficulty:	3 boots
Trail Surface:	Dirt trail
Trail Markings:	None but easy-to-follow
Uses:	Hike, Picnic
Dogs:	OK on leash
Admission:	Free (on the west side of the park); open 9 AM–9 PM
Contact:	Onanda Park
	West Lake Road, Canandaigua, NY 14424
	(585) 394-0315

Onanda Park was first a YWCA camp dating from 1919, then Camp Good Days and Special Times which offered a respite to children with cancer. It became a public park in 1989 through a joint effort of New York State and the city of Canandaigua in an attempt to improve recreational opportunities and swimming access along Canandaigua Lake. Today the park covers 80 acres of land: 7 acres along the lake and 73 acres across West Lake Road, which is where you'll find the hiking trails and Onanda Glen.

Cabins, pavilions, and meeting facilities are available for rent within the park, mostly along the lakeshore. There are also a beach, fishing pier, picnic facilities, playgrounds, basketball, volleyball, and tennis courts on the lakeshore side. Admission is charged on the lakeshore side (free on the uphill side). The word Onanda derives from the Indian word for tall fir or pine tree, a symbol of simplicity and strength.

To view the waterfalls, follow the trails as they wind up the hillside through the woods to observation platforms overlooking the deep gorge and waterfalls that plummet over rock ledges.

Trail Directions
- Head uphill under the wooden sign "Upland Hiking Trail."
- At the first junction, a bench will be to your left. Straight ahead leads to cabins. Turn right (NW).
- At 0.2 mile, reach a "Y" and bear right. The trail continues uphill.
- Reach a "T" and turn right (NW).
- At 0.6 mile, the trail begins bending left.
- Continue bending left along a wooden fence. Reach hemlock overlook.
- At 0.7 mile, reach a "T." A short walk to the right takes you to a raised platform observation deck. The upper waterfall cascades down a mossy rock face into deep Onanda Glen below. Toward the left is a view of Canandaigua Lake through the trees.
- Return from the platform. At the junction bear right, keeping the fence on your right.
- Soon a trail will head off to the left, but continue straight.
- The trail winds downhill.
- Reach a second observation platform at 0.9 mile. Here is the lower waterfall where the water slides down a smooth rock incline.
- The trail bends left.
- Quickly reach a "Y" and bear right.
- Quickly reach a "T" and turn right.
- At 1.0 mile, pass a trail to the left.
- Reach the mowed-grass area with cabins. Canandaigua Lake appears in front of you.
- Before the first cabin, turn left to re-enter the woods.
- Continue straight, heading downhill to the parking area.

Date visited:

Notes:

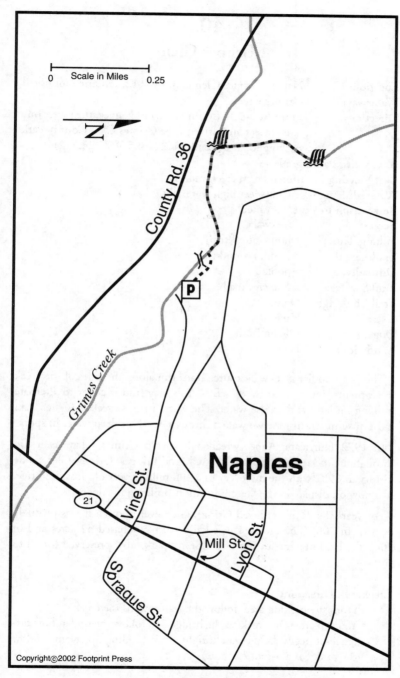

Grimes Glen

40.

Grimes Glen

Location: Naples, Grimes Glen County Park, Ontario County
Waterway: Grimes Creek
Directions: From Route 21 (Main Street) in Naples, turn west on
                   Vine Street and drive to the Grimes Glen County Park
                   parking lot at the end. N42 3.895 W77 24.772)

Alternative Parking: None
Best Viewing Locations: From creekwalk
Waterfall Height: Two 60-feet high waterfalls
Best Season to Visit: Summer
Access: Creekwalk
Hiking Time: 1 hour round trip
Trail Length: 1.2 miles round trip
Difficulty: 4 boots
Trail Surface: Stone creekbed
Trail Markings: None
Uses: Hike
Dogs: OK on leash
Admission: Free

This is a popular creekwalk route. Trails run along the sides of the creek in segments, interrupted by the cliffs. You may find it easier to alternate walking on land and in the water. The water in this creek is higher than most in summer. In June we waded through one-foot deep water in spots.

In 1972 Hurricane Agnes wreaked havoc in Grimes Glen, as it did throughout the region, wiping out trails and bridges. Grimes Glen made history in 1982 with the discovery of a 390 million year old fossilized tree. It is now on display in the State Education Building in Albany.

For years the public enjoyed Grimes Glen even though it was privately owned. In 2005 The Finger Lakes Land trust purchased 32 acres and in 2008 the land became an Ontario County park, now preserved for all to enjoy.

Creekwalk Directions:
- From the parking area, follow the trail toward the creek.
- You can cross the creek on the bridge and follow the trail a short distance or begin the creekwalk right away, heading upstream. (Below the bridge is a 3-foot cascade.)

- Reach the first large waterfall at 0.4 mile. Here a tributary (Springstead Creek) coming into Grimes Glen from the left side plummets in a steep cascade, 60-feet high and 15-feet wide.
- Pass a 2-footer and a 3-footer as you continue upstream.
- At 0.6 mile reach the final fall. Set at a 45 degree angle in the channel, this 60-foot fall funnels through a narrow channel then gushes out midway down. It's set in a deep amphitheater with a pool at the base and a cave in the far wall.
- There is a third major fall above this, but the climb up is very dangerous. We recommend you turn around at this point.

Date visited:

Notes:

One of the Grimes Glen Waterfalls

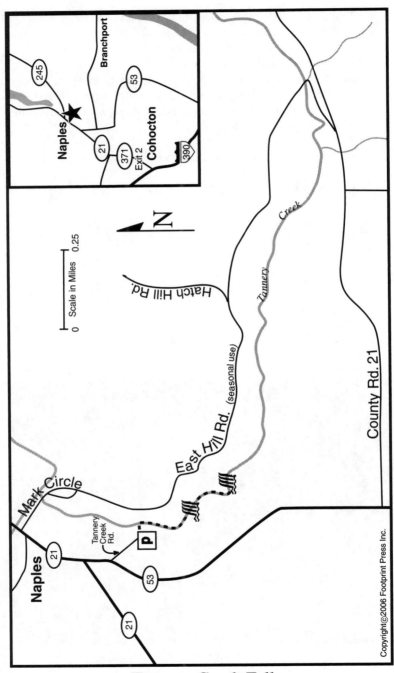

Tannery Creek Falls

41.
Tannery Creek Falls

Location:	Naples, Ontario County
Waterway:	Tannery Creek
Directions:	From Route 21 (Main Street) bear left onto Route 53 at the south end of Naples. Take a quick left onto Tannery Creek Road. Park at the end in the Town of Naples Highway Department area but be sure not to block any of their operations. (N42 36.228 W77 24.433)

Alternative Parking: None

Best Viewing Locations: From Tannery Creek

Waterfall Height: Several 10 to 20-foot falls, the final waterfall is 40-feet high

Best Season to Visit: Summer

Access:	Creekwalk
Hiking Time:	45 minutes round trip
Trail Length:	0.8 mile round trip
Difficulty:	4 boots (falls are more difficult to climb than most creekwalks)
Trail Surface:	Stone creekbed
Trail Markings:	None
Uses:	Hike
Dogs:	OK
Admission:	Free

This creekwalk is more challenging than most. The falls are difficult to climb but well worth the effort. Please exercise caution and do not climb beyond your ability. Remember as you climb up waterfalls, that it is more difficult to climb back down. As you climb, notice the gorge walls. This canyon is framed by tall rock monoliths.

Creekwalk Directions

- Behind the northeast corner of the highway department building is a short trail down to Tannery Creek.
- Enter the creekbed and walk upstream.
- Around the first bend you'll find the first waterfall—a 10-foot gradual cascade that winds sideways as it plummets. It's easy to climb past this waterfall on the left bank.
- The second waterfall, a 10-foot gradual cascade, is at 0.2 mile.
- Next comes a 4-foot gradual cascade. Notice the steep cliff walls that envelop you.

A Waterfall in Tannery Creek

- The first hurdle comes at 0.4 mile. The 20-foot high multi-step cascade is a challenge to climb.
- Just above this waterfall, a 6-foot falls drops in three stages. The top stage is a 3-foot overhung free-fall.
- At 0.4 mile you'll reach a 40-foot waterfall where the creek takes a sharp right bend. At the top is a 15-foot free-fall then a steep cascade to a pool at the base. We recommend you turn around at this point. People have climbed higher but the climb is steep and dangerous.

Date visited:

Notes:

Waterfalls in Chautauqua, Cattaraugus, Allegany and Steuben Counties

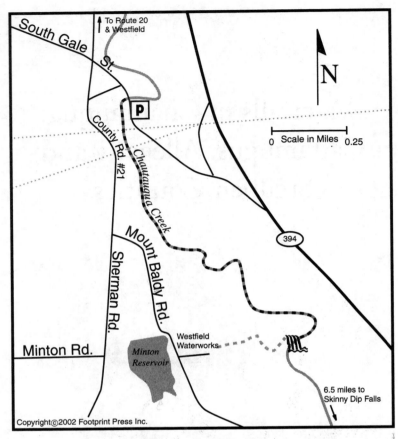

Hawley Dam Falls

42.
Hawley Dam Falls

Location: Westfield, Chautauqua County

Waterway: Chautauqua Creek in Chautauqua Gorge

Directions: From I-90 take Westfield exit #60. Head south on Route 394 into Westfield, then right on Route 20 west. Cross the bridge and take the first left onto Chestnut (County Road 21) which turns into Sherman Road. Turn left (SE) on South Gale Street. Just over the Chautauqua Creek bridge there is a small parking area on the left. (N42 18.491 W79 34.608)

Alternative Parking: None

Best Viewing Locations: From creekbed

Waterfall Height: Estimated at 8-feet high

Best Season to Visit: Summer

Access: Creekwalk

Hiking Time: 2 hours round trip

Trail Length: 2 miles round trip

Difficulty: 3 boots

Trail Surface: Stone and shale creekbed

Trail Markings: None

Uses: Creekwalk, Swim, Camp

Dogs: OK

Admission: Free

Contact: Village of Westfield, Westfield Water Department (716) 326-2561

You can still see remnants of a dam at the crest of this waterfall. It once created a pond to supply inflow water to the Westfield Water Department. Several primitive campsites are available in the flat area near the waterfall that could create a fun weekend adventure. Creekwalk in, camp overnight, then creekwalk out the next day. It's a scenic place. Across the gully rises a 120-foot high cliff and below the waterfall is a swimable pool.

The building off in the trees in the flat area is the Hawley Pumphouse, still in operation. Beyond the pumphouse, 217 steps lead uphill to the Westfield Water Department facilities on posted property.

Creekwalk Directions:
- From the parking area head upstream in the creekbed.

• In 1 mile you'll reach the waterfall, an 8-foot high cascade. (In another 6.5 miles upstream you'd reach Skinny Dip Falls, see page 164.)

Date visited:

Notes:

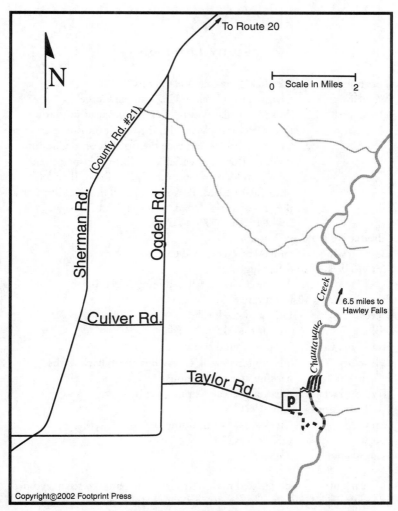

Skinny Dip Falls

43.

Skinny Dip Falls

Location: Westfield, Chautauqua County

Waterway: Chautauqua Creek in Chautauqua Gorge

Directions: From I-90 take Westfield exit #60. Head south on
                        Route 394 into Westfield, then right on Route 20 west.
                        Cross the bridge and take the first left onto Chestnut
                        (County Road 21) which turns into Sherman Road.
                        After 3 miles turn left onto Ogden Road, then left
                        onto Taylor Road. Park in the small dirt parking area at
                        the end of Taylor Road, near the dead end sign.
                        (N42 15.162 W79 34.672)

Alternative Parking: None

Best Viewing Locations: From creekbed

Waterfall Height: 6-feet high
                        A tributary waterfall is about 30-feet high

Best Season to Visit: Summer

Access: Hike and creekwalk

Hiking Time: 1 hour round trip

Trail Length: 1.0 mile round trip

Difficulty: 4 boots (creekwalk is easy but climb back to the
                        parking area is strenuous)

Trail Surface: Dirt roadbed and stone creekbed

Trail Markings: None

Uses: Creekwalk, Swim, Camp

Dogs: OK on leash

Admission: Free

You're entering a designated nudist area so be prepared to see naked people and maybe join in. This is a friendly area, frequented by couples and families. If nudity offends you, pick another waterfall to explore. This creek provides trenches to float in, pools for swimming, and large rocks and flat shale for sunning.

You may be tempted to drive past the dead end sign but we caution against it. The road down into Chautauqua Gorge is very steep and deeply rutted and washed out. Besides, there is no parking space at the bottom. Better to park in the designated parking area and hike down the 0.2 mile.

Once into the gorge, there's a 0.7 mile creekwalk to Skinny Dip Falls, but it's a very easy creekwalk. Sporadically you'll find trails (ATV tracks) parallel to the creek, interrupted by cliffs. Primitive campsites are available near the waterfall and downstream from it a bit.

Trail and Creekwalk Directions:
- From the parking area, follow the dirt road heading east.
- Bear left at the junction (to the right is posted.)
- Continue down the very steep, rutted dirt road.
- Reach the creek at 0.2 mile. Turn left and head downstream. (Stop to take note of landmarks or tie a bandanna to a tree so you can find this trail for your return trip.)
- Around the first bend, you'll see a rock painted yellow "Nudist Area Next One Mile." Look across the creek, into the dark woods to see a 30-foot wispy cascade on a tributary.
- Continue your creek-walk.
- At 0.4 mile you'll find a 5-foot jagged edged waterfall, angled across the stream, followed downstream by a narrow chute.
- Pass a few 1-foot drops then a 3-foot cascade angled in the streambed.
- Continue past a series of small drops then

Chautauqua Creek

through a flat slate bed that beckons you to lie down on a hot summer day.
- At 0.5 mile the water narrows to a channel then cascades over a 4-foot fall to a deep pool. After the pool is a jumble of boulders. You've reached Skinny Dip Falls.
- Enjoy your visit then return upstream. (Or. continue 6.5 miles in the creekbed to the Hawley Dam Falls, see page 162.)

Date visited:

Notes:

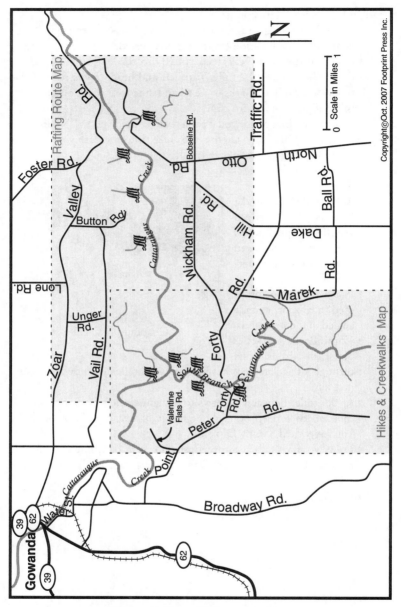

Waterfalls of Zoar Valley

44.
Waterfalls of Zoar Valley

Location:	Gowanda, Cattaraugus County
Waterway:	Cattaraugus Creek - Main Branch & South Branch
Directions:	See details below for 3 separate access areas
Uses:	Hike, Swim, Canoe, Kayak, Raft, Tube, Creekwalk, Fish, Birdwatch
Dogs:	OK on leash
Admission:	Free (closed from sunset to sunrise)
Contact:	DEC, Region 9
	270 Michigan Avenue, Buffalo, NY 14202
	(716) 851-7000
	Zoar Valley Nature Society
	P.O. Box 55, Gowanda, NY 14070
	(716) 380-1430
	www.zoarvalley.org

Zoar Valley is the gorge cut by the Main and South Branches of Cattaraugus Creek. The area was established as a 2,926-acre State Multi-use Area, used for recreation, logging, and wildlife management in the mid-1960s. The total canyon is 12.6 miles long and sports the second highest vertical cliffs in Western New York State (415-feet high). Of more interest to us, it contains 9 waterfalls. The names of these waterfalls aren't official according to DEC or USGS, they're monikers given by local folks over the years. Some waterfalls are even referred to by multiple names.

Back in the 1800s there was a trading post in Zoar Valley. In the late 1960s hippies camped in the valley during warmer months. It became notorious as a nude sunbathing area. Nude sunbathing still occurs here but camping has been outlawed.

Recently, use of the area by humans has skyrocketed and some landowners (outside the bounds of DEC property) are reporting wild parties, drug use, and general abuse of this beautiful land. Please obey all no-trespassing signs and instructions. If abuse continues, we could lose public access to this unique terrain.

For additional information on the geology, archeology, history, flora, and fauna of Zoar Valley, visit the web site of Zoar Valley Nature Society at www.zoarvalley.com.

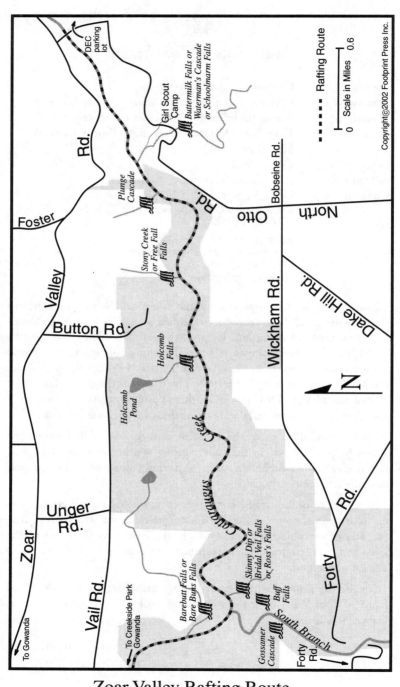

Zoar Valley Rafting Route

Rafting Route
(Plunge Cascade, Stony Creek or Free Fall Falls, Holcomb Falls, and Skinny Dip or Bridal Veil or Ross's Falls)

Waterway: Cattaraugus Creek - Main Branch
Put-in: The DEC fisheries parking lot at the North Otto Road bridge (N42 27.343 W78 48.717)
Take-out: Creekside Park in Gowanda
Best Viewing Locations: From Cattaraugus Creek
Waterfall Height: Several 80-feet high falls
Best Season to Visit: Commercial rafting trips run mid-March through mid-May; adventure trips run throughout the summer (some waterfalls are dry in summer)
Access: Waterway
Trip Time: 2-6 hours depending on water level and trip selected

The river route through Zoar Valley is 9.5 miles. To cover it takes 2 to 5 hours depending on water level and the craft ridden. At high water levels, Cattaraugus Creek can be five miles of white water with class IV rapids. At lower water levels you can experience little ripples and the need to push through low water areas.

Rafting season in Zoar Valley runs from March to late May or early June. March and April are typically white water season. But a rain shower in May can bring on white water also. A fall season runs from September through December.

Two companies run rafting, inflatable kayaking, and 2-person ducky boat trips through Zoar Valley. They take care of the logistics and help assure you run the river only during conditions that meet with your abilities.

Adventure Calls Outfitters, Inc.
PO Box 139, LeRoy, NY 14482
(585) 343-4710 or (888) 270-2410
www.adventure-calls.com

Zoar Valley Canoe & Rafting Company
PO Box 695, Dunkirk, NY 14048
(800) 724-0696
www.zoarvalleyrafting.com

The number of waterfalls seen on these trips varies with the season and with the trip selected. In spring rafting season you're limited to the falls you can see readily from Cattaraugus Creek. In summer on an adventure tour you may be able to combine hikes with your ducky boat trip to see more waterfalls. In fall, with leaves off the trees you can sometimes see waterfalls that are set back from the main channel without hiking. In spring, seasonal falls may be visible. The falls you may see include:

> Plunge Cascade: requires a walk into the woods to see this 80-foot cascade.
>
> Stony Creek or Free Fall Falls: a multi-staged ribbon falls, plunging 80 feet from a cliff into the main creek. You can't miss this one regardless of which trip you select.
>
> Holcomb Falls: requires a walk into the woods to see this 80-foot drop.
>
> Skinny Dip, Bridal Veil, or Ross's Falls: requires a short walk in from the main creek to see this 120-feet high, 50-feet wide, steep cascade.
>
> Barebutt or Bare Buns Falls: an 80-foot cascade that plunges in seven steps, requires a walk in.

You can check current water level data on the Zoar Valley Paddling Club website under River Gauges at www.zoarvalley.com.

Date visited:

Notes:

Drive-by
(Waterman's Cascade, Schoolmarm or Buttermilk Falls)

Waterway: A tributary to Waterman Creek
Directions: From Zoar Valley Road north of Zoar Valley, turn
south on North Otto Road to cross the bridge.
Continue south and west past a Girl Scout camp.
(N42 26.741 W78 49.587)
Best Viewing Locations: From North Otto Road
Waterfall Height: 70-feet high
Best Season to Visit: Year-round
Access: Roadside
Difficulty: 1 boot

This gentle cascade has acquired three names. Some refer to it as Waterman's Cascade. To others it's Buttermilk Falls or Schoolmarm Falls. All have a valid basis. The waterway feeds into Waterman Creek and the falls indeed looks like buttermilk in its creamy froth. Rumor has it a schoolmarm fell to her death here in the 1920s. (See the map for Zoar Valley Rafting Route on page 176.)

Trail Directions:
- Drive southwest on North Otto Road, passing the Girl Scout camp. Slow down as you begin uphill. The falls will be to your left, easily visible in a gully beside the road.

Date visited:

Notes:

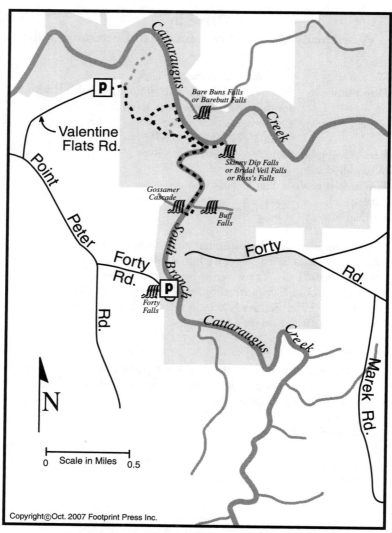

Bare Buns Falls
or Barebutt Falls

Skinny Dip Falls
or Bridal Veil Falls
or Ross's Falls

Gossamer
Cascade

Buff
Falls

Valentine
Flats Rd.

Forty
Rd.

Forty

Rd.

Forty
Falls

South Branch

Cattaraugus Creek

Point Peter Rd.

Marek Rd.

Cattaraugus Creek

N

0   Scale in Miles   0.5

Copyright©Oct. 2007 Footprint Press Inc.

Zoar Valley Hikes & Creekwalks

Hike & Creekwalk via Valentine Flats
(Barebutt or Bare Buns Falls, Skinny Dip or Ross's Falls, Gossamer Cascade, and Buff Falls)

Waterway: Cattaraugus Creek - Main Branch & South Branch

Directions From Gowanda, head southeast on Water Street, then south on Broadway Road. Turn left (E) onto Point Peter Road, then left (E) onto Valentine Flats Road. Drive to the end and park. (N42 26.617 W78 54.248)

Best Viewing Locations: From Cattaraugus Creek

Waterfall Height: 4 waterfalls ranging from 80 to 130-feet high

Best Season to Visit: Summer

Access: Hike and creekwalk

Hiking Time: 4 hour loop

Trail Length: 3.1 mile loop (excluding Barebutt Falls)

Difficulty: 4 boots

Trail Surface: Dirt trails, stony creekbeds

Trail Markings: Aqua green blazes on the trail

Originally called Darby Flats, Valentine Flats has a long history of human use. In 1818 Jacob Balcom and his family built a farm here. To their surprise, they found apple trees on the land, planted by unknown people. Today the 160 acres that sit below the cliffs but above the creekbed are a combination of fields, woods, walnut plantation, and creek shore only accessible to hikers. On Valentine Flats is a naturally occurring pyramid shaped hill that's 120-feet high.

You'll follow a dirt trail down to Valentine Flats. When you reach the confluence of the South and Main Branches of Cattaraugus Creek you'll be at the spot known as Skinny Dip Beach. It's not uncommon to find nude sunbathers in this area. Then begins the creekwalk to reach Skinny Dip Falls (also known as Bridal Veil and Ross's Falls). This is a 120-feet high, 50-feet wide, steep cascade down the cliffs into Cattaraugus Creek. You can stand directly at the base. It dries to a trickle in summer. Next you'll creekwalk to Gossamer Cascade, a 130-feet tall, thin ribbon falls that dumps from the cliff directly into South Branch. Then search out Buff Falls, another 120-feet tall, ribbon waterfall that's hidden in the woods. Finally, if water levels permit, cross Cattaraugus Creek to see the 80-foot cascade that plunges in seven steps called Barebutt Falls (also known as Bare Buns Falls). You have to get close to see this waterfall. Even then, you can only see the lowest two cascade steps. The upper five are hidden high in the cliff side.

Trail and Creekwalk Directions:
- From the parking area, follow the trail into the woods.
- At the "Y" bear right. (Straight leads 0.3 mile, to a viewpoint (called The Point) 120 feet above the cliffs of Zoar Valley.)
- Bear right, following the aqua-green-blazed trail downhill.
- Cross an old landslide area.
- At 0.2 mile pass a trail to the left (this will be your return loop).
- The trail narrows but remains green-blazed.
- Reach the flats after 0.4 mile and continue following the green trail.
- At 0.5 mile, reach a "T" at the base of a unique triangular hill. Turn right to stay on the green trail.
- Reach the South Branch at 0.7 mile. The green trail bends right but continue straight into the creekbed. You'll be at the junction of the Main and South Branches.
- Cross the South Branch (the smaller waterway) and walk upstream along the bank of the Main Branch (Cattaraugus Creek) with cliffs to your right.
- Look for a path into the woods around the corner. Follow it for a short distance to Skinny Dip Falls.
- Return to the confluence of South & Main Branches and begin creekwalking up the South Branch (heading west). (There is a trail through the woods along the south side of the creek that ends in 0.8 mile)
- Round a bend to the left.
- 0.8 mile from the start of South Branch you'll see Gossamer Cascade on your right.
- Cross South Branch and climb the far bank, directly across from Gossamer Cascade.
- Just inside the woods, turn left and follow the dirt trail.
- The trail will peter out, but continue straight, bushwhacking parallel to the South Branch but inside the woods until you hear and see Buff Falls off to your right.
- Return to South Branch and creekwalk back to Main Branch.
- At the confluence, turn left and walk the bank of Main Branch.

Decision Time:
- The object is to find a spot with low water to allow safe crossing of Main Branch. We weren't able to do this with a measure of safety in July. Use your own judgement based on the conditions you find. If it looks risky, do not cross. Instead, skip Barebutt Falls.

To Reach Barebutt Falls:
- Cross Main Branch of Cattaraugus Creek approximately 100 feet downstream from the confluence.

- Head directly into the woods to the edge of the cliff.
- Turn left and follow the cliff edge to Barebutt Falls.
- Cross Main Branch again and climb the bank to find a trail.
- Turn right and follow the trail.

To skip Barebutt Falls:
- From the confluence, follow the trail along the bank of Main Branch.
- At the junction where the green trail turns left, continue straight on an unmarked trail.

Both Routes:
- The trail will loop left and finally meet the green-blazed trail. At the junction turn right to follow the green trail.
- Bear left when there's a choice to return to the parking area.

Date visited:

Notes:

Hike & Creekwalk via Forty Road
(Forty Falls and Little 4-D Falls)

Waterway: Cattaraugus Creek - South Branch

Directions: From Gowanda, head southeast on Water Street, then south on Broadway Road. Turn left (E) onto Point Peter Road, then left (E) on Forty Road. (There is no road sign at the junction. Watch for the Persia School District #4 white building and a yellow "dead end" sign at the corner.) Watch for Forty Falls as you head downhill. Park in the dirt lot at the end of the road. (N42 25.509 W78 53.827)

Best Viewing Locations: From Cattaraugus Creek
Waterfall Height: 75-feet high
Best Season to Visit: Summer
Access: Hike and creekwalk
Hiking Time: 10 minutes round trip
Trail Length: 0.2 mile round trip
Difficulty: 3 boots
Trail Surface: Stony creekbed
Trail Markings: None

You'll pass Forty Falls before leaving your car. The 75-foot falls plunges off a cliff immediately to the right of the bridge as you round a corner on Forty Road, then continues its cascade under the bridge. There's no shoulder to pull off and view the falls so just drive slowly as you descend to the parking area. The old bridge over Forty Falls was damaged in the 1986 flood and has been rebuilt for safe passage.

Trail and Creekwalk Directions:
- From the parking area, head down the path to the creek.
- Walk left (downstream) along the edge of the creek for a few feet to see where the Forty Falls waterway flows to meet South Branch. Look into the woods to see a small ribbon cascade called Little 4-D Falls.
- You can continue downstream from here to view Gossamer Cascade and Buff Falls, or simply return to your car.

Date visited:

Notes:

Deer Lick Falls

Important Information About Upstream Waterfalls:

Do not head upstream from Forty Road. There are several large (and many small) waterfalls upstream, but the land is privately owned and is currently being patrolled due to overuse and abuse. If you head upstream, **you risk getting arrested.**

The first major upstream waterfall is Deer Lick Falls which is an 80-foot-high ribbon cascade that sits in a tributary to the South Branch Cattaraugus Creek. Deer Lick Falls is part of the Deer Lick Conservation Area, owned privately by The Nature Conservancy. Deer Lick Conservation Area has a parking area on Point Peter Road and 11 miles of hiking trails that are currently open to the public. The trails go near, but don't actually get to the falls. Likewise, there is no access to the falls from South Branch Cattaraugus Creek. The terrain is too steep and dangerous to allow access. If trespassing continues to be a problem, Deer Lick Conservation Area may be closed to the public, with visitation by members with valid permits only.

Farther upstream are the 45-foot ribbon cascade with 4 stages called Lower Plumb Brook Falls, and Big Falls (also called The Falls) with an 18-foot free fall into a pool, plus others. The Nature Sanctuary Society of Western New York, Inc. recently purchased this region of South Branch Cattaraugus Creek. According to Richard Rosche, president of the Nature Sanctuary Society, this piece of land has for many years been over-used and abused beyond its limits, as the site of wild parties, pot smoking, drug use, swimming and all sorts of other illegal activity. Therefore, visitation to this area (including Big Falls) is now limited to those carrying current membership cards indicating that they are members of the Nature Sanctuary Society of Western New York, Inc. Group visitation will be limited to those groups who have made prior arrangements with the Preserve Custodian or a Society Officer to be there, and their goals and activities MUST be compatible with those of the Society. At least one member of the group must possess a current membership card. Local law enforcement will charge anyone found on the property, without the membership cards, with criminal trespass charges and they will have to appear in the Persia Town Court and pay a fine.

Membership in the Society is open to all those who are sympathetic to the goals and aims of the organization. Membership dues are $10.00 per year per family/address. Contact Richard C. Rosche, President, Nature Sanctuary Society of Western New York, Inc., 110 Maple Rd., East Aurora, NY 14052, (716) 652-8409, drosche2@verizon.net. Also visit www.zoarvalley.org.

Lower Plumb Brook Falls

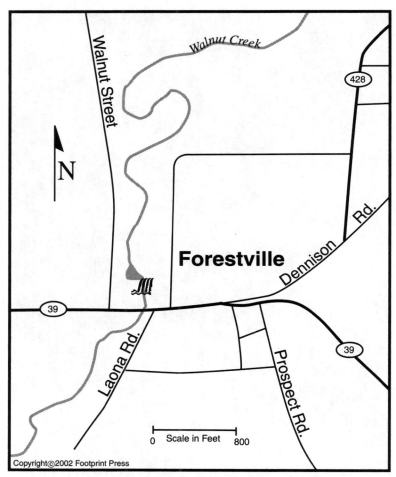

Walnut Falls

45.

Walnut Falls

Location:	Forestville, Chautauqua County
Waterway:	Walnut Creek
Directions:	From Route 39 (Main Street) in Forestville, turn north on Walnut Street, just west of the bridge over
Walnut	Creek. Park along Walnut Street just after a
fire	hydrant. (N42 28.148 W79 10.891)

Alternative Parking: None
Best Viewing Locations: From the sidewalk along Walnut Street
Waterfall Height: Estimated at 40-feet high
Best Season to Visit: Year-round

Access:	Roadside
Difficulty:	1 boot
Trail Surface:	Cement sidewalk
Trail Markings:	None
Uses:	View only
Dogs:	OK
Admission:	Free
Contact:	Village of Forestville
	Village Hall, Chestnut Street
	Forestville, NY 14062

Walnut Falls is the highest waterfall on Walnut Creek. This 40-foot cascade is easily viewable from the sidewalk along Walnut Street. The first sawmill was built here by Jehiel Moor. It stood for more than 100 years before being destroyed by fire in 1929.

Trail Directions:
- Walk the sidewalk along Walnut Street to find the gap in the trees with the best view.

Date visited:

Notes:

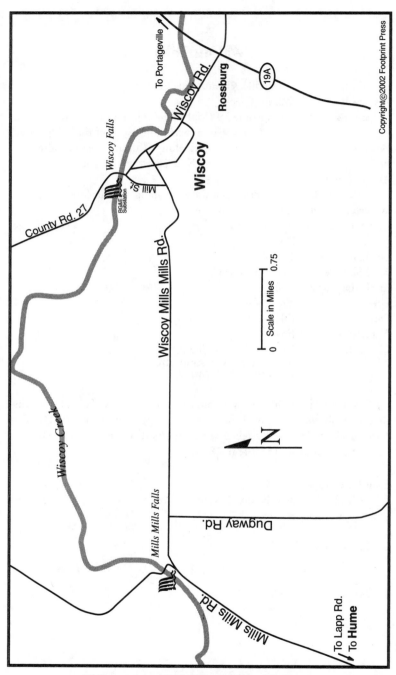

Wiscoy and Mills Mills Falls

46.
Wiscoy Falls

Location:	Wiscoy, Allegany County
Waterway:	Wiscoy Creek
Directions:	From Route 19A south of Letchworth State Park, turn west on Wiscoy Road to Wiscoy. At the end, turn right on Mill Street and park at the old mill building just beyond the bridge over Wiscoy Creek. (N42 30.293 W78 4.943)

Alternative Parking: None
Best Viewing Locations: From the bridge
Waterfall Height: 5 tiers of falls are visible totalling over 40 feet
Best Season to Visit: Year-round

Access:	Roadside
Difficulty:	1 boot
Trail Surface:	Paved bridge
Trail Markings:	None
Uses:	View only
Dogs:	OK
Admission:	Free

Wiscoy is an Indian word meaning "five falls creek or brook." As you stand on the bridge in the Village of Wiscoy, five tiers of waterfall are visible. They start with a pair of jagged edged 2-foot falls, then progress to a 15-foot tall cascade, then a 20-foot cascade. Far into the trees you can see the reflections of moving water from the top tier.

Wiscoy used to be a thriving village. It sported a cabinet shop, hotel, planing mill, cider mill, blacksmith shop, machine shop, gristmill, sawmill, and cutlery. In 1902 a calamitous flood wiped out all the mills.

The red building next to the creek was once a cabinet shop that used a paddlewheel for power. Across the creek is a power plant owned by RG&E.

Directions:
    • Stand on the bridge and look upstream.

Date visited:

Notes:

47.
Mills Mills Falls

Location:	Mills Mills, Allegany County
Waterway:	Wiscoy Creek
Directions:	From Route 19 in Hume head north on Lapp Road. Turn right onto Mills Mills Road and follow it to the bridge over Wiscoy Creek, just after the corner of Wiscoy Mills Mills Road. Park along the road, just before the bridge. (N42 30.046 W78 7.159)

Alternative Parking: None
Best Viewing Locations: From the bridge
Waterfall Height: Dam waterfall is estimated at 10-feet high
Below the dam is a 20-foot series of cascades
Best Season to Visit: Year-round

Access:	Roadside (all land in the area is posted)
Difficulty:	1 boot
Trail Surface:	Paved bridge
Trail Markings:	None
Uses:	View only
Dogs:	OK
Admission:	Free

Roger Mills of Canajoharie, Montgomery County built the first mill on the upper falls of Wiscoy Creek beginning in 1806. First he erected a log cabin home. The following year he dammed the creek and erected his sawmill. In 1808 he added a gristmill, transporting stone and castings from Albany by sleigh. Farmers and Indians came from as far as 40 miles away, hauling their grain by oxen to be ground at the mill. Mills' mills became a center of activity. In addition to the milling services, the Mills offered stock goods for sale, hotel services, and mail distribution. Today, an old sluiceway is still visible across the dam.

Directions:
- Upstream from the bridge is the dam, a free-fall waterfall for 4 feet, followed by a 6-foot cascade.
- Downstream is a series of cascades falling 15 to 20 feet.

Date visited:

Notes:

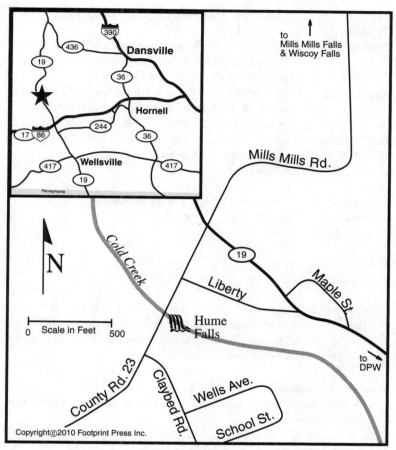

Hume Falls

48.

Hume Falls

Location:	Hume, Allegany County
Waterway:	Cold Creek
Directions:	From Route 19 in Hume head west on County Road 23 / Mills Mills Road. Watch south as you cross Cold Creek. (N42 28.389 W78 8.185)

Alternative Parking: For creekwalking head south on Route 19, 0.5 mile from Mills Mills Road to the DPW area on the west side of the highway. (N42 28.149 W78 7.783)

Best Viewing Locations: From the bridge, or from the base of the falls

Waterfall Height: Approximately 30 feet high

Best Season to Visit: Year-round

Access:	Roadside or Creekwalk
Difficulty:	1 boot from bridge, 3 boots creekwalk
Trail Surface:	Paved bridge, stony creek
Trail Markings:	None
Uses:	View only
Dogs:	OK
Admission:	Free

Hume was formerly called Cold Creek for the waterway that courses through this village. The water in Cold Creek comes from a spring the Indians called Cold Spring. Today, Cold Creek tumbles down this 30-foot cascade almost under the County Road 23 bridge.

Roadside Directions:
- The waterfall can be seen if you look downstream from the County Road 23 bridge.

Creekwalk Directions:
- From the Hume Highway Department lot head down into Cold Creek.
- Walk upstream (N) to the base of Hume Falls.

Date visited:

Notes:

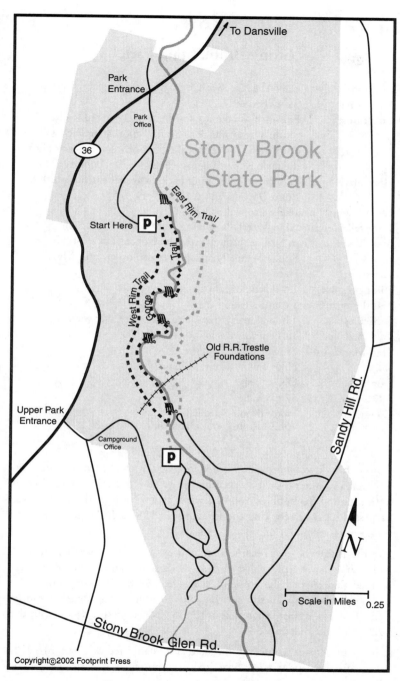

Stony Brook State Park

49.

Stony Brook State Park

Location:	Dansville, Steuben County
Waterway:	Stony Brook
Directions:	From I-390 take the southern of 2 exits to Route 36 south. The entrance to Stony Brook State Park will be on the left. Drive past the park office and bear right to the farthest parking lot. (N42 31.241 W77 41.725)

Alternative Parking: Access to the upper parking area is further south on Route 36 (N42 30.693 W77 41.375)

Best Viewing Locations: From the Gorge Trail

Waterfall Height: Nine waterfalls ranging from 2 to 25-feet high

Best Season to Visit: Spring through Fall (the Gorge Trail closes the Friday before Thanksgiving and opens mid-May)

Access:	Hike
Hiking Time:	1.5 hours round trip
Trail Length:	1.6 miles round trip
Difficulty:	4 boots, many steps, and a slippery, wet walkway
Trail Surface:	Stone walkways and dirt trails
Trail Markings:	Brown signs at trail heads
Uses:	Hike, Swim, Camp, Picnic
Dogs:	OK on leash
Admission:	$7 / vehicle
Contact:	Stony Brook State Park 10820 Route 36S, Dansville, NY 14437 (585) 335-8111

Stony Brook was hunted and fished long ago by the Seneca Indians, and has been a summer tourist destination since 1883. Indians were the first to notice natural gas bubbles from the water in the lower park. The gas was harnessed for use in cooking and for lights. In 1882 a driller unsuccessfully sunk wells looking for oil.

In the 1800s the glen became a popular resort called *Summer Garden*. It had a large dance hall, paths, gardens, swings, and an outdoor theater. A railroad that crossed the gorge on a trestle, 239 feet above, brought the tourists. Today you can still see the concrete abutments along the Gorge Trail. The trestle was dismantled in the 1940s. The resort declined in the 1920s and was abandoned.

Stony Brook was rescued by the state and established as a park in 1928, just before the depression. It benefited from much CCC work. They built lodges, swimming areas, shelters, stairways, and roads. World War II prisoners of war were used for other work projects.

Stony Brook Gorge, like its relatives Enfield Glen and Taughannock Glen, was formed by joint cuts. The stream followed joints in the rock. During floods the water lifted and carried joint-bounded slabs downstream, cutting the gorge in the process.

Along the trail you'll pass brown posts with yellow numbers painted on the top. Pick up a green brochure at the park office to read about the area you're hiking through as noted by the posts. The route described below takes the Gorge Trail out and returns via the Rim Trail. The Rim Trail offers birds-eye views into the gorge and waterfalls far below but it is quite rugged, with lots of steps up and down. For a less strenuous trip, head out and return via the Gorge Trail.

Trail Directions:
- From the parking area, head toward the snack bar/gift shop/changing rooms.
- Behind this building, turn right and pass through the dammed swimming area.
- Continue straight on the Gorge Trail.
- The first waterfall is an L-shaped notch in the rock that water crashes through down a drop of 8 feet. Next to the notch, water glides over a sloped surface.
- Cross the gorge on the first arched stone bridge.
- The next waterfall is a 25-foot gradual drop down a narrow channel.
- Under a bridge is a waterfall that free-falls in two stages from an overhung top for 6 feet then slides 10 feet down a narrow notch.
- The forth waterfall is a 30-foot wide, 30-foot tall, steep cascade.
- Pass a 35-foot wide, 20-foot tall cascade.
- Number 6 is a 3-foot cascade.
- Then comes Hourglass Falls which is no longer an hourglass. The cap rock fell victim to erosion and now forms a sideways slab of rock that channels water to a gradual cascade.
- Pass a 2-foot overhung falls then a 2-foot sluice.
- Pass the footings from the old railroad trestle at 0.6 mile.
- The final falls is hard to see. It's a 25-foot waterfall hidden in the valley.
- At the top of the stairs take a right along a fence to begin on the West Rim Trail (the upper parking area would be 0.15 mile straight ahead, but there are no more waterfalls to see. If you pass post #11, you missed the turn-off to the Rim Trail.)

- Follow the Rim Trail up steps—it has a lot of steps up as well as down.
- At 0.9 mile pass the upper abutments for the old railroad trestle.
- Reach the parking area at 1.6 miles.

Date visited:

Notes:

Waterfalls in Wayne, Yates, Seneca and Cayuga Counties

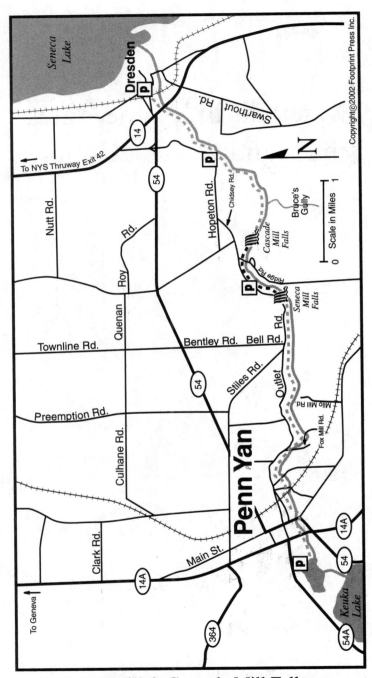

Seneca Mill & Cascade Mill Falls

50.
Seneca Mill Falls & Cascade Mill Falls

Location: Keuka Lake Outlet Trail, Penn Yan, Yates County
Waterway: Keuka Lake Outlet
Directions: From Penn Yan, head east on Route 54. Turn right (S)
                       on Stiles Road. At the end turn left on Outlet Road.
                       Pass Bell Road. Park in a gravel parking area on the
                       right in about 0.5 mile that has an orange metal box
                       labeled "Outlet Trail - Please Sign Register."
                       (N42 39.862 W77 0.151)
Best Viewing Locations: From the Keuka Lake Outlet Trail
Waterfall Height: Seneca Mill Falls is estimated at 45-feet high
                       Cascade Mill Falls is estimated at 20-feet high
Best Season to Visit: Year-round
Access: Hike
Hiking Time: 1.5 hours round trip to both waterfalls
Trail Length: 1.6 miles round trip to Cascade Mill Falls
                       0.7 mile round trip to Seneca Mill Falls
Difficulty: 2 boots
Trail Surface: Dirt trail
Trail Markings: Green and white metal trail signs
Uses: Hike, Bike, Snowshoe, Ski
Dogs: OK on leash
Admission: Free
Contact: Friends of the Outlet
                       PO Box 65, Dresden, NY 14441

In the middle of the nineteenth century, two fingers of water connected the 274-foot drop between Keuka and Seneca Lakes: the Keuka Lake Outlet to power mills, and the Crooked Lake Canal for boat traffic. A dam and guardhouse in Penn Yan controlled the water flow to both. The outlet, which still carries water from one lake to the next, was formed by a ground fault in the Tully limestone allowing water to run between the two lakes. Along its banks are remnants of the many mills which once harnessed the waterpower.

Seneca Mill:

The first white settlers arrived in this area around 1788, attracted by the reliable water source at the outlet. In 1789, the Friends Mill was built at the highest waterfall of Keuka Lake Outlet to grind flour using a 26-foot, overshot flywheel. From then until 1827, the small religious group called the Society of Universal Friends built 12 dams and many mills that helped

Seneca Mill Falls

make the area a thriving community. The mills and shops built near this waterfall produced flour (gristmills), lumber (sawmills), tool handles, linseed oil, plaster, and liquor (distilleries). There were also fulling and carding mills.

In 1825 the Marquis De Lafayette made a triumphal tour with a stop in Geneva. Local militia mustered near the Friend's Mill and fired their muskets and fieldpieces in practice for joining the parade in the general's honor. The sparks ignited the gristmill and linseed mill, burning them to the ground. Joshua Way and Jeremiah Andrews rebuilt the mills and the area became known as Way & Andrew's Hollow.

The various mills in the area changed hands many times over the years. A large papermill called Seneca Mill was built at the site in 1884, using stone salvaged from the canal locks (see below). It utilized water power to produce book paper, heavy wrapping paper and sugar bags. By 1889 Seneca Mill was producing electricity to power the lights in Penn Yan.

Cascade Mill:

Cascade Mill and its dam was built in 1827 by Meredith Mallory. He paid $2,000 for the land surrounding The Cascade, the second highest waterfall on Keuka Lake Outlet. At the time the land was almost inaccessible, deep in the gorge. Mallory built a road down to the site and a bridge over the outlet. His gristmill and sawmill prospered. Other merchants were drawn to the area and it soon had a limekiln, a blacksmith shop, and a cooperage.

Mallory overextended himself through expansion with other mills and by financing his political career and ended up in bankruptcy. Cascade Mill was sold to John Rice who renamed it Croton Mill. In 1866 George Youngs bought the property and converted it into Cascade Paper Manufacturing Company to produce newsprint from straw pulp. However, the paper mill was short-lived and burned in 1869.

The mill lay in ruins and changed hands several times until 1881 when Charles Cave bought it and began producing a light brown wrapping paper used mainly in Cuba to produce cigars. In 1900 Edward Taylor converted the mill into an electrical furnace, using water power to produce carbon bisulfide. Carbon bisulfide was used as a pesticide, as a solvent in the arts, to extract olive oil for soapmaking, to make a cement used in shoemaking, and in the production of artificial silk. The plant was enlarged in 1923 and its name was changed to J.T. Baker Company in 1933. The plant continued operation into the 1960s. In 1997, the Cascade Mills Complex was sold to the Friends of the Outlet.

Crooked Lake Canal and Corkscrew Railway:

In 1833 New York State opened the Crooked Lake Canal to span the six miles between the two lakes and move farm products to eastern markets. The canal was four feet deep and had 28 wooden locks. It took a vessel six hours to journey through the canal. As business boomed in the mills, the state widened and deepened the canal and replaced the wooden locks with stone. But the canal lost money every year of its 44-year history, so in 1877 the state auctioned off all the machinery and stone. Only the towpath remained. In 1844 a railroad was built on the towpath. Initially operated by the Penn Yan and New York Railway Company, it eventually became part of the New York Central System. Railway men called it the "Corkscrew Railway" because of its countless twists and turns. The line operated until 1972 when the tracks were washed out by the flood from Hurricane Agnes.

Keuka Lake Outlet Trail:

A local group interested in recreational use of the ravine convinced the Yates County Legislature to buy the property in 1981. In 1996, the Legislature sold the trail east of Penn Yan to the Friends of the Outlet, Inc., a local not-for-profit group devoted to protecting and preserving the lands and waters of the outlet ravine. The group maintains 5.7 miles of trail and 300 acres of public-access land in the gorge. Trail signs and outhouses were recently added along the route. The entire Keuka Lake Outlet Trail covers 7.0 miles from Penn Yan to Dresden.

For a more complete history, check the website of Friends of the Outlet at www.keukaoutlettrail.org.

The Waterfalls:

The route described below leads east from a parking area to the Cascade Mill Falls for 1.6 miles round trip and west to Seneca Mill Falls for a 0.7 mile round trip. Today, the water shoots out in a two-staged free-fall for 20 feet from rock overhangs at Cascade Mill Falls. Notice the old mill dam just above the waterfall. Seneca Mill Falls, the larger of the two, rushes downhill in three stages. The top is a 15-foot free-fall from an overhung dam. In the middle a natural caprock overhang forms another 15-foot free-fall. The bottom third completes the 15-foot sections with a natural mix of free-falls and sloped cascades.

Trail Directions to Cascade Mill Falls:
- From the Outlet Trail parking area, head left (E) on the trail.
- Cross Ridge Road and continue on the trail.
- Pass the visitor center on the left and continue toward brick buildings (remains of the J. T. Baker Chemical Company).
- Follow the trail around the left of the buildings, then turn right toward the creek, to view Cascade Mill Falls from below.
- In spring you may want to continue east on the trail for another 0.1 mile and peer across Keuka Lake Outlet to Bruce's Gully. Here water drops in three steps through Genesee shale to reach the outlet.

Trail Directions to Seneca Mill Falls:
- From the Outlet Trail parking area, head right (W) on the trail.
- Pass an outhouse and a culvert over a tributary.
- Pass the Sheridan memorial rock and see Seneca Mill Falls to the left. (John Sheridan was a lawyer who negotiated purchase of the land for the Keuka Lake Outlet Preservation Area.)
- Enjoy the view from the observation area at the base of the waterfall then continue uphill to the crest and a picnic area with a covered pavilion.

Date visited:

Notes:

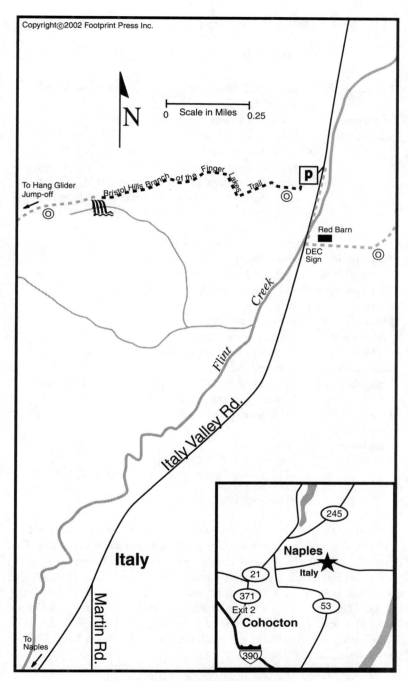

West Italy Hill Waterfall

51.
West Italy Hill Waterfall

Location:	Bristol Hill Branch of the Finger Lakes Trail in Italy Valley, Yates County
Waterway:	Unnamed tributary into Flint Creek
Directions:	From Route 53 south of Naples, take County Route 21. Turn right on County Route 18 (Italy Valley Road). Pass through the town of Italy. Pass a brown sign "Trail to Italy Hill State Forest, NYSDEC" on the right. Turn left onto the next small gravel farm road. Park at the end of the gravel where the Finger Lakes Trail turns right across a field. (N42 37.436 W77 16.899)

Best Viewing Locations: From the Finger Lakes Trail
Waterfall Height: Estimated at 30-feet high
Best Season to Visit: Spring; it's dry in summer

Access:	Hike
Hiking Time:	1 hour round trip
Trail Length:	1.8 miles round trip
Difficulty:	4 boots (a long, steep uphill)
Trail Surface:	Dirt trail
Trail Markings:	Orange blazes and round markers, green and yellow Finger Lakes Trail signs
Uses:	Hike, Snowshoe
Dogs:	OK
Admission:	Free
Contact:	Finger Lakes Trail Conference 6111 Visitor Center Road, Mt. Morris, NY 14510 (585) 658-9320 www.fingerlakestrail.org

Head to this waterfall if you're looking for an aerobic workout with a reward. The hike up the steep hillside will get your heart pounding. The waterfall is somewhat hard to see through trees so very early spring before trees leaf out may be your best viewing time. Once you've reached the waterfall, the main climb is behind you. You can continue on the Finger Lakes Trail past the waterfall for another 1.5 miles to a hang glider jump off point with a panoramic view of Italy Valley. (The Finger Lakes Trail Conference sells detailed maps to all sections of the Finger Lakes Trail at www.fingerlakestrail.org.)

Follow the orange blazes very carefully as you climb up and again upon your return. The trail winds on and off dirt roads and logging lanes, making many turns. It's easy to get mesmerized on an old road and miss the trail as it turns off. You'll pass green, blue, and yellow blazes and boundary markers. Follow only orange markings.

Trail Directions:
- From the gravel farm road follow the orange blazes across the field toward the hill.
- In the woods, the trail traverses the hill diagonally toward the left.
- The orange-blazed trail will turn often. Follow the orange blazes carefully.
- Reach a trail register box at 0.8 mile. Please sign in.
- About 40 steps past the register box you'll see the 30-foot multi-staged cascade in the creekbed to the left.
- Turn around here and retrace your steps or continue 1.5 miles to the view at the hang glider jump-off point.

Date visited:

Notes:

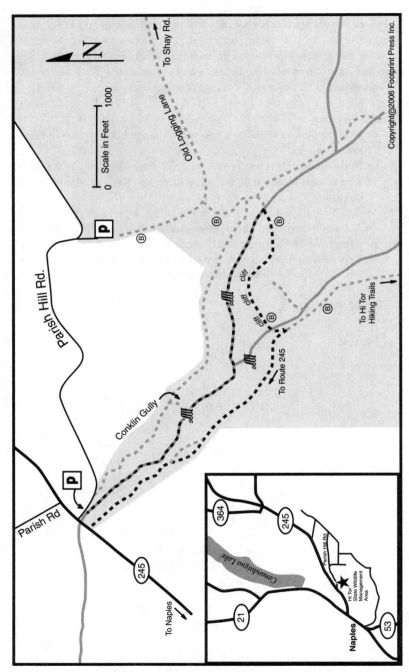

Parish Glen / Conklin Gully

52.
Parish Glen / Conklin Gully

Location: Naples, Hi Tor Wildlife Management Area, Yates County

Waterway: Parish Glen (also called Conklin Gully)

Directions: From Naples, head northeast on Route 245 for 2 miles. Just before Parish Hill Road there is a DEC parking area on the right marked with a brown and yellow sign "Hi Tor Wildlife Management Area, DEC." Park here or turn right onto Parish Hill Road and park on the right at a pull-off area at the first bend in the road. (N42 38.114 W77 22.041)

Best Viewing Locations: From the creekbed

Waterfall Height: Angel Falls: 120-feet high
   Others range from 1 to 33-feet high

Best Season to Visit: Summer; it's a trickle by late summer

Access: Creekwalk and hike

Hiking Time: 1.5 hour loop

Trail Length: 1.9 mile loop

Difficulty: 4 boots (challenging waterfalls to climb)

Trail Surface: Dirt trail and stone creekbed

Trail Markings: None (a blue-blazed trail crosses at the upper end of the gully)

Uses: Hike

Dogs: OK

Admission: Free

Contact: DEC Region 8
   6274 East Avon-Lima Road, Avon, NY 14414
   (585) 226-2466

The locals call this ravine Parish Glen. The Parish family settled in the Naples area in 1789, on roughly a thousand acres that included Parish Glen and Parish Hill (now part of Hi Tor). No one knows where the name Conklin Gully came from, other than that it shows up on USGS topographical maps.

The waterfalls in Parish Glen are challenging to climb. This creekwalk is not for novices or small children. Having said that, it is a spectacular gully with magnificent waterfalls. In summer, even when the creekbed is dry at Route 245 you'll find water higher up and places where the gully narrows forcing you to walk through water. In winter this is a great creekbed to explore with instep crampons.

The waterfalls in Parish Glen are big and numerous. They range from 1-foot ledges to Angel Falls which is a 120-foot drop off the cliff side. Ice climbers use Angel Falls in the winter. The highest waterfalls you'll climb in the gully are approximately 30-feet high. One is best traversed by clinging to trees and roots along a narrow ledge on the cliff wall. The good news is that there's a trail that circles Parish Glen, so the route described below climbs up the creekbed and uses a trail for the return to the parking area. Because of this, you don't have to worry about climbing back down the challenging waterfalls.

Trail Directions:
- From the parking area, walk into the creekbed and head upstream.
- The first small waterfall occurs at 0.2 mile.
- Next comes an 8-foot fall with an overhung caprock.
- Pass a series of 1 to 2-foot ledges.
- At 0.4 mile you'll climb a 2-foot ledge to the base of a long cascade in five steps measuring 15, 6, 6, 3, and 3 feet respectively from the top for a total of 33 feet.
- At the top of this cascade the gully makes a sharp right hand turn in a deep rock amphitheater.
- At 0.5 mile, around a bend you'll reach a 20-foot cascade in 3 stages.
- Watch to the right as a side channel spills over the gorge wall in a 120-foot waterfall called Angel Falls.
- The gully will narrow and you'll climb up one 10-foot cascade after another.
- At 0.6 mile the creek turns left at a huge rock wall. Ahead is a 30-foot gradual cascade in 2 stages. To get up, it's best to climb the far bank and use trees and root handholds to traverse a narrow ledge.
- Continue upstream past an 8-foot cascade. The creekbed will widen.
- The gully takes on a somber hue as the rock sides become wet and dark. Climb two 6-foot falls.
- At 0.8 mile, reach the crossing of the blue-blazed trail. Turn right and follow the blue trail uphill.
- The trail will follow the edge of Parish Glen providing views of the gully from the rim.
- Cross a tributary creek (the one that forms Angel Falls) at 1.2 miles. Continue on the blue-blazed trail.
- Reach a "T" and turn right on an unmarked trail. The first few trees have orange paint circles.
- Reach the Route 245 parking area in 1.9 miles.

Date visited:

Notes:

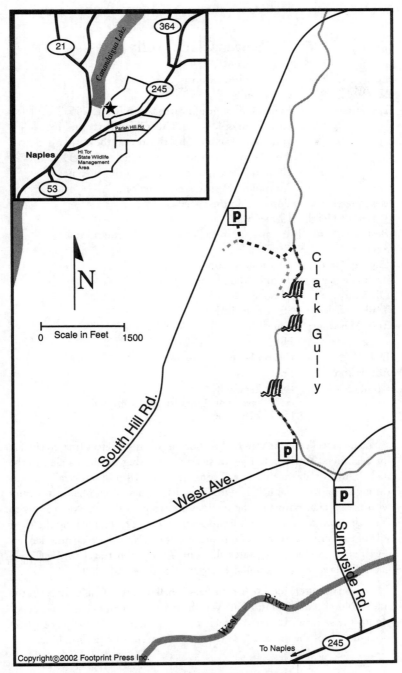

Upper & Lower Clark Gully

53.
Lower Clark Gully

Location:	Naples, Yates County
Waterway:	Clark Gully
Directions:	From Naples, head northeast on Route 245. Turn left onto Sunnyside Road. Cross West River and bear left onto West Avenue. Shortly around the corner park in the dirt road pull-offs on the right. (N 42 39.711 W77 20.023) There is also a DEC parking area near the Sunnyside/West Avenue junction.

Best Viewing Locations: From the creekbed
Waterfall Height: 15-feet high
Best Season to Visit: Early summer; it's a trickle by late summer

Access:	Creekwalk
Hiking Time:	20 minutes round trip
Trail Length:	0.4 mile round trip
Difficulty:	2 boots
Trail Surface:	Stone creekbed
Trail Markings:	None
Uses:	Hike
Dogs:	OK on leash
Admission:	Free
Contact:	DEC Region 8
	6274 East Avon-Lima Road, Avon, NY 14414
	(585) 226-2466

The creekwalk to this waterfall is short and easy—a great first creekwalk for beginners. You'll see a 15-foot steep cascade dug through a cleft in the rock. Directly above this is a 7-foot, then an 18-foot waterfall, all cut through a narrow channel. The three waterfalls may be climbable in winter with instep crampons but the inclines are steep so they are dangerous to climb in summer, even with minimal water flow. The bank along the right side of the waterway is also climbable, but it is extremely steep and dangerous. Better to enjoy this waterfall from below, then travel to the Upper Clark Gully to view additional waterfalls (see page 214).

Former state archeologist Arthur Parker believed that Clark Gully, in the side of Nundawao or South Hill, was the place or origin of the Seneca people. In the southwest, they call such a place sipapu, meaning "place where we came out of the ground." You're treading on historic ground here.

Trail Directions:

- From the dirt pull-off area follow either branch of the trail to the creekbed.
- Head left, upstream in the creekbed.
- In 0.2 mile you'll reach the waterfall—a 15-foot steep cascade dug through a cleft in the rock.

Date visited:

Notes:

54.

Upper Clark Gully

Location:	Naples, Yates County
Waterway:	Clark Gully
Directions:	From Naples, head northeast on Route 245. Turn left onto Sunnyside Road. Cross West River and bear left onto West Avenue. Turn right and head uphill on South Hill Road. Drive 2.4 miles until you see the dirt parking area surrounded by brown wooden posts. (See map on page ???.) (N42 40.399 W77 20.254)

Best Viewing Locations: From the creekbed
Waterfall Height: Two large falls, estimated at 75 and 80-feet high
Best Season to Visit: Early summer; it's a trickle by late summer

Access:	Hike and creekwalk
Hiking Time:	1.5 hours round trip
Trail Length:	1.3 miles round trip
Difficulty:	4 boots
Trail Surface:	Dirt trail and stone creekbed
Trail Markings:	None
Uses:	Hike
Dogs:	OK
Admission:	Free
Contact:	DEC Region 8 6274 East Avon-Lima Road, Avon, NY 14414 (585) 226-2466

Via a 0.4 mile trail hike and a 0.25 mile creekwalk you can reach two impressive waterfalls in a deep gully lined with pine trees and blanketed by brown pine needles. It's both a visual and an aromatic experience as you walk the flat stone creekbed, enveloped by the smell of pine. You'll be walking downstream, so you'll reach each waterfall at its crest. The first waterfall has a steep but fairly easy trail down its left bank. This waterfall is used in winter by ice climbers. Unfortunately, you can't climb to the base of the second waterfall and have to be content with peering at it from the crest—very carefully of course.

Trail Directions:
- From the parking area, follow the grass trail southeast across the field.
- Bear right at each junction until you reach a "T" at the edge of a gully at 0.15 mile.
- Turn left and follow the trail with the gully to your right. (The trail to the right goes a short distance to a field.)
- The trail will head downhill, and you'll see the creekbed off to the left.
- At 0.4 mile take a small side trail to the left. (The main trail continues steeply downhill but terminates at a landslide area and does not offer an entrance to the creekbed below the waterfalls.) The side trail will peter out but continue winding downhill—a gradual old roadbed will lead into the creekbed.
- Mark the trail/creekbed junction with a bandanna so you can find the trail on your return.
- Head to the right, downstream in the creekbed. Notice the pine forest on the creekbanks.
- Pass a series of 1 to 3-foot ledges.
- At 0.5 mile you'll reach the crest of the first big waterfall. It's a 75-feet high steep cascade. There's a fairly easy, but steep path down the bank beside the waterfall on the left. Climb down this path.
- Continue downstream, climbing down a 15-foot cascade.
- This will bring you to the crest of a 20-foot fall followed closely by a 60-foot fall. There is no path beyond this crest so backtrack to the parking lot.

Date visited:

Notes:

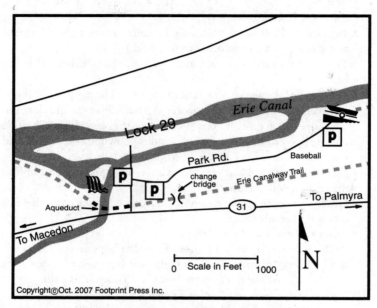

Palmyra-Macedon Aqueduct Falls

55.
Palmyra-Macedon Aqueduct Falls

Location: Palmyra-Macedon Aqueduct Park, Palmyra, Wayne County

Waterway: Erie Canal spilling into Ganargua Creek

Directions: The park is on the north side of Route 31, just west of the village of Palmyra. Park at any parking area within the park. (N43 3.807 W77 14.879)

Best Viewing Locations: From the Erie Canalway Trail

Waterfall Height: Estimated at 15-feet high

Best Season to Visit: Spring, summer, or fall (the canal is drained in the winter)

Access: Short walk

Hiking Time: 4 minutes round trip

Trail Length: 0.1 mile to the waterfall (the Erie Canalway Trail starts here and runs 85 miles west to Lockport)

Difficulty: 1 boot

Trail Surface: Crushed gravel

Trail Markings: Round, Erie Canalway Trail sign

Uses: Hike, Bike, Ski, Picnic, View lock 29

Dogs: OK on leash

Admission: Free

Contact: Palmyra Aqueduct Park, Wayne County Parks Dept.
2685 Route 31, Palmyra, NY 14522
(315) 946-5836

New York State Canal Corporation
1-800-4CANAL4
www.canals.state.ny.us

This is a man-made waterfall that owes its existence to the building of the Erie Canal. When the canal was first built, engineers didn't know how to keep the canal from flooding so they had to segregate it from natural waterways. Aqueducts were built to span creeks that had to be crossed such as Ganargua. The canal waters were carried over the creek in a wooden trough. Eventually as technology improved, flooding could be controlled in other ways and the canal bed was moved into river and creek beds as it was enlarged.

At Palmyra, the original canal flowed through the aqueduct. In its current state, the canal has been moved north slightly and the aqueduct became obsolete. Overflow waters from the canal are now allowed to spill freely into Ganargua Creek.

While you're here, be sure to wander over to the canal for a good view of lock 29. If you head east along the Erie Canalway Trail you'll find the Aldrich Towing Path Change Bridge. A change bridge allowed mules and their drivers to change from one side of the canal to the other. This bridge was salvaged and reconstructed on this site in the early 2000's.

This segment of the Erie Canalway Trail now stretches west to Lockport and east to Newark. Some day it will connect with other segments to join Buffalo to Albany.

Trail Directions:
- The Erie Canalway Trail and the path to the waterfall begins from the entrance road to Palmyra-Macedon Aqueduct Park, heading west parallel to Route 31. Follow the trail for 0.1 mile and you'll come to a bridge over Ganargua Creek. Look right to see the waterfall and remains of the aqueduct.

Date visited:

Notes:

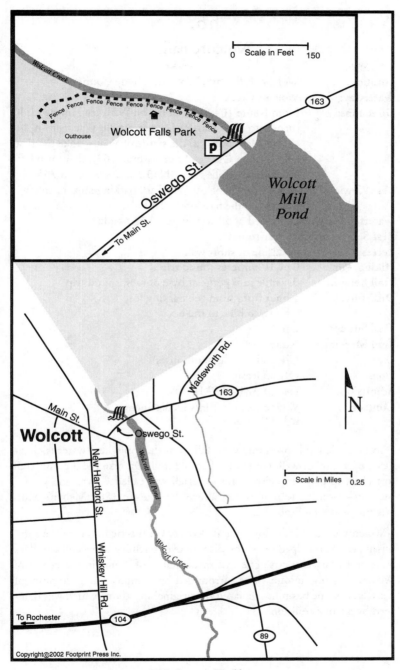

Wolcott Falls

56.

Wolcott Falls

Location: Wolcott Falls Park, Wolcott, Wayne County
Waterway: Wolcott Creek
Directions: From Route 104, head north on Whiskey Hill Road. It turns into New Hartford Street. At 0.8 mile, turn right (E) on Main Street at the statue of Venus. Take the first left (NE) on Oswego Street (Route 163), then turn left into Wolcott Falls Park. (N43 13.278 W76 48.735)
Best Viewing Locations: From Wolcott Falls Park parking area, or follow the trail to the base of the falls
Waterfall Height: Estimated at 50-feet high, 12-feet wide
Best Season to Visit: Year-round
Access: Roadside or short walk
Hiking Time: 0 or 10 minutes round trip
Trail Length: 0.4 mile into gorge at base of falls, round trip
Difficulty: 1 boot from from the parking lot
3 boots to hike to the base
Trail Surface: Dirt
Trail Markings: None
Uses: Hike, Picnic (has outhouses)
Dogs: OK on leash
Admission: Free (9 AM - 9 PM)
Contact: Wayne County Parks Department
(315) 946-5836

You can view this overhung waterfall from the top where water is channeled by a cement wall, remnants of an old mill. Or, take the 0.2 mile trail to feel its spray from below. This waterfall was called Ganadsgo by local Indians—meaning leaping waters above the lake. In 1801 Melvin's Mills gristmill was established here.

Wolcott is named for Governor Wolcott of Connecticut, one of the commissioners who helped settle the dispute over territory between New York State and Massachusetts. The cast metal statue of Venus in the center of Wolcott is truly unique. She's surrounded by nymphs riding dolphins at her feet. A stone basin has replaced the original metal one which was damaged by a truck collision.

Wolcott Falls in winter.

Trail Directions:
- View the falls from the parking lot then head west to the back corner of the park. At a break in the fence you'll find the trail which bears right as it heads downhill to the base of the falls.

Date visited:

Notes:

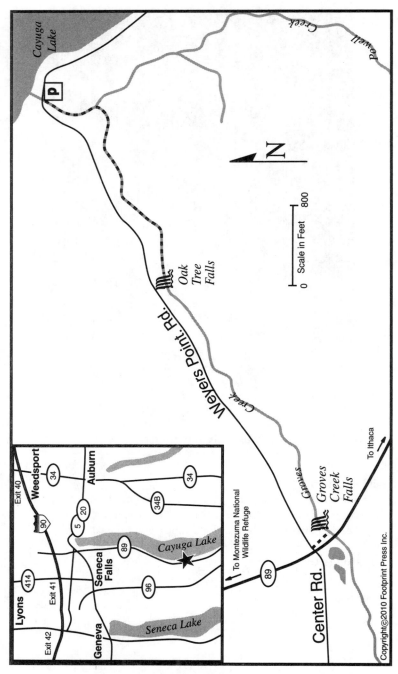

Oak Tree Falls & Groves Creek Falls

57.

Oak Tree Falls & Groves Creek Falls

Location:	Ovid, Seneca County
Waterway:	Groves Creek
Directions:	From Route 89, halfway down on the west side of Cayuga Lake, turn east on Weyers Point Road. Drive to the lakeshore and park along Weyers Point Road just after the road crosses Groves Creek. (N42 40.785 W76 43.364)

Alternative Parking: None
Best Viewing Locations: From the creekbed
Waterfall Height: 60-feet high (Oak Tree Falls)
Best Season to Visit: Summer

Access:	Creekwalk
Hiking Time:	1 hour round trip
Trail Length:	1.0 mile round trip
Difficulty:	3 boots
Trail Surface:	Stone creekbed
Trail Markings:	None
Uses:	Hike
Dogs:	OK
Admission:	Free

We espouse the philosophy that the journey is to be enjoyed in life, not the achievement of goals or end points. On most trails and creekbeds it's important to dally along the way and take in the sights, sounds, and smells that envelop you. Most journeys, that is, except this one. It's an ugly duckling of creekwalks to a magnificent waterfall. The walk is not difficult. There are no precipices to climb along the way, no narrow ledges, no cliff walls dropping rocks. Simply a walk up a rocky creekbed. But, this one is littered with small rocks, weeds, downed trees, and way too much of man's trash. You simply have to endure it for the reward at the end. Oak Tree Falls surges through a notch in a towering cliff and plummets 60 feet down a steep rock face.

In a dry summer, this creek can dry up. So, if you begin up the ugly streambed and don't see any water, it may not be worth continuing upstream - unless you enjoy looking at the geology of dry waterfall ledges.

Trail Directions:
- Enter the creekbed and head upstream.
- Reach a "Y" at 0.1 mile and bear right.
- Oak Tree Falls will loom overhead at 0.5 mile.

Date visited:

Notes:

Location:	Ovid, Seneca County
Waterway:	Groves Creek
Directions:	From Route 89, halfway down on the west side of Cayuga Lake, turn east on Weyers Point Road. Park on the right, near this corner. (N42 40.369 W76 44.334)

Best Viewing Locations: From a short trail

Waterfall Height: 30-feet high, topped with an 8-foot cascade (Groves Creek Falls)

Best Season to Visit: Spring

Access:	Short walk
Hiking Time:	2 minutes
Trail Length:	<0.2 mile round trip
Difficulty:	1 boot
Trail Surface:	Mowed path
Trail Markings:	None
Uses:	Hike
Dogs:	OK
Admission:	Free

Groves Creek Falls can be viewed via a short hike. The mowed path leads to a crossing used by farm vehicles at the crest of a 30-foot waterfall. Above this, toward Route 89 is an 8-foot cascade.

Trail Directions:
- Follow a mowed path south (<0.1 mile) toward the creek. Farm vehicles use this path to cross the creek.

Date visited:

Notes:

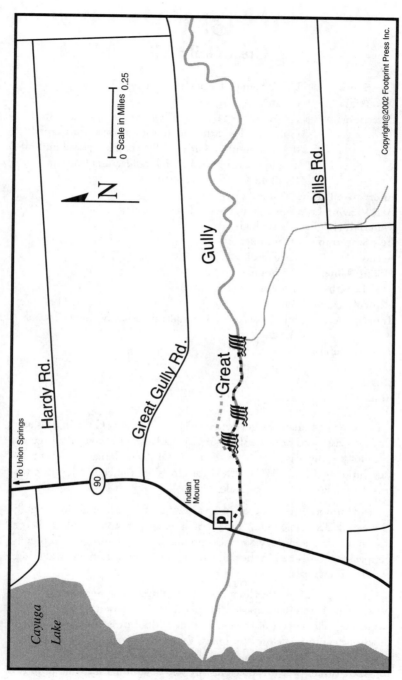

Great Gully Falls

58.

Great Gully Falls

Location:	Union Springs, Great Gully, Cayuga County
Waterway:	Great Gully Creek
Directions:	Follow Route 90 south of Union Springs. Pass Great Gully Road and the Indian Mound and white cross. 0.3 mile south of Great Gully Road is a gravel pull-off area to the left with a gravel trail leading from it. (N42 48.494 W76 42.110)

Alternative Parking: None
Best Viewing Locations: From the creekbed
Waterfall Height: 18-feet high
Best Season to Visit: Summer

Access:	Creekwalk
Hiking Time:	1.5 hours round trip
Trail Length:	1.5 miles round trip
Difficulty:	3 boots
Trail Surface:	Stone creekbed, dirt trails sporadically along edges of the creek
Trail Markings:	None
Uses:	Hike, Swim
Dogs:	OK
Admission:	Free

Two Cayuga Indian villages dotted the banks of Great Gully in days past. Cayuga Castle was near the shore of Cayuga Lake and Cayuga Village was 4 miles to the east. Both were destroyed by colonial forces in the Revolutionary War in 1779. Before this, in 1656, the French Jesuits established a mission at Cayuga Castle.

Early European settlers erected grist, saw, and woolen mills in the gully. None of this is visible today. Today you'll see sugar maple, hemlock, beech, ironwood, oak, and dogwood trees populating the banks of a deep gully. 50 species of birds nest in the gully including the great horned owl, grouse, and hummingbirds.

The full ravine is 4 miles long and 150-feet deep. The small section you'll walk offers 4 waterfalls, most with pools at their base that are good for swimming. The largest of these falls is an 18-foot drop from an overhung limestone caprock. Below it is a massive cavern, 15-feet deep. Please don't enter this cave. Waterfalls are very unstable. In spring a torrent of water 40-feet wide rushes over this precipice. By end of summer it dwindles to two or three ribbons of water. It might be possible to climb above this waterfall if you bring ropes and wear crampons. There is a narrow ledge along the right side as you face the waterfall. Just remember, climbing down is more difficult than climbing up, so do not attempt it without ropes. It's better to enjoy this waterfall from the base, play in its pool and head back downstream.

Creekwalk Directions:
- Follow the gravel path (SE) from the pull-off.
- At the "Y," bear right to view the first waterfall from its base. It's a 10-feet high steep cascade into a deep pool.
- Then backtrack on the trail and take the middle trail to get to the crest of this waterfall. (If you continue following the trail uphill it will dead end in 0.3 mile leaving you high above the creek, out of view of the waterfalls.)
- Enter the creekbed above the first waterfall and walk to the left, upstream.
- The second waterfall, a 6-footer, appears at 0.3 mile.
- At 0.4 mile a 2-footer drops into a deep tub.
- The big falls comes into view at 0.75 mile. Turn around from this point or continue upstream only if you've brought appropriate roping gear.

Date visited:

Notes:

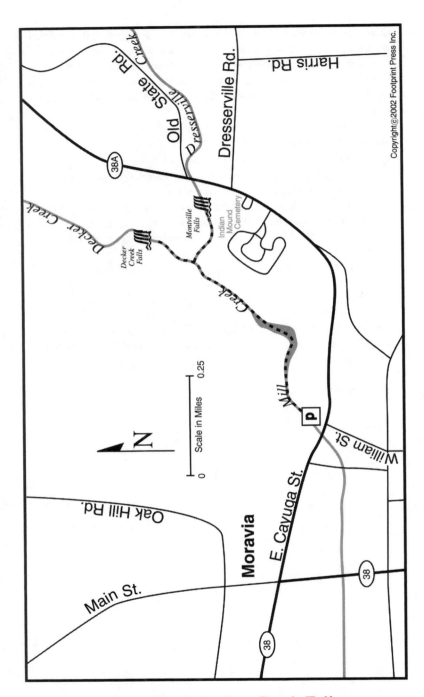

Montville & Decker Creek Falls

59.
Montville and Decker Creek Falls

Location: Moravia, Cayuga County
Waterway: Dresserville and Decker Creeks
Directions: In Moravia, south of Owasco Lake, head east on
                      Route 38A North (E. Cayuga Street). Immediately
                      after the Mill Creek bridge (across from William
                      Street) park behind the red, white and stone block
                      building. (N42 42.745 W76 24.960)
Best Viewing Locations: From the creekbed
Waterfall Height: Montville Falls: 75-feet high
                      Decker Creek Falls: 9 and 6-feet high
Best Season to Visit: Summer
Access: Creekwalk
Hiking Time: 60 minutes round trip
Trail Length: 0.9 mile round trip
Difficulty: 3 boots
Trail Surface: Stone creekbed
Trail Markings: None
Uses: Hike
Dogs: OK
Admission: Free

Decker Creek Falls are two 9 and 6-feet cascades set close together in
Decker Creek. Montville Falls is a massive rock cliff in Dresserville Creek
that sometimes offers a torrent of water. When we visited on a late summer
day after a heavy rainfall, three wisps of water fell across the rock face. The
majority of water was being diverted through the power plant that sits
beside the waterfall. By driving east out of Moravia on Route 38A (N) past
Indian Mound Cemetery, you can see the dam above Montville Falls where
Route 38A crosses Dresserville Creek.

Creekwalk Directions:
- From the parking area, enter the creekbed and turn right, upstream.
- At 0.2 mile you'll reach the junction of Decker Creek and
  Dresserville Creek. Bear left on Decker Creek.
- At 0.4 mile you'll reach the 2 waterfalls in Decker Creek.
- Head back downstream to the Decker Creek and Dresserville Creek
  junction. This time turn left and head up Dresserville Creek.
- At 0.7 mile you'll reach Montville Falls.
- Backtrack to the junction and bear left to follow Mill Creek back to
  the parking area.

Date visited:

Notes:

Montville Falls when most of the water
is diverted to the power plant.

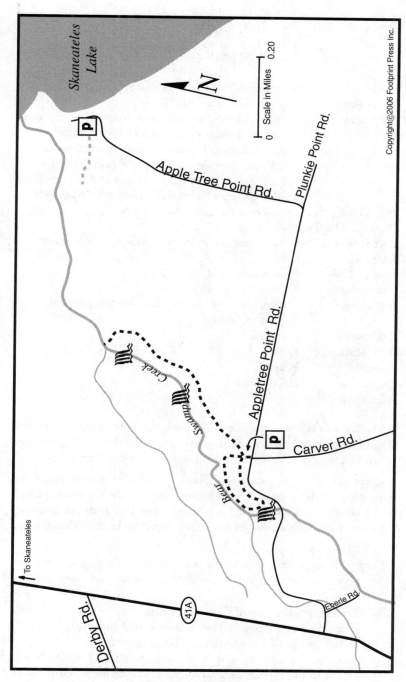

Carpenter Falls

60.
Carpenter Falls

Location:	West side of Skaneateles Lake, Cayuga County
Waterway:	Bear Swamp Creek
Directions:	15 miles south of Skaneateles on Route 41A, turn east on Appletree Point Road (there's a historical maker for Millard Fillmore's homesite at the corner.) Pass the bridge over Bear Swamp Creek and park at the dirt pull-off area on the left at the corner of Appletree Point Road and Carver Road. (N42 48.795 W76 20.487)

Best Viewing Locations: From the trail at base of falls
Waterfall Height: 90-feet high
Best Season to Visit: Early summer; dries to a trickle by late summer

Access:	Hike
Hiking Time:	15 minutes round trip
Trail Length:	0.6 mile round trip
Difficulty:	4 boots (trails are narrow, along steep banks, and very steep in sections)
Trail Surface:	Dirt trails
Trail Markings:	None
Uses:	Hike
Dogs:	OK on leash
Admission:	Free

The trails to this waterfall are not suitable for children or anyone who dislikes heights. Although short, they are narrow and sloped along the edge of a cliff. Everyone should wear hiking boots with a low slip tread.

Carpenter Falls is an awesome display of power. The water is channeled through a notch in the 10-feet thick, overhung Tully limestone caprock and plummets straight down for 80 feet. Then the water continues its downward run over a series of long, flat, sloped rocks through the gorge valley.

Farther down in the gorge as the water races to Skaneateles Lake, are three more significant waterfalls, accessible via another very steep trail.

Trail Directions to the base of Carpenter Falls:
- From the parking area, follow the middle trail (straight).
- In 0.3 mile you'll be at the base of Carpenter Falls.
- You can climb a very steep trail along the edge of the gorge and return to the parking area on the loop trail or for an easier route, just back-track.

Carpenter Falls is a powerful rush of
water even in mid-summer.

Trail Directions to the crest of Carpenter Falls:
- From the parking area, follow the left trail.
- In 0.2 mile you'll be at the crest of Carpenter Falls.
- You can climb down a very steep trail along the edge of the gorge and return to the parking area on the loop trail or for an easier route, just back-track.

Trail Directions to additional waterfalls:
- From the parking area, follow the right trail. (Caution: This route has trail so steep that there are ropes in place to assist in traversing some sections.)
- Pass a 40-foot cascade, a 60-foot free-fall, then a 10-foot cascade before the trail ends at 0.5 mile, and you have to back-track.

Date visited:

Notes:

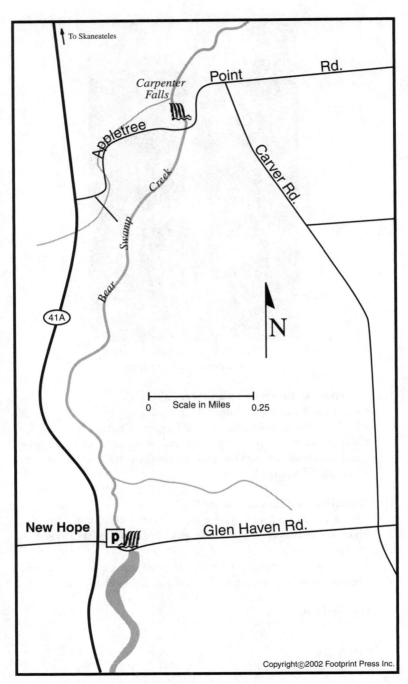

To Skaneateles

Carpenter Falls

Appletree

Point Rd.

Carver Rd.

Creek

Swamp

Bear

41A

N

0 Scale in Miles 0.25

New Hope

P

Glen Haven Rd.

Copyright©2002 Footprint Press Inc.

New Hope Mills Falls

61.
New Hope Mills Falls

Location: New Hope, west side of Skaneateles Lake, Cayuga County
Waterway: Bear Swamp Creek
Directions: 17 miles south of Skaneateles on Route 41A, turn east on Glen Haven Road in New Hope. Turn left into New Hope Mills. (N42 47.867 W76 20.720)

Best Viewing Locations: From New Hope Mills
Waterfall Height: Two dammed falls each 25-feet high
Best Season to Visit: Year-round
Access: Short walk
Hiking Time: 2 minutes round trip
Trail Length: <0.1 mile round trip
Difficulty: 1 boot
Trail Surface: Gravel driveway
Trail Markings: None
Uses: View, Shop
Dogs: OK
Admission: Free
Contact: New Hope Mills
Route 41A, New Hope, Moravia, NY 13118
(315) 497-0783

New Hope Mills was built in 1823. The 26-foot waterwheel on Bear Swamp Creek is no longer in use, but was once one of the oldest and largest in operation in the eastern United States. The mill offers organic flours, pancake mixes, and grains for sale.

The waterfalls are available for viewing any time. The first is under the Glen Haven Road bridge. The second is at the mill. The water is channeled under a covered bridge then plummets 25 feet into a natural chasm. Along with the waterfalls, you can enjoy a goose-filled pond between the two falls, a mill wheel next to the store entrance and the 26-foot waterwheel beside the mill.

Trail Directions:
- From the New Hope Mills parking area, cross the covered bridge to get a good view of the lower waterfall.
- Walk up to the Glen Haven Road bridge to view the upper waterfall.

The mill sits on the edge of Bear Swamp Creek.

Date visited:

Notes:

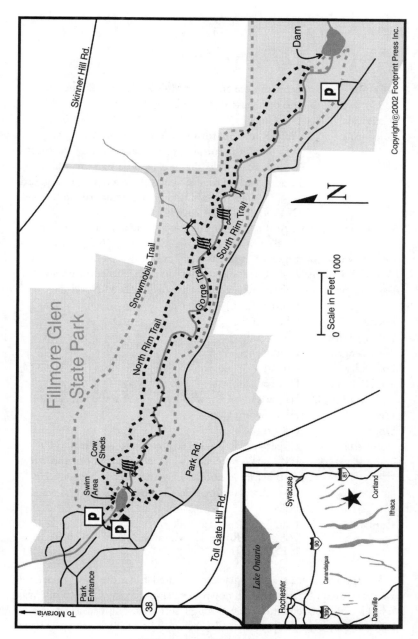

Fillmore Glen Falls

62.

Fillmore Glen Falls

Location: Fillmore Glen State Park, South of Moravia (the south end of Owasco Lake), Cayuga County

Waterway: Dry Creek

Directions: From Route 38, turn east into Fillmore Glen State Park. After the entrance gate, bear right past the camping area road. Take the next left at a sign for "old bath house." Park in the first parking area near the lifeguard and first-aid house and picnic pavilion. (N42 41.929 W76 24.994)

Alternative Parking: At the turn-around loop at the end of South Rim Road, near the dam (N42 41.478 W76 23.606)

Best Viewing Locations: From the Gorge Trail

Waterfall Height: Two 30-feet high waterfalls plus 3 other waterfalls

Best Season to Visit: May through October (trails closed November through April)

Access: Hike

Hiking Time: 2 hour loop

Trail Length: 4 mile loop

Difficulty: 4 boots

Trail Surface: Dirt trail, stone steps and walkways

Trail Markings: Yellow and brown wooden signs at some intersections

Uses: Hike, Swim, Camp

Dogs: OK on leash

Admission: $7 per vehicle is charged from 9:00 AM until 6:00 PM, 7 days per week. The fee is charged only on weekends before Memorial Day and after Labor Day. No fee is charged from mid-October until the first week in May.

Contact: Fillmore Glen State Park
1686 State Route 38, Moravia, NY 13118
(315) 497-0130

Ten thousand years ago as glaciers retreated from the area, their melt waters poured off Summer Hill down steep slopes to the Owasco inlet valley. The torrents cut their way through soft shale, sandstone, and even limestone in their rush to the valley below. The result is the spectacular geologic formation we know today as Fillmore Glen.

The abundant plant life of the gorge caught the attention of physician Dr. Charles Atwood, an amateur botanist. He worked to establish a park in the 1920s. The trails were opened in 1921. In 1925 the 39-acre site was transferred to state ownership.

Today Fillmore Glen State Park covers 938 acres and is managed by the Office of Parks, Recreation, and Historic Preservation. The three trails, each 1.8-miles long, begin in the valley and rise 349 feet to a man-made dam at an elevation of 1,720 feet. The Gorge Trail follows the water's path. The North and South Rim Trails each follow their respective rims. The creek, which flows through the gorge and did the sculpting you're about to see, was given the unlikely name of Dry Creek.

Dry Creek is dammed twice. The first dam at the upper (E) end is to control water flow. The second dam at the lower (W) end creates a swimming hole. Be sure to bring your bathing suit for a dip after a hot climb. Behind the swimming area is the Cow Sheds, a cavern of carved rock formed by the rushing waters and a 30-foot high cascading waterfall. Legend has it that cows from neighboring farms took refuge in the coolness of the rock cavern during hot summer days, hence the name Cow Sheds. It's well worth the short walk to see this unique area.

This park is named after our thirteenth president, Millard Fillmore. He was born in 1800 in a log cabin about five miles from the park. You'll pass a replica of his cabin on your way into the parking area.

Trail Directions:
- From the parking area, head through or around the pavilion, toward the swimming area.
- Pass the dammed swimming area.
- At the "T," turn left and cross an arched stone bridge.
- After the bridge, turn right on a trail to Cow Sheds area.
- At 0.2 mile the trail dead ends at the base of Cow Sheds, a multi-staged cascade set sideways in the channel.
- Turn around and follow the trail back to the bridge.
- Cross the bridge then continue straight, up 138 steps on the Gorge Trail.
- At the top of the hill, bear left to stay on the Gorge Trail.
- Head down 36 steps to an observation area overlooking the Cow Sheds area.
- Turn right and continue upstream on the trail.
- At 0.6 mile cross the first of 8 bridges over Dry Creek. The Civilian Conservation Corps built these walkways in the 1930s.
- Bridge 2 comes quickly then in 0.1 mile cross bridges 3 and 4.
- At the base of the next set of stairs, stop to enjoy the beauty of the waterfalls.

- The trail heads uphill. Watch to the left for a series of small chutes and drops.
- At 1.2 miles, cross bridges 5 and 6 with additional small chutes and drops.
- At 1.3 miles watch across the creek as a tributary cascades from the top of the gorge walls.
- Cross bridge 7 then head uphill.
- At 1.5 miles you'll see a 20-foot and a 4-foot cascade at a bend in the creek.
- Take a natural shower as water trickles over the moss-covered shale ledge along the left of the trail.
- Notice how the water spreads flat on the bedrock and forms a 7-foot high ledge at 1.6 miles.
- Bridge 8 to the right heads to a shelter and the South Rim Trail. Do not cross the bridge. Continue straight, heading uphill.
- At 1.9 miles turn left and head uphill at the "Gorge Trail" sign.
- At 2.0 miles turn left and head uphill on the North Rim Trail through a hemlock and maple forest. (The trail to the right leads to the dam and South Rim Road with an alternate parking lot.)
- At 2.3 miles, bear left. The snowmobile trail is to the right.
- Continue straight at 2.4 miles, past a side trail to the left.
- At 2.8 miles cross a bridge over the tributary stream.
- Continue downhill, passing a side trail to the left.
- At 3.5 miles the trail gets steeper and has steps.
- Pass high above Cow Sheds area. You'll only see the waterfall when leaves are off the trees.
- Pass the swim area and the old bath house.
- At the parking area, turn left and use the pedestrian bridge to cross Dry Creek back to the pavilion parking area.

Date visited:

Notes:

Waterfalls in Schuyler and Tompkins Counties

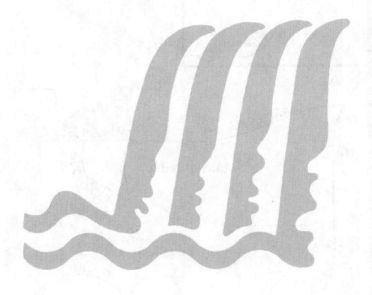

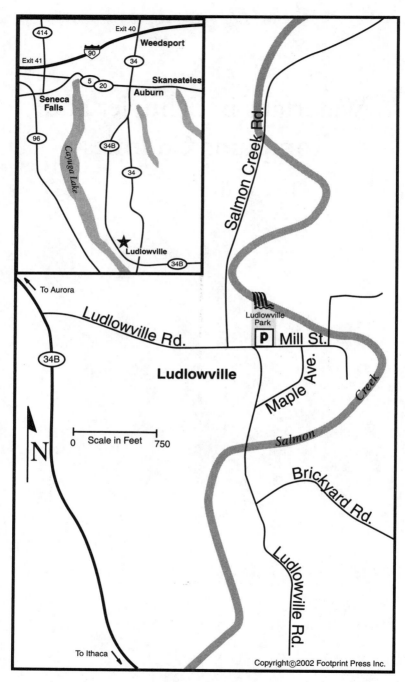

Ludlowville Falls

63.

Ludlowville Falls

Location: Ludlowville Park, Ludlowville, Tompkins County
Waterway: Salmon Creek
Directions: From Ithaca, follow Route 34 north to Route 34B north. Turn right (E) on Ludlowville Road. At a sharp bend, continue straight onto Mill Street. Ludlowville Park will be on the left, marked by a historical marker for "Ludlowville Inn 1792." (N42 33.220 W76 32.235)

Alternative Parking: None
Best Viewing Locations: From along fence at back of park
Waterfall Height: 36-feet high
Best Season to Visit: Year-round; dries to a trickle by late summer
Access: Short walk
Hiking Time: 2 minutes round trip
Trail Length: <0.1 mile round trip
Difficulty: 1 boot
Trail Surface: Mowed grass
Trail Markings: None
Uses: View, Picnic, Playground
Dogs: OK on leash
Admission: Free
Contact: Lansing Parks & Recreation
PO Box 186, Lansing, NY 14882
(607) 533-7388

Like many towns, Ludlowville owes its existence to the waterfalls. Ludlowville became a center of commerce as farmers from miles around brought their wheat to be milled in the gristmill built here in 1795. In 1919 a farmer on the hill bought a combine to grind wheat faster and more efficiently, and thus began the decline of the Ludlowville gristmill. The mill burned down in 1933.

Ludlowville Falls has a 12-foot thick limestone caprock over a large cave. The water tumbles from this ledge, 36 feet to a deep pool. Ice climbers can be seen here in winter, climbing the wall of ice. There are other waterfalls along Salmon Creek, but public access is limited.

Trail Directions:
- From the parking area, cross the mowed grass to the fence line to view the waterfall.

Date visited:

Notes:

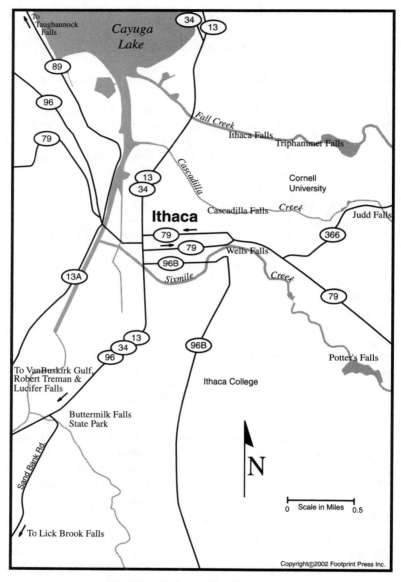

Falls of the Ithaca Area

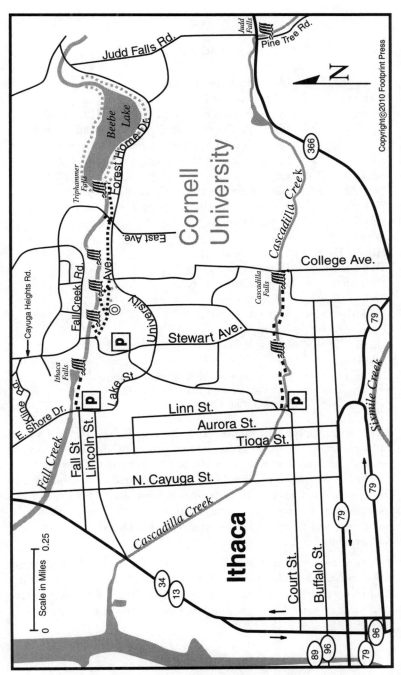

Cascadilla, Ithaca, Judd & Triphammer Falls

64.
Cascadilla Falls

Location:	Ithaca, Tompkins County
Waterway:	Cascadilla Creek
Directions:	In Ithaca, head north on Route 13/34. Turn right (E) on W. Court Street. Park near the end where it meets Linn Street (at the metered spots along E. Court Street). (N42 26.576 W76 29.677)

Alternative Parking: None
Best Viewing Locations: From the trail in Cascadilla Gorge
Waterfall Height: 9 waterfalls, the largest being 50-feet high
Best Season to Visit: Year-round

Access:	Hike
Hiking Time:	1 hour round trip
Trail Length:	1.4 miles round trip
Difficulty:	4 boots, many stairs
Trail Surface:	Stone walkway
Trail Markings:	Sign at entrance only
Uses:	Hiking
Dogs:	OK on leash
Admission:	Free (parking is metered for 2 hour maximum)
Contact:	City of Ithaca, DPW, Parks & Forestry
	245 Pier Road, Ithaca, NY 14850
	www.ci.ithaca.ny.us

Cascadilla Gorge was formed after the last ice age as water carved through layers of sandstone, siltstone, and shale which had been deposited as sand and mud in a shallow sea 400 million years ago. Watch for ripple marks in the sandstone, formed long ago in the shallow sea. You can also find brachiopod fossils, clam-like animals that lived in the sea. More recently the falls and gorge were reshaped by human excavations. The gorge rock was quarried to procure stone for local buildings such as those at Cascadilla Place.

The ravine once began at William's Mill at the center of the village of Ithaca where the first settlers built their cabins. Today it drops 400 feet from Cornell University campus to downtown Ithaca. Cascadilla Gorge's nickname is "Giant's Staircase," appropriate due to the many stairs you'll climb.

Trail Directions:

- From the corner of E. Court & Linn Streets, walk east on the pedestrian walkway parallel to Cascadilla Creek.
- Cross over the creek and continue upstream along the path.
- At <0.1 mile you'll pass the first 20-feet high cascade.
- Steps will lead to the second waterfall—a very long, curving, gradually sloped cascade, which is split in the middle by a small treed island.
- Pass a 10-foot cascade, then a 20-foot cascade through a narrow channel. The Stewart Avenue bridge used to span high overhead. (During our visit in June 2001 welders were dismantling the bridge.)
- At 0.3 mile, cross the creek on an arched stone bridge.
- Pass a 4-foot cascade, then a narrow 2-foot drop, followed by a long, wide cascade.
- Pass a channel to the right which sports a waterfall only in the spring.
- Next comes a 20-foot cascade.
- At 0.6 mile you'll pass a 50-foot high multi-level cascade.
- Finally at 0.7 mile comes 50-feet high Cascadilla Falls. It's under the arched stone bridge of College Avenue.
- Turn around here to walk back down the gorge or continue forward to climb the steps to the Center for Theater Arts at Cornell University.

Date visited:

Notes:

65.

Ithaca Falls

Location:	Ithaca, Tompkins County
Waterway:	Fall Creek (see map on page 245)
Directions:	In Ithaca, head north on Route 13/34. Turn right (E) on Dey Street (to the west it's called Willow Ave.), and take a quick left onto Lincoln Street. At the end, turn left (N) on Lake Street. Park in the two-tiered dirt parking area just south of Fall Creek. (N42 27.142 W76 29.657)

Alternative Parking: None
Best Viewing Locations: From the trail at the base of the falls
Waterfall Height: 150-feet high
Best Season to Visit: Year-round

Access:	Short walk
Hiking Time:	15 minutes round trip
Trail Length:	0.4 mile round trip
Difficulty:	1 boot
Trail Surface:	Dirt
Trail Markings:	None
Uses:	Hike, Picnic, Swim
Dogs:	OK on leash
Admission:	Free
Contact:	City of Ithaca, DPW, Parks & Forestry 245 Pier Road, Ithaca, NY 14850 www.ci.ithaca.ny.us

Ithaca Falls is the final hurrah as Fall Creek rushes toward Cayuga Lake. It's at the end of a 1-mile long gorge at the base of the Portage Escarpment, that sports a total of 6 waterfalls (see page 244 for access to the others.). This one is a frothy beauty—worthy of the much overused name "Buttermilk Falls." Thank goodness this one was given another name. It stands proud at 150-feet high and 175-feet wide.

Back in the late 1800s it was 156-feet high and only 86-feet wide, evidence of ongoing erosive forces. The water was used to power numerous mills, beginning with the first in 1814. A wooden flume attached to the cliffs carried water from above the falls to the mills. Ithaca winters made this mode of transporting water difficult to sustain so in 1830 a tunnel was blasted through the rock.

Look at the gorge walls near Ithaca Falls to find a fossiliferous rock outcrop that contains the brachiopod *Warrenalla laevis*. The fossils in this thin

Ithaca Falls

rock bed are distinctive enough to be used as a marker for the base of the Ithaca Formation of rock.

You can glimpse this waterfall from your car on Lake Street but by far the best view is to walk the short trail to its base. Along the way, you'll pass a round tube in an old stone wall. This is what remains of the abandoned Ithaca Gun Company. In summer Ithaca Falls is a favorite spot for locals to frolic in the water and sit under the waterfall spray.

Trail Directions:
- From the parking area head north along Lake Road.
- After the large factory tube set in stonework, turn right and head down to the creek on a trail.
- Pass a small waterfall on the right—a tributary into Fall Creek.
- You'll begin to hear and see Ithaca Falls as you reach the creek.
- Follow the trail along the creek to Ithaca Falls.

Date visited:

Notes:

66.
Triphammer, Forest, Foaming, and Rocky Falls

Location: Ithaca, Tompkins County

Waterway: Fall Creek (see map on page 245)

Directions: At the Routes 34/13 junction northeast of Ithaca, head south on East Shore Drive. Turn left on Kline Road (a steep, narrow climb) then right on Needham Place. At the end turn right on Cayuga Heights Road. Bear right to cross Fall Creek on the Stewart Avenue bridge. Look for a parking spot on the right along Stewart Avenue. (N42 27.098 W76 29.461)

Alternative Parking: None

Best Viewing Locations: From the Cayuga Trail along Fall Creek

Waterfall Height: Triphammer Falls is estimated at 55-feet high
Forest Falls is estimated at 20-feet high
Foaming Falls is estimated at 15-feet high
Rocky Falls is estimated at 25-feet high

Best Season to Visit: Year-round (one side trip section of the trail is closed in winter)

Access: Hike

Hiking Time: 1 hour round trip

Trail Length: 2 miles round trip

Difficulty: 4 boots

Trail Surface: Paved sidewalks, dirt trails, and many steps

Trail Markings: Orange blazes and markers along the Cayuga Trail

Uses: Hike

Dogs: OK on leash

Admission: Free (you may have to pay a parking meter)

Contact: Cayuga Trails Club
PO Box 754, Ithaca, NY 14851-0754
email: ctc@lightlink.com
www.lightlink.com/ctc/

Named for the mighty pulsing beat it produces, Triphammer Falls sits below the dam that creates Beebe Lake on the edge of the Cornell University campus. At its south side sits the now crumbling Hydraulic Laboratory which was built in 1897. Construction of this stone building and the dam and canal used to divert the water cost about $20,000. Equipment used in the laboratory cost another $30,000. The pedestrian bridge overlooking Triphammer Falls was built in 1997 to connect the central and north Cornell campuses. It replaced a 35-year-old bridge which had been closed in 1995 due to structural damage.

Fall Creek is one of the hanging valleys left high above Cayuga Lake when the glaciers scoured the north-south valleys but left the east-west tributaries relatively unscathed. Since the glaciers receded, spring water surges have carved out the softer shales and left waterfalls where harder limestones existed.

On the route described, you'll see Triphammer Falls as the culmination of your journey. Along the way, you'll get to see three other significant cascades in Fall Creek, by following a section of Cayuga

Forest Falls in Fall Creek Gorge

Trail. (See the back cover for a picture of a Fall Creek waterfall.) This trail was built beginning in 1964 by the Cayuga Trails Club using Cornell University lands. The entire trail is 6 miles long from the Stewart Avenue bridge to NY Route 13.

Trail Directions:
- Walk back up Stewart Avenue to the Stewart Avenue bridge. (The bridge has pedestrian sidewalks on both sides, making waterfall viewing safe and easy.) To the west is the crest of Ithaca Falls. Upstream, to the east, is a 20-foot high, multi-staged cascade called Forest Falls, set deep in the Fall Creek gorge.
- At the southeast corner of the bridge, head into the hemlock and maple woods on the Cayuga Trail. Look for the plastic, orange diamond marker.
- Reach a "Y," at 0.1 mile and bear left into the gorge. (This side trail is closed in winter.)

- Continue down 123 steps to creek level at 0.2 mile. You'll be at the base of a 15-foot multi-tiered cascade with a concave crest called Foaming Falls. High above is a pedestrian suspension bridge. Upstream is a stone power building and another waterfall.
- Climb back up the stairs and turn left to continue on the Cayuga Trail.
- At the next junction turn left. It will lead to the pedestrian bridge. (Straight leads to University Avenue, right leads to a parking lot.)
- Walk out on the pedestrian bridge to get a better view of the waterfall by the power plant. Rocky Falls is a 25-foot gradual cascade set in a bend of Fall Creek.
- Don't cross the bridge. Instead, return to the Cayuga Trail and climb 89 steps to University Avenue.
- Turn left and follow the University Avenue sidewalk to the East Avenue bridge at 0.8 mile.
- Cross East Avenue and turn left onto the East Avenue bridge. Upstream is your first view of Triphammer Falls below Beebe Lake.
- Don't cross the East Avenue bridge. Return to the University Avenue corner and head left on the Forest Home Drive sidewalk.
- Follow the orange marked trail to the left at 0.8 mile.
- At the "T," turn left (the orange marked trail turns right) to the pedestrian bridge to get a closer look at Triphammer Falls. Can you find the potholes at the bottom of the falls? Notice the Hydraulic Laboratory (now crumbling) built into the side of the cliff.
- Reverse the route to return to your car. (Or extend your hike with a 1 mile walk around Beebe Lake.)

Date visited:

Notes:

67.
Judd Falls

Location: Ithaca, Tompkins County
Waterway: Cascadilla Creek (see maps on pages 244 & 245)
Directions: From Route 366 at the eastern edge of Ithaca, turn south on Judd Falls Road and park along the edge of the road, before the railroad bridge which now carries the East Ithaca Recreationway Trail.
(N42 26.599 W76 28.206)

Alternative Parking: None
Best Viewing Locations: From Judd Falls Road
Waterfall Height: Estimated at 12-feet high
Best Season to Visit: Year-round
Access: Roadside
Difficulty: 1 boot
Uses: View only
Dogs: OK on leash
Admission: Free

Reuben Judd operated a water powered woolen mill on this site from 1832 until 1858. It has also been home to a lead pipe factory and a chair factory. Today it sits next to a busy road and is traversed above by the East Ithaca Recreationway Trail (see *Take Your Bike - Family Rides in New York's Finger Lakes Region*).

Judd Falls is a gradual cascade that travels 12 feet down a series of small drops.

Trail Directions:

• From Judd Falls Road, cross over to creekside to view the waterfall.

Date visited:

Notes:

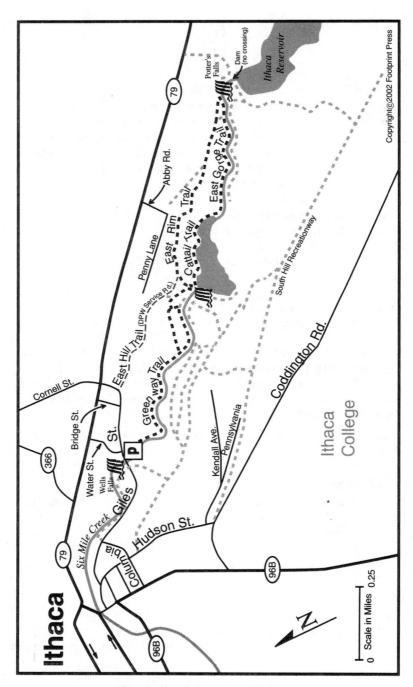

Potter's & Wells Falls

68.
Wells Falls
(a.k.a. Business Man's Lunch Falls, Van Nattas Cascade, and First Dam)

Location:	Ithaca, Tompkins County
Waterway:	Six Mile Creek
Directions:	In Ithaca, take Route 79 east, past Route 366. Turn right onto Giles Street. Just before the bridge over Six Mile Creek, turn left into a parking area. It's marked by a brown sign "Mulholland Wildflower Preserve" and a white sign "VanNattas Dam Watershed Area." (N42 25.960 W76 29.054)

Alternative Parking: None
Best Viewing Locations: From a trail at the base of the waterfall
Waterfall Height: A 20-foot dam on top of a 3-tiered waterfall totaling 35 feet
Best Season to Visit: Year-round

Access:	Hike
Hiking Time:	30 minutes round trip
Trail Length:	0.6 mile round trip
Difficulty:	3 boots
Trail Surface:	Dirt
Trail Markings:	None
Uses:	Hike
Dogs:	OK on leash, clean up after pet
Admission:	Free, closed 10PM - 4 AM
Contact:	City of Ithaca, DPW, Parks & Forestry 245 Pier Road, Ithaca, NY 14850 www.ci.ithaca.ny.us

Wells Falls alludes to the fact that water has worn round holes or wells into the rock. It sits directly below VanNattas Dam. Beside the waterfall sits a crumbling old power plant. The dam creates a 30-foot free-fall followed by 3 natural cascades 5, 15, and 15 feet respectively. It drops into a large pool where Six Mile Creek bends at the base of a huge stone wall. Listen for the echo off this wall as your eyes feast on the glorious sights.

From the end of the trail at the base of Wells Falls be sure to look downstream, across the creek, to see water plummeting 70 feet down the far cliff wall. This area is inviting, but the creek is still used as Ithaca's water source —hence the no-swimming rule.

Wells Falls in late summer.

See Waterfall #69 (page 257) for a description of the hike east from this parking area to Potter's Falls.

Trail Directions:
- From the parking area, walk up the entrance road and cross Giles Street.
- Turn left and cross the Giles Street bridge.
- Pass the first trail after the guard rail. (You can follow it to see the waterfall from a side view, but this route to the base is much steeper.)
- At 0.1 mile turn right onto the trail at the red and blue fire hydrant.
- Follow the trail downhill. It will curve right at the base of a tall rock wall and end at the base of Wells Falls at 0.3 mile.

Date visited:

Notes:

69.

Potter's Falls (or Green Tree Falls)

Location: Ithaca, Tompkins County

Waterway: Six Mile Creek (see maps on pages 244 & 254)

Directions: In Ithaca, take Route 79 east, past Route 366. Turn right onto Giles Street. Just before the bridge over Six Mile Creek, turn left into a parking area. It's marked by a brown sign "Mulholland Wildflower Preserve" and a white sign "VanNattas Dam Watershed Area." (N42 25.960 W76 29.054)

Alternative Parking: None

Best Viewing Locations: From the East Gorge Trail

Waterfall Height: Potter's Falls is a 25-foot high jagged edged cascade Two dam waterfalls are 8 and 30-feet high respectively

Best Season to Visit: Year-round

Access: Hike

Hiking Time: 2.5 hours round trip

Trail Length: 4.8 miles round trip

Difficulty: 4 boots

Trail Surface: Dirt

Trail Markings: Sign at entrance only

Uses: Hike

Dogs: OK on leash, clean up after pet

Admission: Free, closed 10PM - 4 AM

Contact: City of Ithaca, DPW, Parks & Forestry
245 Pier Road, Ithaca, NY 14850
www.ci.ithaca.ny.us

Six Mile Creek, particularly above the dam and at Potter's Falls, is a notorious nude sunbathing and skinny dip area. But beware, swimming is not allowed here. The area is patrolled by the Gorge Rangers who can arrest swimmers. Too bad, the allure is almost too much to resist.

Even so, the walk to this waterfall is a very pleasant hike through woods. In spring you'll see waterfalls in tributaries as well as Six Mile Creek. Along the creek bed and deep in the woods you'll find many old water pipes dating from the early 1900s. This creek is still used as Ithaca's water source—hence the no-swimming rule.

Across Giles Street is the VanNattas Dam, which creates a waterfall above a natural waterfall called Wells Falls or Business Man's Lunch Falls. See waterfall #68 (page 254).

Potter's Falls

Trail Directions:
- From the parking area head south across a wooden bridge toward the creek.
- Walk upstream on a mulched trail (Greenway Trail), parallel to the creek.
- At 0.5 mile, pass a side trail to the left. Continue straight.
- At 0.6 mile, look across the creek at a wide dirt area. In spring a waterfall tumbles down to Six Mile Creek. Also look upstream on Six Mile Creek to see your first small waterfall.
- The side loop trail comes in on the left, but continue straight.
- The trail will narrow. Continue straight until you can see a small dam with an 8-foot cascade. Just beyond it is a larger dam with a 30-foot free-fall waterfall. (The two dams help minimize siltation problems in the drinking water.) This is as far as you can go on this trail.
- Backtrack to the last side trail and turn right, away from the creek.
- Shortly, in the woods, turn right and take the trail uphill, heading north.
- Reach a junction at 1.1 miles and turn right (E).
- At 1.2 miles cross a tributary creek (with waterfalls in spring).

- Pass the two dam falls far below.
- At the reservoir, turn left and head uphill. (The trail straight ahead will be part of your return loop.)
- At 1.5 miles turn right (E) onto an old gravel roadway (East Rim Trail).
- The roadway disappears and the trail narrows above a swampy reservoir pond.
- At 1.7 miles, cross a gully (with waterfalls in spring) on an old waterpipe.
- Climb a steep hill to get a great view from the end of the swampy reservoir pond.
- At the top of the hill, continue straight, downhill. (A trail to the left leads to houses.)
- At 2 miles, cross a gully that sports a 12-foot waterfall even in mid-June.
- Continue straight as a trail merges from houses.
- With the creek in view, turn left onto a side trail to stay upland on a trail that leads to Potter's Falls.
- The trail ends at Potter's Falls at 2.4 miles.

To Return:
- Put your back to the waterfall and turn left to take the trail down at water level (East Gorge Trail).
- Continue straight, passing several small side trails.
- At 2.8 miles pass a gully with a waterfall.
- Continue straight at water level (Cattail Trail), passing the swampy reservoir pond.
- At 3.4 miles climb a hill to get around the dam.
- Cross a gully at 3.7 miles (with waterfalls in spring).
- At 3.8 miles, turn left at a junction and head downhill.
- At the base of the hill, bear right, then turn right onto a wide dirt trail.
- Turn right when you reach the water's edge and follow this trail (Greenway Trail) back to the parking area.

Date visited:

Notes:

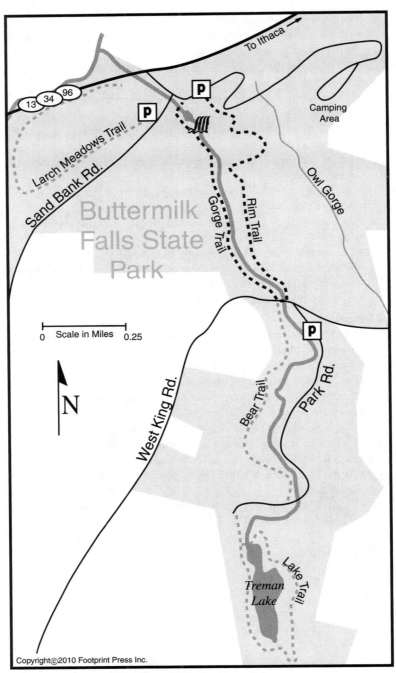

Buttermilk Falls - Ithaca

70.
Buttermilk Falls - Ithaca

Location: Buttermilk Falls State Park, Ithaca, Tompkins County
Waterway: Buttermilk Creek in Buttermilk Glen
Directions: From Ithaca's central business district, head south for 2 miles on Route 13/34/96. Buttermilk Falls State Park will be on the left. Park just beyond the entrance toll gate. (N42 25.039 W76 31.273)
Alternative Parking: The upper park entrance on West King Road (N42 24.565 W76 30.734)
Best Viewing Locations: Buttermilk Falls can be viewed from its base near the entrance to the park (even from Routes 13/34/96). Many additional waterfalls are viewed via the Gorge Trail.
Waterfall Height: 180-feet high
Best Season to Visit: Spring, summer & fall (trails close November through April)
Access: Short walk (wheelchair accessible) for Buttermilk Falls Hike to see at least 10 other waterfalls
Hiking Time: 1 hour loop
Trail Length: 1.6 mile loop
Difficulty: 4 boots, many stairs
Trail Surface: Dirt, stone, and old pavement
Trail Markings: Brown signs at trailheads
Uses: Hike, Swim
Dogs: OK on leash (please clean up after pets)
Admission: $7 / vehicle, mid-April through mid-October
Contact: Buttermilk Falls State Park
c/o Robert H. Treman State Park
R.D. #10, Ithaca, NY 14850
(607) 273-5761
www.nysparks.state.ny.us/

You'll see Buttermilk Falls the minute you drive into this state park. It looms above as a frothy white cascade, 80-feet wide. It's comprised of two segments, called First Fall and Second Fall, each approximately 90-feet high. At the base is a dammed swimming area. Buttermilk Creek drops 500 feet in a series of waterfalls and rapids, on its way to Cayuga Inlet. Above Buttermilk Falls, the gorge widens to an amphitheater where rocks project in a semicircle forming Pulpit Rock and Pulpit Falls. Farther up, you'll find Pinnacle Rock, also called Monument Rock or Steeple Rock. This 50-feet high stone pillar stands in the center of the glen, detached from the sides. Pinnacle Rock has worn down at a rate of one inch per century.

In the 1700s the Sapony Indians lived in the village of Coreorgonel near Buttermilk Falls. They had 25 log cabins surrounded by farm fields and orchards. The Indians fled before General John Sullivan's Continental Army during the Revolutionary War. The army burned Coreorgonel on September 4th, 1779.

Early European settlers constructed dams and mills along Buttermilk Creek. VanOrman's Dam was built in the gorge in 1872 and supplied water to Ithaca until 1903. This dam no longer exists. In 1875 Scott's Dam was built in the upper park area for a grist mill. It too is gone.

In 1924 Robert and Laura Treman donated 154 acres, including Buttermilk Gorge to New York State. Today the park covers 751 acres.

The hike described below climbs up the Gorge Trail and returns via the Rim Trail. After an initial climb, you will walk through the gorge almost at water level. All the waterfalls will be viewable from the Gorge Trail. The Rim Trail is a pleasant walk through the woods but offers no spectacular views.

While on the Gorge Trail, watch for potholes drilled in the rock, where no waterfall exists today. This is evidence that the falls are migrating uphill as the forces of erosion work their magic. At one time each pothole was at the base of a roaring waterfall. Loose stones in the eddies of the waterfall wore the round holes in the rock.

If you don't get your fill of waterfalls by hiking the Gorge Trail, go visit Owl Creek. Drive toward the camping area. Before the bridge on the road is a small parking area. From here, follow a very short dirt path to see a series of small cascades.

Trail Directions:
- From the parking area, head south across the entrance area to cross a bridge over Buttermilk Creek. It's marked with a brown sign with yellow letters "Gorge Trail." After the bridge turn left on the Gorge Trail. (Or, head toward Buttermilk Falls and cross Buttermilk Creek on the dam that creates the swimming area.)
- Begin the climb of what will be many stone steps, beside Buttermilk Falls.
- At the next waterfall (approximately a 25-footer), notice the narrow notch the water has cut through the rock cliffs.
- As you reach a fence, peer over it to see two deep holes drilled by the water.

- Climb past one, then a second three-tiered waterfall.
- At 0.5 mile you'll pass a shelter then quickly pass a bridge over the gorge. Continue straight.
- Watch for a waterfall to your right as water plunges to join Buttermilk Creek.
- Pass a two-tiered waterfall, approximately 25-feet high.
- At 0.7 mile, reach Pinnacle Rock. Look for the pothole at its base, a sign that a waterfall once existed here.
- Pass a 15-foot waterfall.
- Climb to a bridge and turn left to cross the bridge. You're near the upper park entrance. (Or, turnaround and follow the Gorge Trail back down.)
- After the bridge, turn left onto the Rim Trail.
- Pass a cut-off trail on the left and continue straight, downhill.
- Pass an overlook (not a great view).
- Continue downhill to the parking area.

Date visited:

Notes:

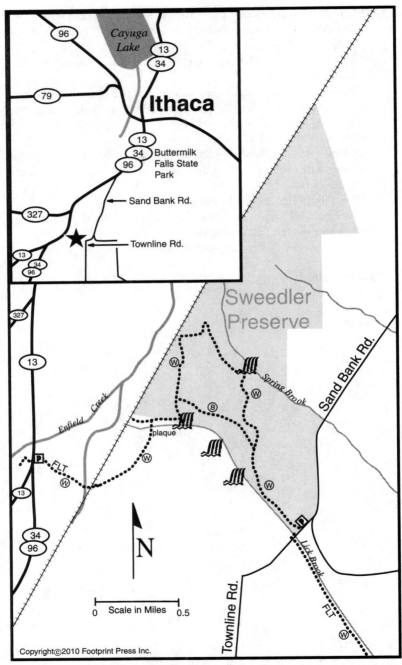

Lick Brook Falls

71.
Lick Brook Falls

Location: Sweedler Preserve, south of Ithaca, Tompkins County
Waterway: Lick Brook
Directions: From Ithaca, head south on Route 13/34/96. Just south of Buttermilk Falls State Park, turn left (S) on Sand Bank Road. Bear right onto Town Line Road. Park on the right side of the road near the Finger Lakes Trail sign. (N42 23.743 W76 31.997)
Alternative Parking: Parking area adjacent to confluence of Routes 13 and 34/96 (N42 23.898 W76 32.762)
Best Viewing Locations: From the Finger Lakes Trail
Waterfall Height: 3 major waterfalls, estimated at 50 to 140 feet, plus many smaller falls
Best Season to Visit: Spring or after heavy rain; it dries to a trickle in summer
Winter ice climbing through the Cornell Outdoor Education program only
Access: Hike
Hiking Time: 1 hour loop
Trail Length: 1.4 mile loop
Difficulty: 4 boots, very steep
Trail Surface: Dirt
Trail Markings: White and blue blazes
Uses: Hike, Snowshoe
Dogs: OK on leash
Admission: Free
Contact: Finger Lakes Land Trust
202 East Court Street, Ithaca, NY 14850
(607) 275-9487
www.fllt.org

Cayuga Trails Club
PO Box 754, Ithaca, NY 14851
www.lightlink.com/ctc
email: ctc@lightlink.com

Finger Lakes Trail Conference
6111 Visitor Center Road, Mt. Morris, NY 14510
(585) 658-9320
www.fingerlakestrail.org

Like much of the land in the Finger Lakes region, most of the Sweedler Preserve was cleared for farming after the Revolutionary War. But poor soil led to abandonment of the farms and their return to forest. Since the

1800s, Lick Brook has been a popular picnic and hiking spot, primarily because of the many waterfalls. The Finger Lakes Land Trust acquired this unique land through a swap and bargain sale in 1993. Owners Moss and Kristin Sweedler traded their Lick Brook land for a plot with a pond where their dogs could swim. By selling the Lick Brook land for far below market value, the Sweedlers helped preserve this beautiful land and did us all an immense favor.

In its plummet to Cayuga Inlet, Lick Brook has carved a deep gorge with dangerous cliffs. Please stay on the trail, away from cliff edges. In 2001, the Finger Lakes Trail was rerouted to provide a gentler climb up the hillside. White blazes denote the current Finger Lakes Trail. The steep trail along the edge of Lick Brook is now a blue-blazed side trail. To best view the waterfalls the trail directions instruct you to hike to the bottom of the valley following the white-blazed Finger Lakes Trail, then watch for waterfalls on your way back uphill along the blue-blazed trail. This will facilitate seeing the waterfalls without leaving the trail.

Ice climbing is permitted only through the Cornell Outdoor Education Program. See web site www.coe.cornell.edu/ or call (607) 255-6183.

Trail Directions:
- From the parking area along Town Line Road, head downhill (NW), following the white blazes. At first the descent will be gradual, then it will get steeper.
- Watch for the white-blazed trail to turn right. Continue following the white blazes to Spring Brook which is loaded with small waterfalls (it flows best in spring).
- At Spring Brook, turn left and follow the trail downhill, still marked by white blazes.
- When you reach the valley floor, follow the white blazes as they turn left toward Lick Brook.
- Leave the main trail to walk into the Lick Brook stream bed (if the water is low enough) to get a view of the bottom waterfall. It's a steep cascade, approximately 50-feet high.
- Now, return to the trail and follow the blue-blazed trail steeply up the hill, watching to the right for a never ending procession of waterfalls.
- Next in line will be a long cascade. Its first 15 feet are gradual followed by 25 feet of steep cascade.
- The third waterfall is the big one. It's tall with published estimates ranging from 93 to 140 feet. The falls is a narrow wisp in a large arched amphitheater. It's possible to view only the top portion.
- Continue uphill, passing many small waterfalls.

- Continue straight as the blazes turn to white and you pass the white trail to the left.
- Cross a wooden bridge near a 15-foot cascade.
- Next up will be a 15-foot gradual cascade, then a 12-foot table top with a shear drop, and finally a 15-foot ribbon cascade.
- You'll reach the parking area gasping for breath but sated with the beauty of Lick Brook.

Date visited:

Notes:

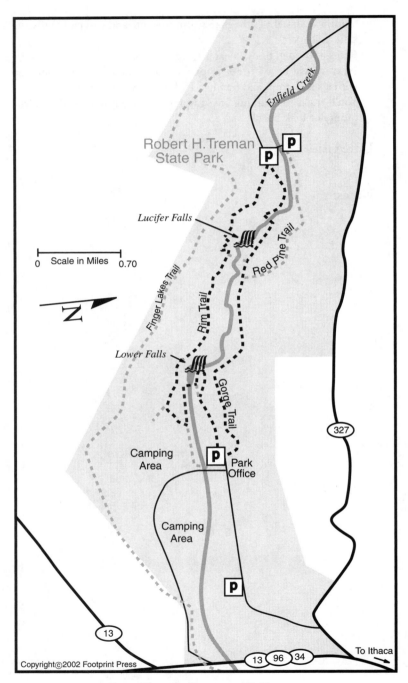

Lucifer & Lower Falls

72.

Lucifer & Lower Falls

Location: Robert H. Treman State Park, south of Ithaca, Tompkins County

Waterway: Enfield Creek in Enfield Glen

Directions: From Ithaca, head south for 3 miles on Route 13/34/96. Turn right onto Route 327. Robert H. Treman State Park will be on the left. Park in the main lot, just past the park office. (N42 23.871 W76 33.433)

Alternative Parking: There is an upper park entrance with a parking area off NYS Route 327, three miles from the lower entrance. (N42 24.137 W76 35.385)

Best Viewing Locations: From the Gorge Trail

Waterfall Height: Lucifer Falls is 115-feet high

Lower or Enfield Falls is estimated at 70-feet high

Best Season to Visit: Spring, summer or fall (trails are closed November 10th through mid-April)

Access: Hike

Hiking Time: 3 hour loop

Trail Length: 5.3 mile loop

Difficulty: 4 boots, many stairs

Trail Surface: Dirt, stone, and old pavement

Trail Markings: Brown signs at trailheads

Uses: Hike, Swim in pool below Lower Falls

Dogs: OK on leash (please clean up after pets)

Admission: $7 / vehicle

Contact: Robert H. Treman State Park
R.D. #10, Ithaca, NY 14850
(607) 273-3440
www.nysparks.state.ny.us/

Enfield Glen is three miles long and sports two major waterfalls and many smaller cascades. It's unique in that it's actually three glens interwoven. The middle gorge is a wide, deep section with forested slopes. It was formed by massive water flows between glacier visits. The upper and lower gorges are younger and have more rugged sections. They were eroded by the creek after the last glacier. The lower gorge has been closed since a flood in 1935.

Where the middle and upper glens meet we find Lucifer Falls. The water turns left at its base because of joint plane fissures in the rock. The alcove at the plunge basin is called Devil's Kitchen. In pioneer days raucous barbeques

Lower Falls

were held near this waterfall. A party of tourists during this time dubbed it Lucifer Falls.

The other major waterfall found here is Lower Falls (also called Enfield Falls). This is a jutting "pulpit" or bastion type of waterfall which is common in the Finger Lake gorges. It resulted from even erosion of a shale bed without a strong capstone, resulting in a convex, crescent shape.

Throughout Enfield Glen, look for straight troughs that resemble millraces. Erosion of this gorge was governed by rectangular joint planes in the rock beds. Over time water worked into the joints and widened them into fissures.

Early in the history of Enfield Gulf, it was simply known as The Gulf. In 1839 Isaac Rumsey built a gristmill and house in the upper gorge. Corn and wheat were ground at the mill until 1917, part of a hamlet known then as Enfield Falls. You can still tour the mill which is located near the upper parking area.

Robert H. Treman was an Ithaca banker who bought the Enfield Glen land and built paths and stone bridges to blend with the natural setting. He donated the land to New York State in 1920.

The route described below takes you out on the Gorge Trail and returns via the Rim Trail. But here, Gorge and Rim Trails are misnomers. Both trails wander high to the rim and down to water level. On the Gorge Trail, you start by climbing high and can hear but not see the waterfalls below. Waterfalling on this portion of trail is strictly an auditory experience.

However, have patience. Eventually the trail dips to water level and you get to see many spectacular waterfalls.

Trail Directions:
- From the parking lot head up the path nearest the park office. "Up" is the operative word. There are lots of steps and a steep climb.
- You'll hear the waterfalls far below, but you can't see them yet.
- Cross a wooden bridge at 0.6 mile.
- The trail now descends so you can see Enfield Creek and the waterfalls but shortly takes you back up a long flight of steps.
- At 1.1 miles reach an outcrop, overlooking an 8-feet high free-falling waterfall with a "W" shaped caprock.
- Reach water level via a stone stairway and continue on a dirt path through fields of vinca and day lilies.
- Cross another wooden bridge at 1.4 miles. If you're here in spring, look to the right to see a waterfall.

The upper portion of Lucifer Falls

- At 1.5 miles, climb steps next to a 10-feet high waterfall, where one half is a cascade and the other half is free-falling.
- Cross a third wooden bridge at 1.7 miles.
- A stone walkway will take you past towering stone cliffs.
- Pass the intersection with Red Pine Trail at 1.9 miles. Continue straight.
- Pass a waterfall covering the full width of the channel. Its top is a 10-foot free-fall to a cascading bottom.
- Pass a waterfall with a jagged edge.
- At 2.1 miles, pass a bridge across Enfield Glen. Continue straight.
- More steps to climb, but your reward is Lucifer Falls at 2.3 miles. The four segments start with a cascading top, followed by two free-falling sections, and terminating in a long cascade. If the wind is blowing watch for the third section to get tossed aside.
- Round the bend to another spectacular waterfall—a multi-staged cascade.
- At 2.4 miles, climb more steps to cross the gorge on a stone bridge, high above a flume.
- Pass yet another waterfall.
- Continue straight, passing a bridge across the gorge.
- Pass a drinking fountain just before the junction with the Rim Trail.
- At 2.6 miles, turn left onto the Rim Trail. (To your right is the upper parking area and the mill.)
- Cross a wooden bridge and climb.
- Pass a service road.
- Continue downhill.
- Continue straight, past steps to the left that lead to a viewing area.
- The next viewpoint gives you a lofty view of Lucifer Falls.
- A knee-killer—lots of stone steps, switchbacking down into the gully.
- At 3.3 miles, turn right. The sign at this junction is misleading. (Straight takes you over the gorge to the Gorge Trail.)
- Cross a wooden bridge at 3.6 miles.
- Climb back to the rim.
- Next is a long, gradual downhill.
- At 4.7 miles, bear left to continue steeply downhill on the Rim Trail.
- You'll get an upper view of Lower Falls.
- Steps will take you down to the cabin area at 5.0 miles.
- Continue straight through the cabin area, to the edge of Enfield Creek.
- Turn left on the trail with the creek to your right.

- Pass a 4-foot crescent shaped cascade and get another glimpse of Lower Falls.
- Cross the bridge over Enfield Creek (which dams the swimming area in summer) and bear left up steps to a lookout next to Lower Falls.
- Turn around on the paved path to pass the bath house and return to the parking area.

Date visited:

Notes:

An unnamed waterfall in Robert Treman State Park.

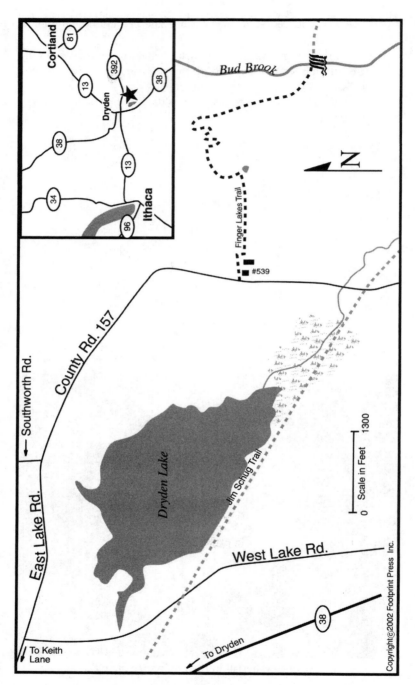

Bud Brook Falls

73.

Bud Brook Falls

Location:	South of Dryden, Tompkins County
Waterway:	Bud Brook
Directions:	From Dryden, head south on Route 38. Take the first left (E) onto Keith Lane. At the end of Keith Lane, turn right (S) on County Road 157 (also called East Lake Road). Park along the road, just north of house #539 where you see a yellow and green Finger Lakes Trail sign. There is room for one car only. Please don't park in or block the driveway. (N42 27.573 W76 15.679)

Alternative Parking: Parking for the nearby Jim Schug Trail accommodates a few cars, about 0.2 miles south of the Finger Lakes Trail.

Best Viewing Locations: From the banks of Bud Brook

Waterfall Height: About 12 small falls ranging from 1 to 3-feet high

Best Season to Visit: Year-round

Access:	Hike
Hiking Time:	1.5 hours round trip
Trail Length:	2.4 miles round trip
Difficulty:	4 boots
Trail Surface:	Dirt
Trail Markings:	White blazes
Uses:	Hike, Snowshoe
Dogs:	OK on leash
Admission:	Free
Contact:	Finger Lakes Trail Conference 6111 Visitor Center Road, Mt. Morris, NY 14510 (585) 658-9320 www.fingerlakestrail.org

The hike to Bud Brook will get your heart pumping—a good aerobic workout. You'll climb through a forest, cross fields and pasture lands and gain a vista of the valley below from a high vantage point. Your reward will be at least a dozen small drops in a babbling brook.

Trail Directions:
- From County Road 157, head east across a field on the Finger Lakes Trail.
- Follow the white blazes around the edge of a field and cross a stile at 0.3 mile.
- Continue east toward the forested hill.

Bud Brook Falls

- Head uphill (N) on an old dirt road.
- Watch for, then take a right turn off the dirt road, halfway up the hill. Head uphill (SE).
- Follow the white blazes carefully; the trail makes many turns.
- At 0.6 mile, pause a moment to sign the trail register.
- At 0.8 mile the trail flattens out at the top of the hill.
- Begin the steep descent down the backside of the hill.
- At 1.1 miles, turn left before the cow pasture with a beautiful valley view.

- Cross Bud Brook at 1.2 miles, but do not climb the next stile.
- Turn right to follow the edge of the brook downstream. You'll find a series of small but pretty waterfalls.

Date visited:

Notes:

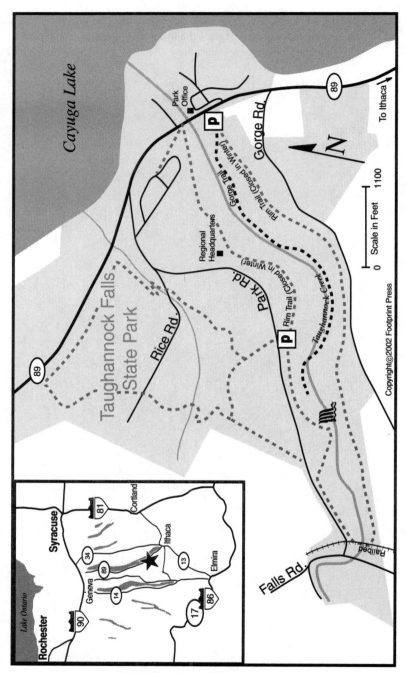

Taughannock Falls

74.
Taughannock Falls

Location: Taughannock Falls State Park, Trumansburg, Tompkins County

Waterway: Taughannock Creek

Directions: From Ithaca, take Route 89 north for 8 miles. The parking lot for the trails and waterfall will be on your left as you head north. (N42 32.711 W76 35.922)

Alternative Parking: Additional parking is available on the east (Cayuga Lake) side of Route 89.

Best Viewing Locations: From the Gorge Trail
From the overlook on Park Road

Waterfall Height: 215-feet high

Best Season to Visit: Year-round; creek becomes a trickle by late summer

Access: Hike or roadside or wheelchair

Hiking Time: 45 minutes round trip

Trail Length: 1.5 miles round trip

Difficulty: 1 boot

Trail Surface: Dirt trail

Trail Markings: Wooden "Gorge Trail" sign

Uses: Hike, Snowshoe

Dogs: OK on leash

Admission: $8 / vehicle May through September

Contact: Taughannock Falls State Park
PO Box 1055, Trumansburg, NY 14886
(607) 387-6739

This impressive waterfall is easy to see whichever route you choose. The first option is a drive to an overlook where you can view the falls from the rim of the gorge. Or, choose the wide, flat trail that leads to the base of the waterfall via an easy 0.75 mile hike (each way). Signs along the trail teach of the history and geology of the area. Both viewpoints are wheelchair accessible. The hardest part of this waterfall is pronouncing its name "tau-han-nock."

The water plummets down a sheer cliff wall through a small notch in the rock. In spring it's a mighty roar. In summer it whispers with only a narrow wisp of water. In winter it forms a unique ice sculpture. Until 1894 the water came over the brink, projecting at a right angle. A fierce electric storm shook loose a square block of hard sandstone leaving the falls to tumble from a recess at the brink. The capstone is Sherburne flagstone, underlaid with 200 feet of weak Geneseo shales. Above the crest rises another 50 feet of Ithaca shales. The hard, flat base of the gorge is Tully limestone.

Taughannock Gorge is the closest of any Finger Lakes gorge to being a canyon. It has a level basin between 400-feet high cliffs. The waterfall forms a 30-foot deep plunge pool at its base.

Park literature claims that this 215-feet high waterfall is higher than Niagara Falls—which is true. It's 31 feet higher then Niagara. But it also claims it to be the highest waterfall in the eastern US. Well, not exactly. Inspiration Falls in Letchworth State Park beats it by 135 feet.

There are only speculations about the origin of the name Taughannock. One legend attributes it to the Native American word "Taghkanic" meaning "great fall in the woods." Another, more elaborate legend tells of a chieftain of the Delaware tribes named Taughannock who lost his life in a battle over land with the Cayuga Indians. His body was hurled into the gorge near the falls, which have born his name ever since. Evidence has been found of Native American villages on Taughannock Point. The Cayuga and Seneca Indians, two tribes in the 6-Nation Confederacy of the Iroquois, were driven out of the area after the Revolutionary War.

In the 19th century, a railroad station was built near the upper gorge. Sandstone was quarried upstream, shaped in a mill near the railroad, and shipped to New York City to make sidewalks. Luxury hotels were built on both sides of the gorge near the falls. Tourists came by steamboat to stay at Taughannock House, Cataract House, and J. S. Halsey's Hotel which once had a stairway into the gorge.

Taughannock State Park opened in 1925 with 64 acres of land. Today it covers 745 acres. The main recreation area of the park, east of Route 89 is land formed as a delta by the material eroded by Taughannock Creek.

Directions to the Overlook:
- Pass the main parking areas for Taughannock State Park as you head north on Route 89 then turn west onto Park Road.
- Bear left to stay on Park Road.
- Pass the regional headquarters building for the park.
- Park at the overlook parking area on the left.

Trail Directions:
- From the parking area on the west side of Route 89, head up the Gorge Trail.

- In less than 0.1 mile you'll see the first waterfall. It's a sheer drop 15 feet over a 10-foot thick limestone caprock to a pool below. (Swimming is not allowed here.)
- As you continue west on the trail, notice the absolutely flat rock creekbed.
- At 0.2 mile you'll pass a 3-foot drop across the creekbed then several 1 to 2-foot drops.
- Cross the wooden bridge over Taughannock Creek and Taughannock Falls will come into view.
- The trail ends at a viewpoint below the waterfall at 0.75 mile.

Date visited:

Notes:

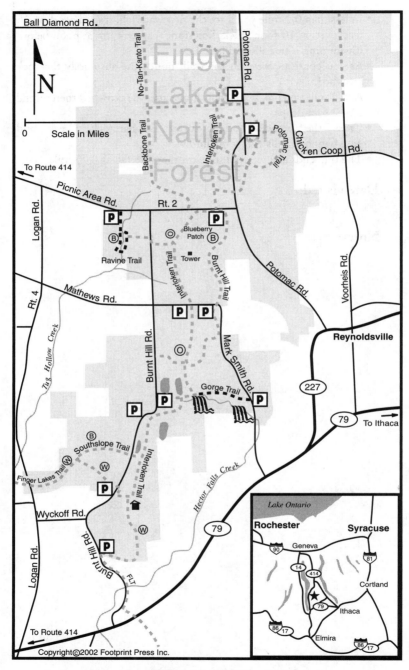

Gorge & Ravine Trail Falls

75.
Gorge Trail Falls

Location: Finger Lakes National Forest, Schuyler County
Waterway: Hector Falls Creek
Directions: From Route 414 along the east shore of Seneca Lake, head east on Route 79. Turn north on Mark Smith Road. Cross Hector Falls Creek as you enter the Finger Lakes National Forest. In 0.1 mile, park in the parking area on the right at the sign "Gorge Trail & Interloken Trail." (Note: Mark Smith Road is seasonal—not plowed in winter.) (N42 27.257 W76 47.169)
Alternative Parking: The Gorge Trail parking area on Burnt Hill Road (N42 27.305 W76 48.361)
Best Viewing Locations: From Mark Smith Road and the Gorge Trail
Waterfall Height: Mark Smith Road Falls: 6 and 3-feet high
Gorge Trail Falls: 1 and 4-feet high
Best Season to Visit: Spring; creek dries by late summer (road closed in winter; beware of hunters in fall)
Access: Hike
Hiking Time: 30 minutes round trip
Trail Length: 0.8 mile round trip
Difficulty: 3 boots
Trail Surface: Dirt trail
Trail Markings: Blue blazes
Uses: Hike, Snowshoe, Camp
Dogs: OK
Admission: Free
Contact: Finger Lakes National Forest
5218 State Route 414, Hector, NY 14841
(607) 546-4470

The Finger Lakes National Forest encompasses 16,000 acres of land and has over 30 miles of interconnecting hiking trails. Hiking during hunting season is not recommended since the national forest is open to hunting.

On foot, you can explore the deep forests and steep hills of this varied countryside. The forest contains a five-acre blueberry patch. What better treat on any excursion than devouring a handful of freshly picked blueberries? July and August are the best months to find ripe blueberries. This forest also offers overnight camping and a privately owned bed-and-breakfast nearby (Red House Country Inn B&B, 607-546-8566), making it a perfect weekend getaway. Contact the Finger Lakes National Forest for additional information on camping.

The segment of trail described here is a minor portion of the trails available in this forest. The waterfalls it leads you to are relatively minor but pretty just the same. The walk to the waterfalls is as much a part of the adventure as the waterfalls themselves.

The Iroquois Indians originally inhabited the area around the Finger Lakes National Forest. In 1790 the area was divided into 600-acre military lots and distributed among Revolutionary War veterans as payment for their services. These early settlers cleared the land for production of hay and small grains such as buckwheat. As New York City grew, a strong market for these products developed, encouraging more intensive agriculture. The farmers prospered until the middle of the nineteenth century, when a series of events occurred. These included the popularity of motorized transportation in urban centers (reducing the number of horses to be fed), gradual depletion of the soil resource, and competition from midwestern agriculture due to the opening of the Erie Canal.

Between 1890 and the Great Depression, over a million acres of farmland were abandoned in south central New York State. In the 1930s it was obvious that farmers in many parts of the country could no longer make a living from their exhausted land. Environmental damage worsened as they cultivated the land more and more intensively to make ends meet. Several pieces of legislation were passed, including the Emergency Relief Act of 1933 and the Bankhead-Jones Farm Tenant Act of 1937, to address these problems. A new government agency, the Resettlement Administration, was formed to carry out the new laws. This agency not only directed the relocation of farmers to better land or other jobs, but also coordinated the purchase of marginal farmland by the federal government.

Between 1938 and 1941, over 100 farms were purchased in the Finger Lakes National Forest area and administered by the Soil Conservation Service. Because this was done on a willing-seller, willing-buyer basis, the resulting federal ownership resembled a patchwork quilt. The land was named the Hector Land Use Area and was planted with conifers and turned into grazing fields to stabilize the soil. Individual livestock owners were allowed to graze animals on the pasture land to show how less intensive agriculture could still make productive use of the land.

By the 1950s many of the objectives of the Hector Land Use Area had been met, and the public was becoming interested in the concept of multiple uses of public land. In 1954 administration responsibilities were transferred to the U.S. Forest Service. The name was changed to the Hector Ranger District, Finger Lakes National Forest, in 1985.

Today this National Forest is used for recreation, hunting, forestry, grazing of private livestock, preservation of wildlife habitat, and education and research. It is a treasure available for us all to enjoy.

Trail Directions:

- The first waterfall viewing occurs on your drive in. As you enter Finger Lakes National Forest (or leave it) watch to the west to see two waterfalls in Hector Falls Creek. These are on private property so are only viewable from the road.
- From the parking area, follow the blue-blazed trail uphill.
- The gorge will appear to your left. Periodically peer over the edge to see if you can see any of the many waterfalls far below. This will obviously be easier when leaves are off the trees.
- You'll see the creekbed when the trail heads downhill and a 4-foot waterfall with a V-shaped crest will come into view.
- Beyond this are some 1-foot ledges.
- Once you've reached creek level at 0.4 mile, turn around unless you plan to hike additional trails in the Finger Lakes National Forest.

Date visited:

Notes:

76.
Ravine Trail Falls

Location:	Finger Lakes National Forest, Schuyler County
Waterway:	Tug Hollow Creek (see map on page 282)
Directions:	From Route 414 along the east shore of Seneca Lake, head east on County Route 2 (Picnic Area Road). The parking area for the Ravine Trail is on the right, past County Road 4 (Logan Road) and 0.3 mile before the Burnt Hill Road intersection. (N42 29.043 W76 48.791)

Alternative Parking: None
Best Viewing Locations: From the Ravine Trail
Waterfall Height: A series of ledges ranging from 1 to 4-feet high
Best Season to Visit: Spring; creek dries by late summer (beware of hunters in fall)

Access:	Hike
Hiking Time:	30 minute loop
Trail Length:	0.9 mile loop
Difficulty:	3 boots
Trail Surface:	Dirt trail
Trail Markings:	Blue blazes
Uses:	Hike, Snowshoe, Camp
Dogs:	OK
Admission:	Free
Contact:	Finger Lakes National Forest 5218 State Route 414, Hector, NY 14841 (607) 546-4470

This short loop follows the Ravine Trail where Tug Hollow Creek dug its way to a bed of flat slate slabs. The biggest climb is in and out of this ravine. The waterfalls will come into view as you cross bridges, cross tributaries, and hike along the top edge of the ravine. See the Gorge Trail Falls #75 on page 283 for a history of the Finger Lakes National Forest.

Across Picnic Area Road from the parking lot is the Updike Historical Site. A short walk on the trail takes you to the remains of a once prosperous farm, which was owned by the Updike family for generations. It was originally built by Renselaer and Orvilla Updike in 1852 and passed to their son Alvah and his wife Harriet in 1902. The stone house foundation and concrete slab from the barn are still visible.

Trail Directions:

- From the parking area, start the blue-blazed trail near the brown "Ravine Loop Trail" sign.
- Pass a register box at 0.1 mile then bear left at the "Y."
- Cross a wooden bridge. Stop to enjoy the 2 to 3-foot drops on both sides of the bridge.
- At 0.3 mile, look into the ravine to your right to see a 2-foot fall with a jagged edge.
- The trail turns left, then heads down into a side ravine on the left.
- At 0.4 mile, cross a tributary at the bottom of the side ravine then follow the trail as it turns right.
- Cross Tug Hollow Creek and look in both directions to see waterfalls.
- The trail turns right along the opposite side of the creek. Keep an eye to the right to catch glimpses of waterfalls.
- Cross a small wooden bridge at 0.6 mile.
- Reach the trail junction at 0.7 mile and continue straight to the parking area.

Date visited:

Notes:

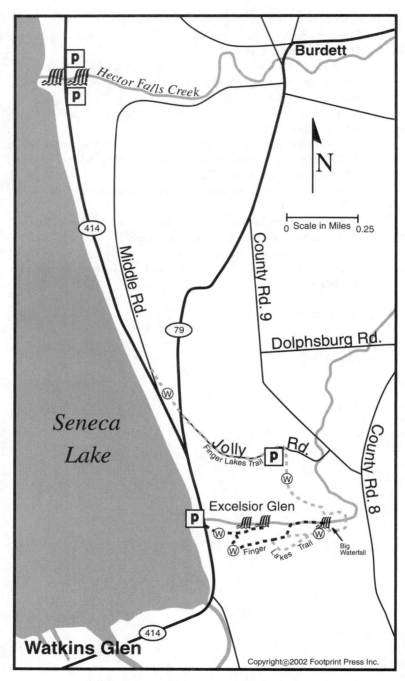

Excelsior Glen and Hector Falls

77.

Hector Falls

Location: Watkins Glen, Schuyler County
Waterway: Hector Falls Creek
Directions: From Watkins Glen, take Route 414 north for two miles. There is a sign for Hector Falls just before the bridge. Parallel parking is allowed before and after the bridge. Obey the posted signs. (N42 23.714 W76 51.080)
Alternative Parking: None
Best Viewing Locations: From roadside
Waterfall Height: 165-feet high
Best Season to Visit: Year-round
Access: Roadside or waterway (from Seneca Lake)
Difficulty: 1 boot
Trail Markings: Road sign
Uses: View only
Dogs: OK on leash
Admission: Free
Contact: Schuyler County Visitors Center
100 N. Franklin Street, Watkins Glen, NY 14891
1-800-607-4552
www.schuylerny.com

Our first reaction to viewing this hanging valley waterfall was—wow, it's beautiful, but it's not 165-feet high. Then we realized, as you stand on the highway bridge you're only seeing a portion of this great waterfall. It continues under the bridge and through private property for its full journey in three major steps to Seneca Lake. For a better perspective, rent a kayak or jet ski in Watkins Glen and see Hector Falls from Seneca Lake.

Hector Falls was known earlier as Factory Falls because of the mills, foundry, and potash works that once clustered here. Industrial use first began in 1801 when Samuel A. Seely erected a woolen mill—the first in Schuyler County.

Trail Directions:
• View Hector Falls from the Route 414 bridge.

Date visited:

Notes:

78.
Excelsior Glen Falls

Location: Watkins Glen, Schuyler County
Waterway: Excelsior Glen (see map on page 288)
Directions: From Watkins Glen, take Route 414 north. As the
                  road bends left around the south end of Seneca Lake,
                  watch for a bridge over Excelsior Glen. Park along
                  Route 414. (N42 23.461 W76 51.335)
Alternative Parking: Jolly Road at the FLT trailhead
                  (N42 23.737 W76 50.976)
Best Viewing Locations: From the creekbed
Waterfall Height: 3 major falls ranging from 30 to 100-feet high
Best Season to Visit: Early summer; dries in late summer
Access: Hike and creekwalk
Hiking Time: 1 hour round trip
Trail Length: 1.2 miles round trip
Difficulty: 4 boots
Trail Surface: Dirt trails and rock creekbed
Trail Markings: White blazes on Finger Lakes Trail,
                  otherwise no markings
Uses: Hike
Dogs: OK on leash
Admission: Free
Contact: Finger Lakes Trail Conference
                  6111 Visitor Center Road, Mt. Morris, NY 14510
                  (585) 658-9320
                  www.fingerlakestrail.org

You can reach the lower two waterfalls from hiking trails, but to see the largest—a 100-foot steep cascade that falls in three tiers, you need to walk in the creekbed. Ice climbers use this waterfall in the winter. It's not one of the prettiest creekwalks. The stream bed is weedy and riddled with downed trees. However, the waterfalls are spectacular and worth the steep climb.

Trail & Creekwalk Directions:
- From Route 414 head uphill on the east side of Excelsior Glen following the white blazes of the Finger Lakes Trail.
- In <0.1 mile, continue straight on an unmarked trail. (The FLT will switchback toward the right. There's a register box at this junction.)
- You'll quickly see the first waterfall cut a narrow notch through the rock gorge. A boulder is stuck in the notch. Continue up the trail.

(If the water level is low you may be able to creekwalk from above the first waterfall to the base of the second waterfall.)

- At 0.08 mile the trail will end at the crest of the second waterfall—a 30-foot steep cascade across the width of the channel.
- Back-track to the register box and follow the white-blazed Finger Lakes Trail. (If you diligently follow the white blazes, they will lead uphill for 0.6 mile to cross Excelsior Glen at a 15-foot two-tiered waterfall above the big waterfall.)
- 0.07 mile above the register box continue straight on an unmarked trail as the FLT bears right.
- In another 0.03 mile (0.23 miles traveled in total so far) turn left on an unmarked side trail.
- Reach the creekbed and head upstream at 0.3 mile. Be sure to flag this trail entrance to the creekbed, so you can find it on the way out. (There are sporadic trails along the edge of the creek that you can follow.)
- Pass a series of small waterfalls.
- At 0.6 mile you'll reach the base of the big waterfall.

Date visited:

Notes:

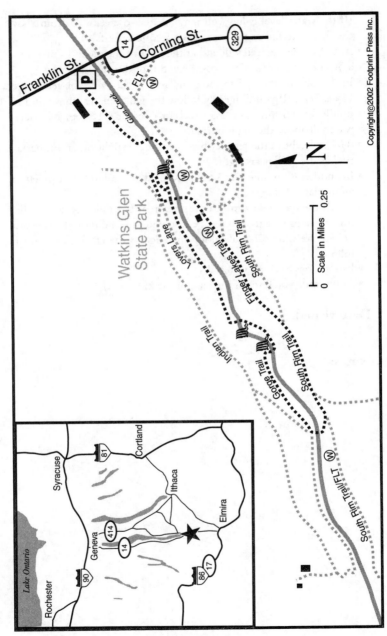

Watkins Glen

79.
Watkins Glen
(Cavern Cascade, Central Cascade, Rainbow Falls, Pluto Falls)

Location: Watkins Glen State Park, South end of Seneca Lake, Schuyler County

Waterway: Glen Creek

Directions: Route 14 becomes Franklin Street in Watkins Glen. The pay parking area for Watkins Glen State Park is between 9th and 10th Streets on the west side of Franklin Street. (N42 22.552 W76 52.271)

Alternative Parking: Anywhere within the town of Watkins Glen

Best Viewing Locations: From the Gorge Trail

Waterfall Height: 19 waterfalls, highest is Central Cascade which is 60-feet high

Best Season to Visit: Mid-May through October (closed in winter)

Access: Hike

Hiking Time: 1.5 hour loop

Trail Length: 3 mile loop

Difficulty: 4 boots

Trail Surface: Stone and dirt trails

Trail Markings: Some brown and yellow signs. White blazes on the Finger Lakes Trail portion.

Uses: Hike

Dogs: Pets NOT allowed on Gorge Trail

Admission: Free if you park in town and walk. (Parking at the trailhead costs $8 per vehicle from the 3rd Saturday in June through Labor Day)

Contact: Watkins Glen State Park
P.O. Box 304, Watkins Glen, NY 14891-0304
(607) 535-4511

Finger Lakes Trail Conference
6111 Visitor Center Road, Mt. Morris, NY 14510
(585) 658-9320
www.fingerlakestrail.org

Whether it's a first time visit, or a repeat hike, you're in for a treat at this park. The strenuous trails wander through rock tunnels, behind waterfalls, over bridges above the gorge, and most importantly, alongside an incredibly spectacular gorge full of water cuts and waterfalls. There are many steps to climb, so you'll get a good aerobic workout in a short time, and you may get wet from waterfall spray. The Gorge Trail is closed

November 10 when ice and snow make the journey dangerous, and is reopened in early May once it is deemed safer.

The glen began to form 12,000 years ago at the end of the ice age. Great continental glaciers from Canada excavated an immense trough in an ancient river valley, leaving behind 35-mile long Seneca Lake, the deepest of the Finger Lakes. Glen Creek has poured down the glacially steepened valley ever since, slowly eroding the weak sedimentary rock. Today Glen Creek descends 400 feet in two miles, creating 19 waterfalls and 300-feet cliffs. It is New York's finest example of a pothole type gorge. Swirling currents of rapidly descending water created borings called potholes. They were enlarged by stones and gravel caught in the swirls and became deep, round kettles in the bedrock. The potholes are sometimes connected by long, narrow passages. Some of them break through and merge, looking like hourglasses.

Locals called this area Big Gully and named the waterway Mill Creek because of the sawmills and gristmills that made use of its water. The town of Watkins Glen was laid out by a former New York druggist, Dr. Samuel Watkins. He called his town Salubria, and later Jefferson. The NYS Legislature renamed the town as a tribute to Watkins after his death in 1851.

Morvalden Ells, a journalist from Elmira, opened Watkins Glen as a private tourist resort in 1863. Gradually the mills and dams were removed and wooden steps and rails were changed to concrete walkways and iron guardrails. The rock tunnels you'll walk through were hand-cut in the early 1900s. The area became a state park in 1906, purchased for just over $46,000. In 1935 a flood destroyed most of the walkways and railings. The state used natural stone masonry to rebuild them.

The route described below follows the Gorge Trail west from the lower entrance, loops back on the Finger Lakes Trail, crosses the gorge on a suspension bridge, and continues back through the gorge to the beginning point.

Trail Directions:
- From the parking area, head up stairs through a rock tunnel.
- Cross Sentry Bridge, 52 feet above the water. Notice the hole cut in the rock directly in front of the bridge. In the mid 1800s, water behind a dam passed through this flume tunnel, down a wooden trough, and over the waterwheel of a flour mill in what is now the parking area.
- Stay on the Gorge Trail, passing stairs to the left.
- Walk behind Cavern Cascade waterfall, then into a spiral tunnel.

- The suspension bridge overhead and the stairway to the right will be part of your return loop. Stay on the Gorge Trail.
- Climb though another tunnel stairway. You've entered the narrows with a unique micro-climate. It is shady, cool, and moist most of the time, almost like a rainforest.
- At 0.6 mile, pass stairs to the right that lead to Lover's Lane.
- Climb stairs and a pass through a tunnel. Then cross the bridge over Central Cascade, which plunges more than 60 feet.
- Walk under Rainbow Falls. If you're lucky enough to be here on a sunny, late afternoon, see if you can spot the rainbow.
- At 0.8 mile, cross another bridge, then walk under Pluto Falls, named for the ancient Roman lord of the underworld. Little can grow in this dark, narrow passage.
- At 1.1 miles, cross Mile Point bridge to the Finger Lakes Trail. (The Gorge Trail continues straight for another 0.4 mile. To the right is Indian Trail.)
- Climb stairs to a "T." Turn left on the Finger Lakes Trail.
- Follow the white blazes past a trail to the right which leads to the camping area.
- Pass a shelter.
- Cross a cement bridge.
- Bear left at the "Y."
- At the next "Y" bear right, following white blazes through a picnic area.
- Pass a building and road to the right. Continue following white blazes.
- Turn left to return to the Gorge Trail at the small lily pond.
- Cross a suspension bridge 85 feet over the creek. During the great flood of 1935, the water rose to within five feet of this bridge.
- Turn right following the "main entrance" sign.
- Turn right and head down stairs.
- Turn left and continue down, following the Gorge Trail back to the parking area.

Date visited:

Notes:

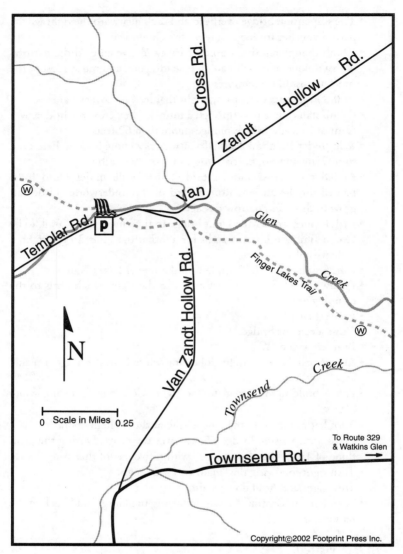

Twin Falls

80.

Twin Falls

Location:	Dix, Schuyler County
Waterway:	Glen Creek
Directions:	From Watkins Glen take Route 329 west. Continue straight on Townsend Road. Turn right onto Van Zandt Hollow Road, then left onto Templar Road. In 0.18 mile pull off on the right (on an abandoned road) at the Finger Lakes Trail crossing. (N42.36880 W76.958697)

Alternative Parking: None

Best Viewing Locations: From the creekbed at the base of the falls

Waterfall Height: Upper waterfall: 15-feet high

Lower waterfall: 10-feet high

Best Season to Visit: Year-round

Access:	Short walk
Hiking Time:	30 minutes round trip
Trail Length:	<0.1 mile round trip
Difficulty:	2 boots to see the upper falls
	4 boots to see the lower falls
Trail Surface:	Dirt trails and rock creekbed
Trail Markings:	White blazes and green and yellow Finger Lakes Trail signs
Uses:	Hike, Swim, Snowshoe
Dogs:	OK
Admission:	Free
Contact:	Finger Lakes Trail Conference 6111 Visitor Center Road, Mt. Morris, NY 14510 (585) 658-9320 www.fingerlakestrail.org

From the trail junction at Templar Road, follow the trail down to the creek crossing. This is called Ebenezer's Crossing and sits at the crest of the upper waterfall of the Twin Falls. FLT trail maintainer Fred Yahn says he and his brother dubbed this waterfall Twin Falls back in the mid-fifties. As you'll see, it's an appropriate name so we'll help to immortalize it here. Both drops are steep cascades. The upper falls is 15-feet high and the lower one 10-feet high, culminating in a deep pool.

Trail Directions:

- View the upper fall from the trail.
- Cross the creek and follow a steep trail down the far bank to reach the base of the lower waterfall.

Date visited:

Notes:

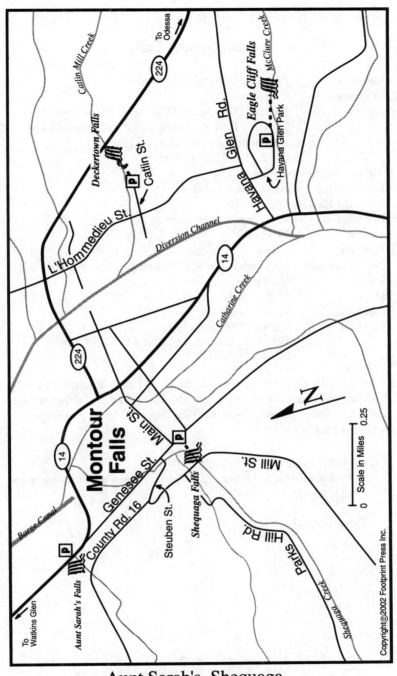

Aunt Sarah's, Shequaga,
Deckertown, and Eagle Cliff Falls 299

81.
Aunt Sarah's Falls

Location: Montour Falls, Schuyler County
Waterway: Unnamed
Directions: Located along Route 14 at the northern edge of
Montour Falls. A parking area is available across from
the waterfall on the east side of Route 14.
(N42 21.143 W76 51.331)
Alternative Parking: None
Best Viewing Locations: From Route 14
Waterfall Height: 90-feet high
Best Season to Visit: Spring; dries in summer
Access: Roadside
Difficulty: 1 boot
Trail Markings: Near sign for village "Welcome to Montour Falls"
Uses: View only
Dogs: OK on leash
Admission: Free
Contact: Village of Montour Falls
408 W. Main Street, Montour Falls, NY 14865
(607) 535-7367

Aunt Sarah's Falls free-falls for its first 30 feet then bounces off a ledge and fans out to double its original width. This waterfall changes dramatically throughout the year, from a spring torrent to an impressive wall of sculptured ice in winter.

Trail Directions:
- Park across from the waterfall so you can view this impressive cascade leisurely.

Date visited:

Notes:

82.
Shequaga Falls

Location: Montour Falls, Schuyler County
Waterway: Shequaga Creek (see map on page 299)
Directions: From Route 14 (N. Catharine Street) in Montour Falls, turn southeast on Genesee Street. Pass Main Street West on the left and Shequaga Falls will appear on the right. (N42 20.704 W76 50.991)
Alternative Parking: None
Best Viewing Locations: From a small park on Genesee Street
Waterfall Height: 156-feet high
Best Season to Visit: Year-round; dries to a trickle by late summer
Access: Roadside, short walk
Difficulty: 1 boot
Trail Surface: Pavement
Trail Markings: She-Qua-Ga Falls sign
Uses: View only
Dogs: OK on leash
Admission: Free
Contact: Village of Montour Falls
408 W. Main Street, Montour Falls, NY 14865
(607) 535-7367

The Indian name for this waterfall is She-Qua-Ga meaning "tumbling waters." You'll sometimes see it spelled Chequagua. It's illuminated at night as it flows right to the doorstep of Montour Falls. A small park sits at its base. Once you've viewed Shequaga Falls from its base, consider driving to its crest. The falls begin above the Shequaga Creek bridge across Mill Street before they plummet to the village of Montour Falls.

In the late 1700s Louis Philippe from France's royal family was exiled to the United States. While staying in the Finger Lakes area he sketched this waterfall. His sketch now hangs in the Louvre Museum in Paris. Louis Philippe became King Louis XVIII of France, the "citizen king," and reigned from 1830 to 1848.

Directions to the Base:
- Park on Genesee Street and walk through the park to the base of the waterfall.

Directions to the Crest:

- Head northwest on Genesee Street then turn left on Steuben Street (County Route 16).
- Take the first left onto Mills Street (a sharp horseshoe bend).
- Drive slowly over the Shequagua Creek bridge to see the crest. You are not allowed to park and walk on the bridge.

Date visited:

Notes:

83.
Deckertown Falls

Location:	Montour Falls, Schuyler County
Waterway:	Catlin Mill Creek (see map on page 299)
Directions:	From Route 14 in Montour Falls, turn east onto Route 224. Cross the Diversion Channel bridge and take the next right onto L'Hommedieu Street. Cross a small creek then turn left on Catlin Street, marked by a "dead-end" sign. Park at the end of this street. (N42 20.600 W76 49.860)

Alternative Parking: None
Best Viewing Locations: From the creekbed and from a trail
Waterfall Height: Three falls 25, 10 and 75-feet high
Best Season to Visit: Year-round

Access:	Short walk and/or creekwalk
Hiking Time:	2 minutes round trip to the lower falls
Trail Length:	0.1 mile round trip to lower falls
	0.3 mile round trip to upper falls
Difficulty:	2 boots to lower falls
	4 boots to upper falls
Trail Surface:	Dirt trails and rock creekbed
Trail Markings:	None
Uses:	Hike, Fish
Dogs:	OK on leash
Admission:	Free
Contact:	Village of Montour Falls
	408 W. Main Street, Montour Falls, NY 14865
	(607) 535-7367

The water level in Catlin Mill Creek will determine if you can see Deckertown Falls and keep your feet dry. In late summer we were able to stone hop and get to the base, but in higher water conditions it would require a wet creekwalk. Also, access to this waterfall may be impeded by local dogs. Although we didn't encounter any, we've heard reports of mean dogs on Catlin Street.

Walking in this creekbed, you're in a narrow gorge cut through layers of shale. The waterfall is a narrow cascade through a notch in the gorge with 25-feet and 10-feet drops. An upper falls, 75-feet high, is located higher in the gorge, under the Route 224 bridge. To reach this requires a very steep trail climb.

As is true with most waterfalls in the area, settlers used Deckertown Falls for mills. The original Deckertown Gristmill was purchased in 1885 by Coral and Chauncey Meeks. It burned in 1887 and was rebuilt as Phoenix Roller Mill. Records show it burned and was rebuilt several more times over the years.

Trail & Creekwalk Directions to the Lower Falls:
- From the parking area, follow the trail and bear left to Catlin Mill Creek.
- Follow the creekbed to the base of the waterfall.

Trail Directions to the Upper Falls:
- From the parking area, follow the trail and bear left toward Catlin Mill Creek.
- Continue on the unmarked trail parallel to the creekbed, climbing sharply uphill.
- You'll reach the crest of the lower falls and gain a view of the deep upper gorge.
- Once the upper falls is in view, turn around and head back down. Do not attempt to get close to the upper falls. The dirt path becomes extremely dangerous—a narrow overhanging ledge. Also, the upper portion of this gorge is private, posted land.

Date visited:

Notes:

84.

Eagle Cliff Falls

Location:	Montour Falls, Schuyler County
Waterway:	McClure Creek in Havana Glen (see map on page 299)
Directions:	From Route 14 at the south end of Montour Falls, turn east onto Havana Glen Road then right into Havana Glen Park. Parking is at the end of the road in Havana Glen Park. (N42 20.146 W76 49.768)

Alternative Parking: None
Best Viewing Locations: From a trail to the waterfall
Waterfall Height: 41-feet high
Best Season to Visit: Year-round

Access:	Short walk
Hiking Time:	10 minutes round trip
Trail Length:	0.2 mile round trip
Difficulty:	3 boots
Trail Surface:	Dirt and rock
Trail Markings:	None
Uses:	Camp
Dogs:	OK on leash in park, but prohibited on gorge trail
Admission:	$2/vehicle May 15 through October 15
Contact:	Havana Glen Park (owned by Town of Montour) Havana Glen Road, PO Box 57 Montour Falls, NY 14865 (607) 535-9476

Havana Glen is a deep gorge with steep shale cliffs. In summer you can stand in the water at the base of the waterfall surrounded by the rock amphitheater. In spring the torrent of water free-falls, 41 feet down and 20-feet wide at the crest, through a notch in the rock walls.

Montour Falls was once called Havana, but the name was changed in 1900 because of the Spanish-American War when any name connected with Cuba was considered deleterious. Montour comes from Catharine Montour (of French & Indian descent), the last ruler of the Seneca Indians who once lived here. Her village was destroyed by General John Sullivan's troops in 1779 during the Revolutionary War.

Trail Directions:
- From the parking area, head up the glen along a walkway with a railing.

- Climb a series of steps.
- Walk in the streambed to reach the base of the falls at 0.12 mile. (In summer you can do this and stay dry.)

Date visited:

Notes:

Waterfalls in Chemung, Tioga, Broome, Cortland and Chenango Counties

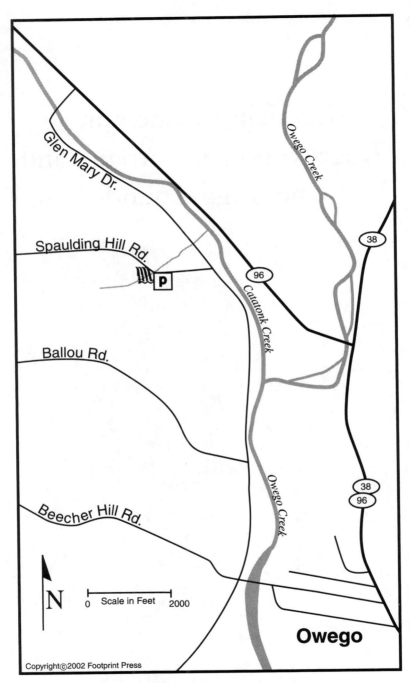

Buttermilk Falls - Owego

85.
Buttermilk Falls - Owego

Location: Owego, Tioga County
Waterway: Unnamed tributary to Catatonk Creek
Directions: From Owego, head north on Route 38/96. Turn left
                   (NE) on Route 96. Take the second left onto Glen
                   Mary Drive. Turn left to stay on Glen Mary Drive.
                   Turn right (W) on Spaulding Hill Road. Park in the
                   small dirt pull-off area on the left, just before crossing
                   the tributary. (N42 7.920 W76 17.219)
Alternative parking: Another dirt pull-off after the tributary crossing
Best Viewing Locations: From the trail at the base of the falls
Waterfall Height: 50-feet high
Best Season to Visit: Spring runoff and rainy seasons are best. In mid-
                   June we found only a trickle of water.
Hiking Time: 2 minutes round trip
Trail Length: <0.1 mile round trip
Access: Short walk
Difficulty: 1 boot
Trail Surface: Dirt trail
Trail Markings: None except a sign at the trailhead
Uses: Viewing only
Dogs: OK
Admission: Free

Buttermilk Falls can be viewed from Spaulding Hill Road but it's best to walk the short trail to its base. The waterfall is a multi-stepped cascade in a peaceful tree-lined gully. You may want to wear bug repellent to visit this waterfall. We got buzzed during our visit.

Trail Directions:

- From the parking area, follow the dirt trail for 93 steps to the base of the waterfall.

Date visited:

Notes:

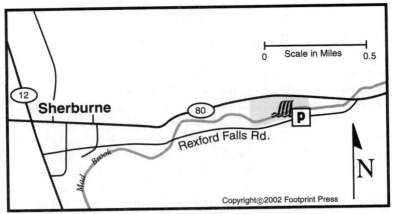

Rexford Falls

86.
Rexford Falls

Location: Sherburne, Chenango County
Waterway: Mad Brook
Directions: From Sherburne located at the corner of Routes 12 and 80, head east on Route 80 for 1.5 miles. You'll pass a sign for Rexford Falls on the right but continue and turn right onto Rexford Falls Road. Park in 0.2 mile at a dirt pull-off area on the right.
(N42 40.711 W75 28.364)
Alternative parking: Park along Route 80 at the Rexford Falls sign
Best Viewing Locations: From the bridge over Mad Brook and from the stream bank just below the waterfall
Waterfall Height: Estimated at 75-feet high
Best Season to Visit: Spring
Hiking Time: 2 minutes round trip
Trail Length: <0.1 mile round trip
Access: Short walk
Difficulty: 1 boot
Trail Surface: Dirt trail
Trail Markings: None

Uses:	Hike, Picnic
Dogs:	OK
Admission:	Free
Contact:	Town of Sherburne
	1 Canal Street, Box 860, Sherburne, NY 13460
	(607) 674-4481
	email: sherbtwn@clarityconnect.com

A pedestrian bridge spans the deep Mad Brook gorge at the crest of Rexford Falls providing an easy-to-reach vantage point. It leads to the undeveloped park along Route 80. The only amenity is an in-need-of-repair outhouse.

Mad Brook flows through a long, gradual shoot then drops into the deep gorge at Rexford Falls.

Trail Directions:

- From the Rexford Falls Road parking area, follow the short trail through a pine forest to the pedestrian bridge over Mad Brook to drink in your fill of this wild waterfall.
- Continue exploring by following the bank of the gorge on the parking area side. If you're visiting in early spring, look across the gorge just below the waterfall to see a narrow ribbon tributary plummeting full distance from Route 80 to the base of the gorge.

Date visited:

Notes:

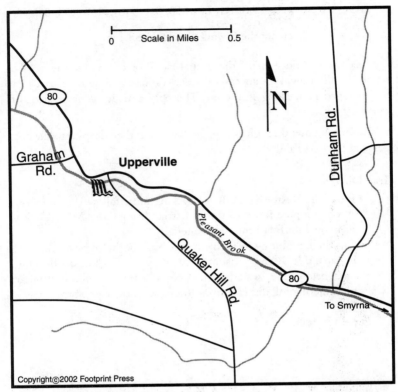

Scale in Miles

0　　　　　　　　0.5

N

80

Graham Rd.

Upperville

Dunham Rd.

Pleasant Brook

Quaker Hill Rd.

80

To Smyrna

Copyright©2002 Footprint Press

Upperville Falls

87.
Upperville Falls

Location: Upperville, Chenango County
Waterway: Pleasant Brook
Directions: Upperville is west of Smyrna on Route 80. From Route 80 in Upperville, turn south on Quaker Hill Road. Park on the left just after the bridge over Pleasant Brook. (N42 41.983 W75 36.964)
Alternative parking: None
Best Viewing Locations: From the Quaker Hill Road bridge
Waterfall Height: Estimated at 8-feet high
Best Season to Visit: Year-round
Access: Roadside
Difficulty: 1 boot
Trail Surface: Paved road
Trail Markings: None
Uses: View only
Dogs: OK
Admission: Free

Look right as you drive over Quaker Hill Road bridge to see the falls or park beyond the bridge and walk back for a more leisurely viewing. Pleasant Brook reaches the caprock ledge and free-falls about 8 feet. As with many small towns throughout the region, Upperville probably owes its existence to this waterfall and the mills which once utilized its power.

Date visited:

Notes:

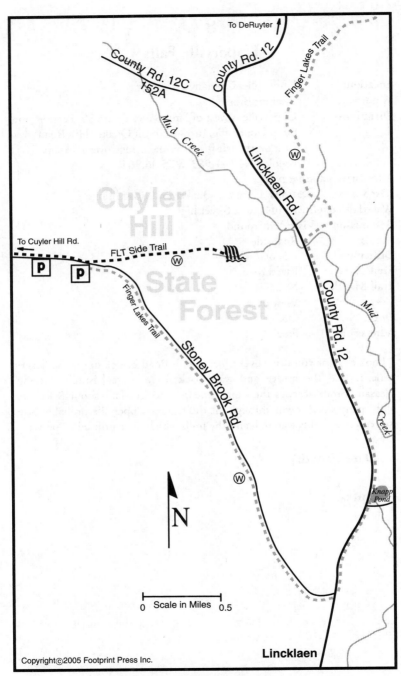

To DeRuyter

County Rd. 12

County Rd. 12C
152A

Finger Lakes Trail

Mud Creek

Lincklaen Rd.

Cuyler
Hill

To Cuyler Hill Rd.

FLT Side Trail

P P

Finger Lakes Trail

State
Forest

Stoney Brook Rd.

County Rd. 12

Mud

Creek

Knapp
Pond

W

W

W

N

Scale in Miles
0   0.5

Lincklaen

Chippewa Falls

88.
Chippewa Falls

Location: Cuyler Hill State Forest, Lincklaen, Cortland County (near the Chenango County border)

Waterway: A tributary into Mud Creek

Directions: In the northwest corner of Chenango County, head north on County Road 12 through the village of Lincklaen. Turn left onto Stoney Brook Road (a seasonal, hard-packed gravel road that is not plowed in winter). Enter Cuyler Hill State Forest and watch right for a 12 x 12-inch yellow Finger Lakes Trail sign marking the FLT side trail. Parking is along a grass shoulder with room for 4 to 5 cars. (N42 42.462 W75 54.661) In winter the closest parking is along Cuyler Hill Road.

Alternative parking: A pull-off parking area about 0.25-mile west of the trail-head as Stoney brook Road enters Cuyler Hill State Forest.

Best Viewing Locations: From the Finger Lakes Trail side trail

Waterfall Height: Estimated at 200-feet high

Best Season to Visit: Spring; dries in summer

Hiking Time: 1.5 hour round trip

Trail Length: 3 miles round trip

Access: Hike, Snowshoe

Difficulty: 2 boots, with a short steep descent to the falls

Trail Surface: A woods floor with no discernable trail

Trail Markings: White blazes

Uses: Hike

Dogs: OK

Admission: Free

Contact: Finger Lakes Trail Conference
6111 Visitor Center Road, Mt. Morris, NY 14510
(585) 658-9320
www.fingerlakestrail.org

We visited this waterfall in mid-April. Water oozed from the land and the trail was still dotted with patches of snow. Our boots quickly soaked through but our reward was a lush waterfall. A ribbon of water starts its cascade above the trail. Then just after passing the trail, it crests and plunges about 20 feet, only to return to its ribbon cascade for as far as the eye can see down the hillside.

The Finger Lakes Trail used to continue from this side trail to Lincklaen Road but access through the private land was revoked, so the Finger Lakes Trail now follows the roads in this area. Fortunately, this side trail still exists, allowing access to Chippewa Falls.

Don't be lured by the orange blazes near the waterfall. They simply mark the border of posted property. They don't designate a trail to better waterfall sighting opportunities. And, please don't continue downhill on the old trail toward Lincklaen Road. Return to Stoney Brook Road after enjoying the waterfall.

Trail Directions:
- Follow the trail off Stoney Brook Road up a small incline and pass a trail register.
- Follow the white blazes along an old logging road.
- Stay on the trail as it circumvents a small private land plot.
- A relatively short but steep descent will lead you to the falls.

Date visited:

Notes:

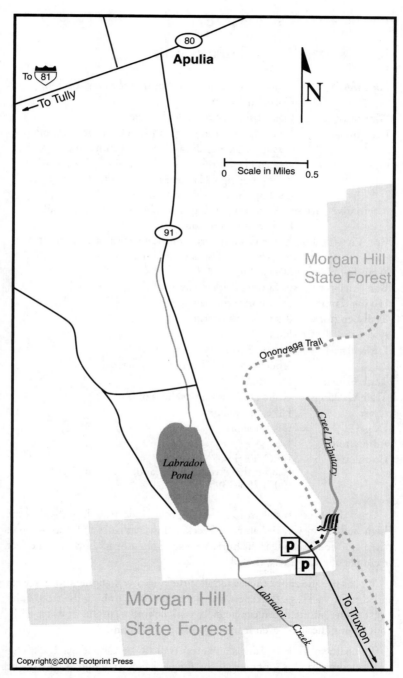

Tinkers Falls

89.
Tinkers Falls

Location: Labrador Hollow State Nature Preserve, Truxton, Cortland County

Waterway: Creel Tributary to Labrador Creek

Directions: From Apulia head south on Route 91 for 3.25 miles, passing the Onondaga/Cortland county line. A parking area will be on the right (W). (N42 46.794 W76 2.149) A sign "Tinkers Falls 1/4 mile" marks the trail head on the east side of Route 91.

Alternative parking: A second parking area is beyond the guard rail, farther south on Route 91.

Best Viewing Locations: From the trail, or the adventurous can climb a steep bank and walk behind the falls

Waterfall Height: 80-feet high

Best Season to Visit: Spring; dries in summer

Hiking Time: 15 minutes round trip

Trail Length: 0.5 mile round trip

Access: Short walk

Difficulty: 1 boot if you stay on the trail
4 boots to climb behind the waterfall

Trail Surface: Dirt trail

Trail Markings: None except a sign at the trailhead

Uses: Hike, Snowshoe

Dogs: OK on leash

Admission: Free

Contact: DEC, Region 7
1285 Fisher Avenue, Cortland, NY 13045-1090
(607) 753-3095

Creel Tributary rushes through a 0.5 mile wide trough with 700-feet high walls on its way to Labrador Creek. Midway it takes a 50-foot free-fall then a 30-foot cascade in its hurry to reach Labrador Hollow. It's a perfect example of a hanging waterfall.

What's unique about this waterfall is the huge overhanging caprock with a ledge for walking 2/3 of the way up the falls. By climbing the steep bank next to the waterfall you can actually walk behind a curtain of water without feeling the spray even in spring run-off conditions.

The path to Tinkers Falls is an access trail to the Onondaga Trail. This 23-mile-long trail is a branch of the Finger Lakes Trail and is part of the

A trail leads behind Tinkers Falls.
Snow still clings to the edges,
well into summer.

North Country Trail that will eventually reach all the way to North Dakota.

Trail Directions:

- Cross Route 91 from the parking areas and follow the well-trodden trail parallel to the creek.
- In 0.25 mile the trail will end and you'll have a great view of Tinkers Falls.
- But the adventurous needn't stop here. Cross the stream and continue toward the waterfall on the opposite bank. (In spring run-off conditions it's impossible to keep your boots dry.)
- Just before the waterfall, climb the bank and follow the ledge behind the falls. It's a wide, easy to walk ledge, and there's lots of space to walk behind the wall of water.

Date visited:

Notes:

Waterfalls in Onondaga, Madison and Oneida Counties

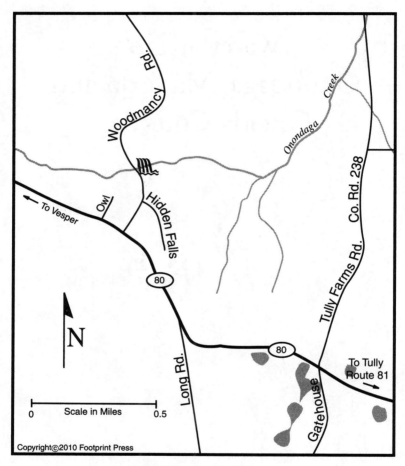

Fellows Falls

90.
Fellows Falls

Location: Tully, Onondaga County
Waterway: Onondaga Creek
Directions: Exit Route 81 at Tully and head west on Route 80.
Pass Tully Farms Road, Long Road, and turn right
onto Woodmancy Road. Shortly after Hidden Falls
Road you'll cross a bridge over the waterway. Park just
past the bridge. (N42 48.944 W76 9.745)
Best Viewing Locations: From Woodmancy Road
Waterfall Height: Estimated at 40-feet high
Best Season to Visit: Year-round
Access: Roadside
Difficulty: 1 boot
Uses: View only
Dogs: OK on leash
Admission: Free

The creek crosses under Woodmancy Road then immediately cascades
40 feet. Slightly downstream a second fall drops 20 feet in a much more
gradual cascade. Both falls can be seen from Woodmancy Road.

Date visited:

Notes:

Fellows Falls

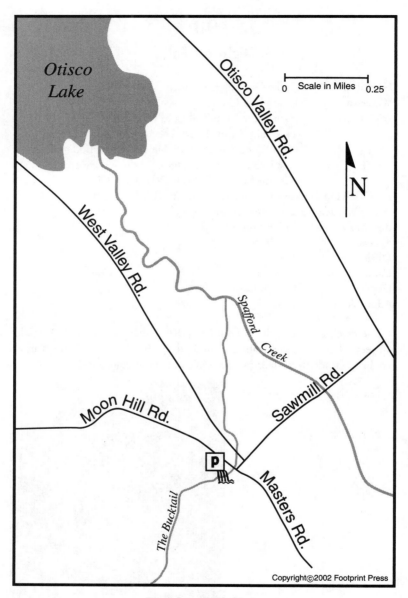

Bucktail Falls

91.
Bucktail Falls

Location:	Spafford, Onondaga County
Waterway:	The Bucktail
Directions:	From Otisco Valley Road at the south end of Otisco Lake, turn southwest on Sawmill Road. At the end, turn right onto Moon Hill Road and quickly see the dirt parking area just after the creek crossing on the left. (N42 49.360 W76 14.463)

Alternative parking: Along the shoulder of Masters Road
Best Viewing Locations: From the base of the waterfall
Waterfall Height: Estimated at 35-feet high
Best Season to Visit: Year-round

Access:	Short walk
Hiking Time:	1 minute round trip
Trail Length:	<0.1 mile round trip
Difficulty:	1 boot
Trail Surface:	Dirt
Trail Markings:	None
Uses:	View only
Dogs:	OK on leash
Admission:	Free

Set in a moss and fern covered glen, the water free-falls at a 45 degree angle in the creekbed, then rolls over tight layers of shale for the rest of its journey. A very easy, short walk on a dirt trail takes you to the base of this idyllic waterfall. Take bug spray if you plan to stay any length of time. Bugs also find this an appealing location. Or, visit in winter when bugs are not a problem, and the waterfall is partially frozen over forming a wintertime spectacle. (Note: Although not posted, this falls is on private property, so a respectful visit is essential.)

Trail Directions:
- From the parking area, follow the short dirt trail to the base of the waterfall.

Date visited:

Notes:

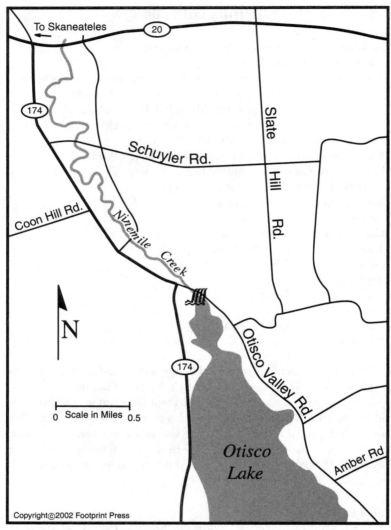

Otisco Lake Overflow

92.
Otisco Lake Overflow

Location: Marietta, Onondaga County
Waterway: Ninemile Creek
Directions: From Route 174 at the north end of Otisco Lake, turn
                 southeast on Otisco Valley Road. The waterfall is
                 immediately to the right. (N42 54.267 W76 18.722)
Alternative parking: None
Best Viewing Locations: Drive-by
Waterfall Height: A 15-foot dam forms a steep cascade
Best Season to Visit: Spring or after heavy rain
Access: Roadside
Difficulty: 1 boot
Uses: View only
Dogs: OK
Admission: Free
Contact: Onondaga County Water Authority
                 200 Northern Concourse, PO Box 9
                 Syracuse, NY 13211-0009
                 (315) 455-7061

Otisco Lake is the most easterly of the Finger Lakes and seventh in size of the eleven lakes. Its outlet is Ninemile Creek which flows north to Onondaga Lake. The name Otisco was bestowed by Native Americans and means "the place where the waters dry up." It's thought to be a reference to the shallow south end that was little more then a swamp before the lake was dammed and flooded to raise water levels in 1868 and 1910.

The Onondaga County Water Authority was created in 1951 to meet the water supply needs of the Syracuse region. They took over the Otisco Lake System which had been privately owned by the New York Water Service Company, to rehabilitate and enlarge the system. The other water source for Syracuse is Skaneateles Lake.

Drive-by Directions:
- Driving south on Route 174, turn left onto Otisco Valley Road and look right to see the waterfall.

Date visited:

Notes:

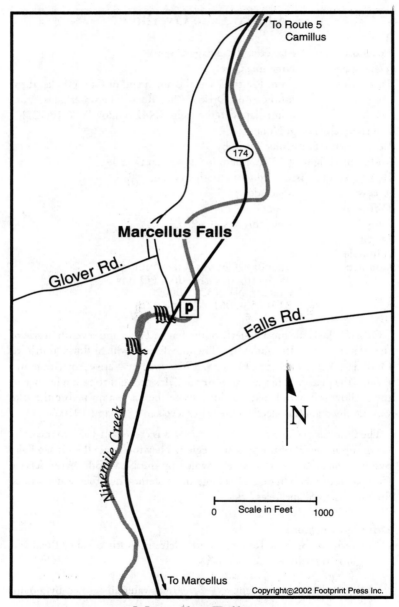

To Route 5
Camillus

174

Marcellus Falls

Glover Rd.

P

Falls Rd.

N

Ninemile Creek

0   Scale in Feet   1000

To Marcellus

Copyright©2002 Footprint Press Inc.

Marcellus Falls

93.
Marcellus Falls

Location:	Marcellus Falls, Onondaga County
Waterway:	Ninemile Creek
Directions:	From Route 5 west of Syracuse, turn south on Route 174 in Camillus. Route 174 runs through Marcellus Falls and past the waterfalls. There is public parking on the left (E) side of Route 174 just before Marcellus Falls marked by a brown and yellow sign "Ninemile Creek Public Fishing Stream." (N43 0.383 W76 20.103)

Alternative parking: None
Best Viewing Locations: From bridge and drive-by
Waterfall Height: A 10-foot dam followed by a series of cascades
A 10-foot steep cascade
Best Season to Visit: Year-round

Access:	Short walk or roadside
Hiking Time:	30 minutes round trip walking
Trail Length:	0.8 mile round trip from parking area to both falls
Difficulty:	1 boot
Trail Surface:	Paved road
Trail Markings:	None
Uses:	View only
Dogs:	OK
Admission:	Free

These 2 waterfalls can be partially viewed in a drive-by, or for more leisurely viewing, park at the fishing access and walk 0.2 mile to the first waterfall and another 0.2 mile to the second.

The town of Marcellus Falls began in 1801 as a settlement called Union Village. From its very beginning, it was a manufacturing settlement. Ninemile Creek once sported 25 mill sites. In 1808 a crude sawmill was erected and a gristmill was added in 1824. Today the second waterfall is behind the Martisco Paper Company.

Drive-by Directions:
- Driving south on Route 174, slow down as you enter Marcellus Falls. Look to the right to see the first waterfall formed by a dam. The cascades below the dam will be obscured under the bridge.

- Continue south 0.2 mile and keep looking right. Just before Martisco Paper Company you'll catch a glimpse of the second waterfall.

Trail Directions:
- From the parking area, walk south along Route 174. (It has wide shoulders.)
- From the bridge, look to the right to see the first waterfall formed by a dam. Look down to view cascades under the bridge.
- Continue south 0.2 mile and keep looking right. Just before Martisco Paper Company, you'll see the second waterfall.

Date visited:

Notes:

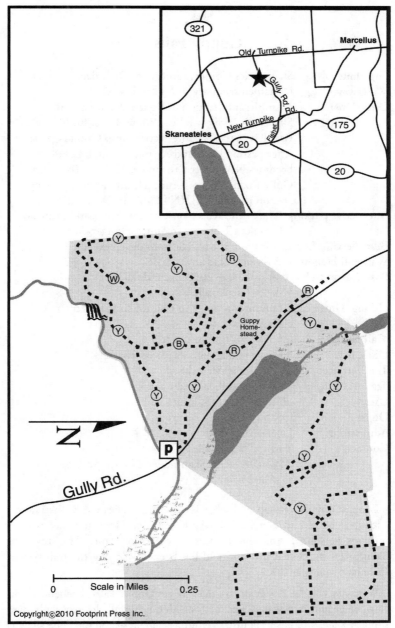

Guppy Falls

94.
Guppy Falls

Location: Skaneateles Conservation Area, Onondaga County

Waterway: Unnamed tributary to Ninemile Creek

Directions: From the intersection of Routes 20 and 321 in Skaneateles, follow follow Route 2 east for 0.3 mile. Bear left at the "Y" intersection onto Onondaga Street. After passing Highland Avenue, Onondaga Street becomes New Seneca Turnpike. Turn left (N) onto Gully Road. In 1 mile turn left into a small parking area on the left (W). (N42.968202 W76.389951)

Alternative parking: The Skaneateles Conservation Area parking area off Old Seneca Turnpike (requires a longer hike)

Best Viewing Locations: From the trail or from the creekbed

Waterfall Height: A 23-foot cascade over shale

Best Season to Visit: Spring, early summer, and fall, or after rain

Access: Hike or Creekwalk

Hiking Time: 30 minutes round trip trail walking, longer to creekwalk

Trail Length: 0.5 mile via trail round trip

Difficulty: 1 boot to hike, 3 boots to creekwalk

Trail Surface: dirt trail, rocky creekbed

Trail Markings: Trail signs and colored markers

Uses: Hike, picnic, fish, hunt

Dogs: OK on leash

Admission: Free

Contact: Town of Skaneateles
24 Jordan Street,Skaneateles, NY 13152
(315) 685-3473

Look at any older map and what is now the Skaneateles Conservation Area may be labeled as a US Military Reservation. The land was used by military personnel from local bases as recreation land. The Town of Skaneateles purchased the land and has been developing the trail system since its opening in 2001.

Water flow in the feeder stream that houses Guppy Falls is dependent on snow melt and rain water. The 23-foot high waterfall slopes steeply over slippery shale and has a slightly overhung segment at the top. The shale is developed in the Skaneateles Formation of the Hamilton Group and dates from 390 to 415 million years ago.

The homestead and namesake of this property was William Guppy who emigrated from England in the early 1850's. He and his wife Ann operated a dairy farm here and raised eight children.

A color pdf file of the Skaneateles Conservation Area trails is available at http://www.townofskaneateles.com/pub/docs/sca.map.pdf

Trail Directions:
- From the parking area, head northwest on the trail parallel to Gully Road.
- At the intersection, turn left onto the yellow Rudl Trail.
- Bear left at the blue trail intersection to stay on the yellow trail.
- Reach the Guppy Falls overlook.
- You can retrace your path back to the parking lot or continue down the trail following any of the trails that loop back (yellow, white, or red).

Creekwalking Directions:
- From the parking area, walk southeast along Gully Road to the creek bed.
- Walk upstream in the creekbed until you reach the waterfall. You'll pass several small cascades along the way. (Please do not climb the gully walls.)

Date visited:

Notes:

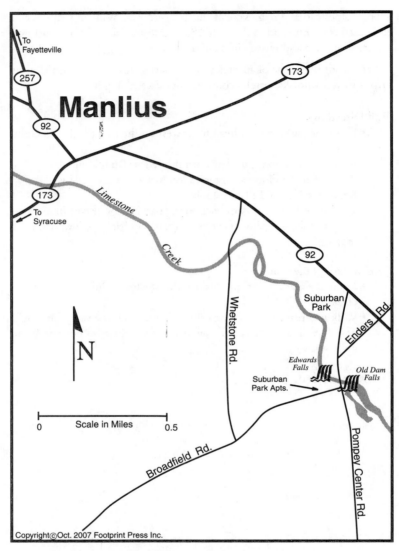

Old Dam & Edwards Falls

95.
Old Dam and Edwards Falls

Location: Manlius, Onondaga County
Waterway: Limestone Creek
Directions: Old Dam Falls: From Route 92 south of Manlius, turn
                     right (S) on Pompey Center Road. Drive slowly and
                     look east as you cross the Limestone Creek bridge.
                     (N42 59.364 W75 57.653) Parking is prohibited in
                     the area.
                     Edwards Falls: From Route 92 south of Manlius, turn
                     right (S) into the Suburban Park apartment complex.
                     (N42 59.743 W75 57.735)/
Alternative parking: None
Best Viewing Locations: Roadside (from parking lot for Edwards Falls and
                     drive-by only for Old Dam Falls)
Waterfall Height: Edwards Falls: 70-feet high
                     Old Dam Falls: 30-feet high
Best Season to Visit: Year-round
Access: Roadside
Difficulty: 1 boot
Trail Markings: None
Uses: View only
Dogs: OK
Admission: Free
Contact: Village of Manlius
                     One Elmbrook Drive West, Manlius, NY 13104
                     (315) 682-9171

Limestone Creek and this area around Edwards Falls was once a very active mill area. Colonel Elijah Phillips built the first sawmill here in 1792, followed by a gristmill in 1796. The Suburban Trolley Line once terminated here, bringing tourists to enjoy the impressive, 70-foot, straight drop waterfall. In 1809 a major flood wiped out bridges, dams, and mills along Limestone Creek.

In 2001 an apartment complex called Suburban Park was built between Route 92 and Limestone Creek. You can view Edwards Falls from the parking lot (it's about 1,000 feet upstream). In 2007 a landslide into Limestone Creek occurred behind the apartment buildings, creating very unsafe conditions.

Upstream a short distance is the Old Dam Falls. This one is viewable only as a drive-by. It's a shame we can't park and savor this waterfall like we

Old Dam Falls

can so many others. It's a curtain of water, dropping 30 feet in a sheer cliff free-fall, 90-feet wide. Well worth a slow drive by.

Manlius has two other waterfalls that are inaccessible to the public. Brickyard Falls is surrounded by private residential property between Watervale and Gibbs Roads. Broadfield Falls' crest can be seen from Broadfield Road (east of Gibbs Road) but the full beauty of it can only be enjoyed by the adjacent property owners.

Directions to Edwards Falls:
  • View from the Suburban Park apartment complex parking lot.

Directions to Old Dam Falls:
  • Look as you drive slowly past this waterfall.

Date visited:

Notes:

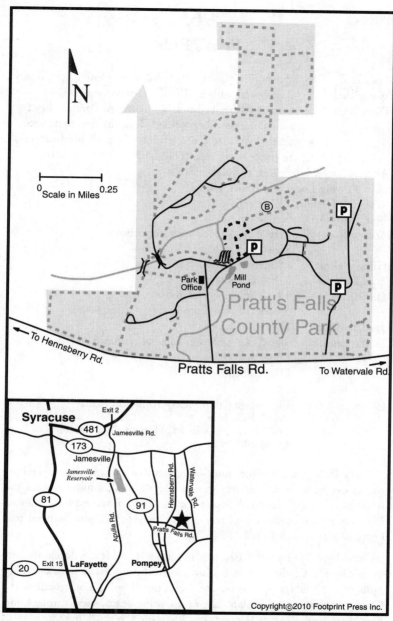

Pratt's Falls

96.
Pratt's Falls

Location: Pratt's Falls County Park, Manlius, Onondaga County
Waterway: A Tributary of West Branch Limestone Creek
Directions: From I-81 head east on Route 20. At Pompey, head
                  north on Hennsberry Road. Take the first right onto
                  Pratts Fall Road. Turn left into the park and bear right
                  to the parking area. (N42 55.889 W75 59.580)
Alternative parking: Near the park office
Best Viewing Locations: Short walk
Waterfall Height: 137-feet high
Best Season to Visit: Year-round
Access: Very short walk to view from above
                  Short walk to view from below
Hiking Time: 15 minutes round trip
Trail Length: 0.4 mile round trip
Difficulty: 1 boot to view from above
                  3 boots to view from below
Trail Surface: Dirt with stairs
Trail Markings: Sign "Trail to Lower Falls" at trailhead
Uses: Hike, Picnic, Snowshoe, Ski
Dogs: OK on leash
Admission: $1 / vehicle
Contact: Onondaga County Department of Parks
                  Pratt's Falls Park
                  7671 Pratts Falls Road, Manlius, NY 13104
                  (315) 682-5934

Pratt's Falls is a 137-foot, multi-tiered, milky cascade that sometimes freezes over in winter. This area was an early Indian camping ground and home to Onondaga County's first sawmill in 1796. It was built by Manoah Pratt on a rock overlooking Pratt's Falls. The sawmill was changed to a gristmill and operated until 1874.

Onondaga County purchased the land in 1931 and it was developed into a park by the Civilian Conservation Corps during the depression. They built roads, bridges, stairways, and buildings. During construction, the CCC crews unearthed Indian skeletons, trading beads, axes, a stone knife, bear claws, and other implements of Indian life. The park has lots of trails and is active year-round for hiking and cross-country skiing.

In 1998 Pratt's Falls became famous when Onondaga Community College geology professor Meg Harris and her students discovered a new species of insect fossil in the gorge. Dubbed *Kennacryphaeus Harrisae*, the 245-million-year-old trilobite predates the dinosaurs. Trilobites lived on the ocean bottom and ate mud. They ranged from 1 to 5 inches long. Harris' species has a jagged fringe along the bottom that distinguishes it from other trilobites.

To view Pratt's Falls, you can walk to an observation platform at the crest and follow the fence line for a very short, easy walk to get a face-on view of this pretty waterfall. If you're energetic, continue on the trail that uses several flights of stairs and leads to a look-out near the base of the waterfall. This waterfall is impressive from any angle. When the mist is in the air and the sunlight is at the right angle, rainbows dance across the waterfall.

Trail Directions:
- From the parking area, head west through the trees, along the road to the viewing platform at the crest of the waterfall.
- Then follow the fence line back toward the parking area and keep looking toward the falls to catch some great views.
- Continue around the edge of the trees until you reach the trailhead sign. (Don't take the dirt trail that heads straight down the hill—you'd only encourage erosion.)
- Bear left whenever you have a choice and keep heading downhill on flights of steps.
- The trail dead-ends in 0.2 mile at the falls overlook.

Date visited:

Notes:

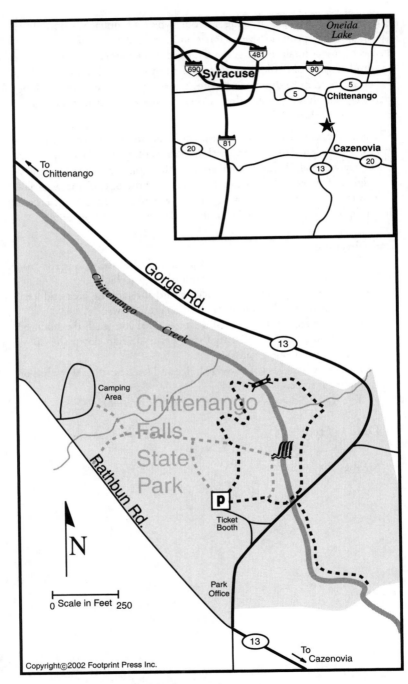

Chittenango Falls

97.

Chittenango Falls

Location:	Chittenango Falls State Park, Madison County
Waterway:	Chittenango Creek
Directions:	From Cazenovia at the south end of Cazenovia Lake, head north for 4.5 miles on Gorge Road (NY Route 13) to the park entrance. Follow signs through the entrance gate to the parking area. (N42 58.664 W75 50.536)

Alternative parking: None

Best Viewing Locations: From the top overlook, midway down the steps and the bridge at base of the waterfall

Waterfall Height: 167-feet high

Best Season to Visit: Year-round

Access:	Hike
Hiking Time:	1 hour loop
Trail Length:	1.1 mile loop
Difficulty:	4 boots, many steps
Trail Surface:	Paved & dirt trail
Trail Markings:	Brown wooden signs
Uses:	Hike, Camp
Dogs:	OK on leash
Admission:	$3 / vehicle weekdays, $5 weekends and holidays. Free off-season.
Contact:	Chittenango Falls State Park 2300 Rathbun Road, Cazenovia, NY 13035 (315) 655-9620

Chittenango Creek flows north from Cazenovia Lake to Oneida Lake. At Chittenango Falls State Park it plunges off the Allegany Plateau, cutting through Onondaga limestone. The water takes a single large leap for half its total distance then cascades in a series of smaller steps. With spring runoff, it makes a mighty roar as water is shot off ledges at various angles.

This was an active industrial area in the mid-1800s. Stone foundations of old factories, water channels, and buildings can still be found. The first European owner was John Lincklaen, the founder of Cazenovia, in 1797. He sold the land in 1813 to Studson Benson who industrialized the area. William's Stone Quarry, H.L. Jones Paper Mill, Foster's sawmill and others used power generated from the waterfall. In 1866, 40 acres were sold on auction to Reverend George Boardman who gave the tract to his son Derrick. The son was approached by a gunpowder maker to sell the land, but he offered it instead for less to Mrs. Helen L. Fairchild if she'd dedicate it to public use. Mrs. Fairchild formed the Chittenango Falls Park Association in 1887 to raise funds and operated the area until 1922. Then, worried about liability near the waterfall, she asked the state to take it over. They did, and today it's Chittenango Falls State Park, open to us all. The Civilian Conservation Corps built the shelter and flagstone path you'll walk.

While the 167-foot waterfall is the main feature of the park, Chittenango Falls is also home to and protects endangered wildlife and plants. The rare Chittenango Ovate Amber snail is found here as are Hart's Tongue fern and Roseroot, also rare species. Please do not disturb or remove any plants, wildlife, fossils, or rocks from the park.

Trail Directions:
- From the parking area, follow the brown sign "Falls Overlook & Trails" which will lead down 26 steps.
- Pass a pavilion on the left and continue straight toward the wooden fence.
- Continue down 32 steps.
- Turn right and proceed down 62 more steps to a landing with your first view of Chittenango Falls at 0.2 mile.
- Continue down 26 steps then follow a guard rail to water level.
- Cross Chittenango Creek on a wood and metal bridge at 0.3 mile. (You can return to the parking lot from here or continue forward.)
- Climb 37 steps uphill on the dirt trail.
- At 0.5 mile, cross a tributary on a wooden bridge.
- Switchback up the hill, climbing 27 more steps.
- Bear right at 0.6 mile to enjoy an upper overlook.
- Climb up another 15 steps.
- At 0.7 mile you can climb to the road and circle back to the parking lot or continue on the path, under the road bridge where you'll pass a 2-foot overhung waterfall then a series of small drops above the bridge.
- The trail winds through the woods with side trails to the right that lead to overlooks for a series of small falls.
- The trail ends at 0.8 mile as designated by the "end of trail" sign.
- Follow the trail back to cross under the road bridge.
- Bear right to climb the stairs up to the bridge and follow the pedestrian walkway.
- At the "T," turn left to return to the parking area.

Date visited:

Notes:

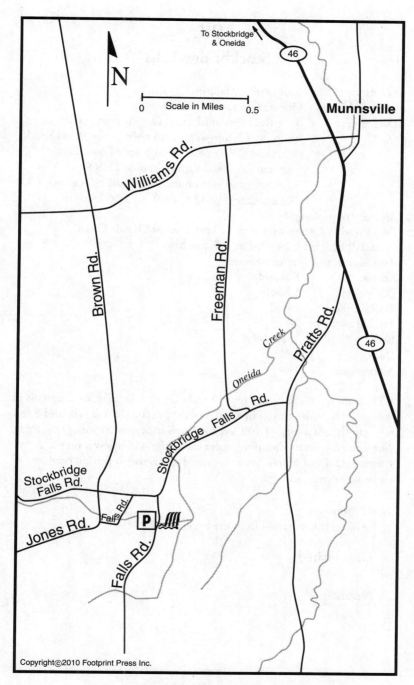

Stockbridge Falls

98.

Stockbridge Falls

Location:	Munnsville, Madison County
Waterway:	Oneida Creek
Directions:	Take Route 46 south from Oneida through Stockbridge and Munnsville. Turn right (S) on Pratts Road, then right (W) on Stockbridge Falls Road. Pass Freeman Road and turn right onto Falls Road. View Stockbridge Falls from the Falls Road bridge over Oneida Creek. (N42 57.069 W75 36.242)

Alternative parking: None
Best Viewing Locations: From the bridge across Oneida Creek
Waterfall Height: Estimated at 100-feet high
Best Season to Visit: Year-round

Access:	Roadside
Difficulty:	1 boot
Trail Surface:	Paved
Trail Markings:	None
Uses:	View only
Dogs:	OK
Admission:	Free

The view from the bridge over Oneida Creek is unique for waterfalls in the area. The water travels in a series of drops (10, 15, 6, 2, 10, and 5 feet respectively) for a total of 100 feet over pink rock spotted with green algae. The water continues dropping under the bridge and below it on the downstream side. Even if you don't see posted signs, this is private property, so please don't trespass.

Trail Directions:
• View this waterfall from the bridge.

Date visited:

Notes:

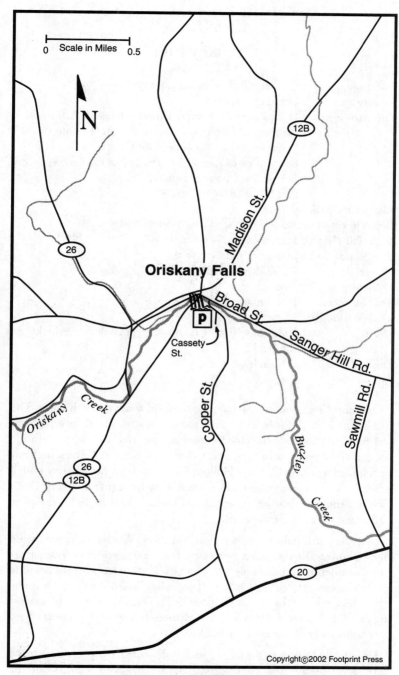

Oriskany Falls

99.
Oriskany Falls

Location:	Oriskany Falls, Oneida County
Waterway:	Oriskany Creek
Directions:	From Route 20, head north on Routes 26/12B into the town of Oriskany Falls. Turn right (E) onto Broad Street then right (S) again onto Cassety Street. The falls will be to your right as you cross the Cassety Street Bridge. Park along the street. (N42 56.318 W75 27.637)

Alternative parking: None
Best Viewing Locations: From the Cassety Street bridge
Waterfall Height: Estimated at 20-feet high
Best Season to Visit: Year-round

Access:	Roadside, wheelchair
Difficulty:	1 boot
Trail Surface:	Paved road
Trail Markings:	None
Uses:	View only (fishing is allowed from a deck overlooking the creek)
Dogs:	OK on leash
Admission:	Free

Oriskany Creek and its waterfalls are what drew settlers to this area. The first sawmill was built in 1794 by Thomas Cassety, a land surveyor who was hired to subdivide the land because he had lived for awhile with the Indians and knew how to negotiate with them successfully. The settlement he founded was called Cassety Hollow. Two years later, Mr. Cassety built a gristmill. Unfortunately, this was washed away by spring floods in 1807. The settlement's name was changed to Oriskany Falls in 1829, the same year a post office branch opened.

Over the years, mills flourished along the creek. Woolen mills producing fine cashmeres, flannels, and yarns were built, along with tanneries, gristmills, distilleries, and sawmills. Oriskany Falls prospered with the opening of the Chenango Canal in 1836. This waterway linked Binghamton to the Erie Canal at Utica, by way of Oriskany Falls. For forty years until its closing in 1876, the canal allowed for the efficient transport of products from area farms and mills to far away markets.

A major flood occurred in 1917 as a wall of water broke through the flood gates of the mill ponds above town. The flood washed out the

Cooper Street bridge and area railroad tracks, and damaged property all along the creek.

Today, the water of Oriskany Creek passes under Madison Street in the middle of town then angles toward the center of the waterway as it cascades down a series of small steps. A second man-made falls with approximately a 6-foot sheer drop can be seen below the Cassety Street bridge. A small paved walkway provides wheelchair access to a deck overlooking this waterfall. The deck is labeled as the "Hinman Memorial Fishing Access Site" by the DEC.

Date visited:

Notes:

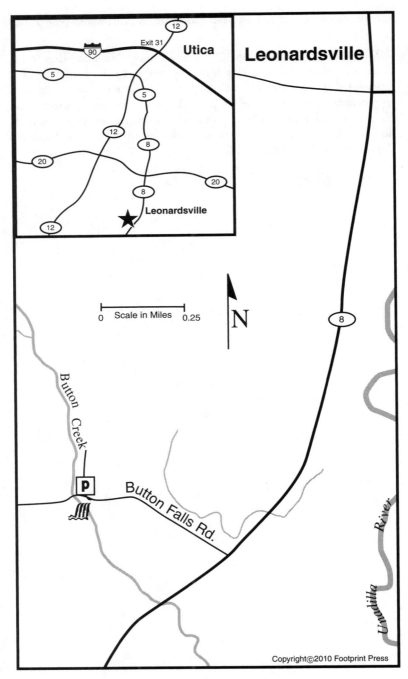

Button Falls

100.
Button Falls

Location: South of Leonardsville, Madison County
Waterway: Button Creek
Directions: Head south on Route 8 through Leonardsville. Turn right (W) onto Button Falls Road. Park along the road, before the bridge, 0.4 mile in from Route 8. (N42 47.501 W75 16.151)
Alternative parking: None
Best Viewing Locations: From the roadside.
Waterfall Height: Estimated at 40-feet high
Best Season to Visit: Year-round (easier to see when leaves are off trees)
Trail Length: <0.1 mile to the crest of the falls
Access: Roadside to view the top of the falls
Difficulty: 1 boot roadside
Trail Surface: None, woods
Trail Markings: None
Uses: View only
Dogs: OK on leash
Admission: Free

You can see the crest of the upper section of Button Falls from Button Falls Road, but to get a full view you must bushwhack through the woods and past posted signs, so a road-only view is recommended.

The creek passes under Button Falls Road then plummets through a narrow rock fissure for two drops. The first is about 2-feet high, the second approximately 8 feet. The falls then drops again through another narrow fissure and cascades approximately 40 feet down a rock face.

Date visited:

Notes:

Definitions

Aqueduct: A man-made trough to carry canal water over a natural waterway such as a creek. The aqueduct was usually made from stone archways with wood lining the trough.

Brachiopods: Clam-like organisms that lived long ago in shallow seas.

Bushwhack: To travel through woods without the aid of a trail.

Caprock: A hard rock, usually limestone or sandstone, which forms the top plate of a waterfall because of its resistance to erosion.

CCC: Civilian Conservation Corps - a federal public works project during the depression which was responsible for the construction of stairways, trails, and buildings in many of our state parks.

Change bridge: A bridge over a canal where mules crossed the canal to continue towing from a towpath on the opposite side of the canal.

Concretion: Solid, rounded masses of mineral matter that occur in sedimentary rock. They have a different composition from the rock in which they are found, such as a limestone concretion found in a bed of shale. Concretions form around a nucleus that commonly is a fragment of fossil shell, bone or plant material.

Crampons: Metal spikes attached to the bottom of boots to prevent slipping when climbing or walking on ice. Some crampons cover the full sole, instep crampons cover only the arch area of the bottom of the boot.

Dam: A barrier constructed across a waterway to control the flow or raise the level of water.

DEC: Department of Environmental Conservation

Dolomite: A stone similar to limestone but more durable because it contains magnesium.

Escarpment: A long, more or less continuous cliff or slope separating relatively flat land into two levels. Also called a scarp.

Esker: A ridge of debris formed when a river flowed under a glacier in an icy tunnel. Rocky material accumulated on the tunnel beds, and when the glacier melted, a ridge of rubble remained.

Definitions

Fossil: Any remains, trace, or imprint of a plant or animal naturally preserved in sediments or rocks from past geologic time.

Glacial erratics:Boulders transported by a glacier that generally differ from the bedrock underneath.

Glen: An old Scottish Gaelic word meaning valley. It typically refers to a wide, gentle valley, but in New York State, glen is used synonymous with gorge and gulf, referring to a deep, narrow canyon cut by a stream at the site of a hanging valley.

Gorge: (see Glen)

Gulf: (see Glen)

Hanging valley: A small glacial valley left hanging high above the floor of a larger, deeper glacial valley.

Height: Total vertical drop of the waterfall or of a close series of waterfalls.

Instep crampons: (see Crampons)

Joints: Smooth, vertical fractures in rock.

Kames: Hills formed by rivers that flowed on top of a glacier and spilled over the edge depositing soil into huge piles.

Kettle: A small pond sitting in a depression, created when a large block of ice separated from a glacier. Water running off of the glacier deposited gravel and debris all around the ice block. The block melted, leaving behind a rough circular depression.

Limestone: A sedimentary rock chiefly composed of the mineral calcite.

Millrace: The channel, often made of wood or stone, that directs the water entering or leaving a mill.

Millstone: One of a pair of cylindrical stones used in a mill for grinding grain.

Mudboil: Volcano-like cones of sand and silt that boil out of the earth. They may erupt and form a large cone in several days and then cease flowing, or they may discharge for several years.

Definitions

Niagara Escarpment: An outcropping of Lockport dolomite (a type of limestone) that forms cliffs from Rochester through Niagara Falls and the Bruce Peninsula to Michigan.

OSHA: The acronym for Occupational Safety and Health Administration, the government agency that oversees workplace safety issues.

Pool: A deep or still place in a stream.

Pothole: A rounded hole ground into streambed rock by sand and gravel in swirling eddies.

Plunge pool: A deep section of a stream at the base of a waterfall, carved by the force of water plunging over the waterfall.

Race: A channel built to carry water.

Sandstone: Sedimentary rock composed of consolidated sand.

Scarp: (see Escarpment)

Scree: A slope (generally < 60 degrees) of loose rock debris at the base of a steep incline or cliff.

Shale: A sedimentary rock mainly composed of clay or very fine material in thin layers.

Siltstone: A sedimentary rock composed of a fine-grained sediment.

Slate: A low-grade metamorphic rock formed from shale and characterized by flat cleavage plates.

Sluiceway: An artificial channel, especially one for carrying off excess water.

Snow bridge: A covering of snow with air or water below it. If a snow bridge is thin enough, stepping on it can cause your foot to crash through into the air or water below.

Spillway: A channel for an overflow of water, as from a reservoir or canal.

Stile: A set of steps for crossing a fence or wall.

Suffrage: The right or privilege of voting or exercising the right to vote.

Talus: A sloping mass (generally > 60 degrees) of rock debris at the base of a cliff.

Definitions

Terminal moraine: An accumulation of boulders, stones, or other debris carried and deposited by a glacier at it's farthest point of migration.

Topo map: Short for topographic map. It's a map showing elevation changes using gradient lines.

USGS: United States Geological Survey, the branch of government that produces topographic maps.

Waterwheel: A large wooden wheel placed at the edge of a moving stream. Water collects in buckets or paddles on the wheel and turns the wheel. Waterwheels powered many mills.

Width: The distance from one stream bank to another along the crest (or top edge) of the waterfall.

Waste weir: A dam along the edge of a canal that allows overflow water to dissipate to a side waterway. A type of spillway.

Weir: A dam placed across a river or canal to raise or divert the water, as for a millrace, or to regulate or measure the flow.

Waterfall Web Sites

Eastern Waterfall Guide:
www.aria-database.com/waterfall
Great Lakes Waterfalls
www.gowaterfalling.com
NY Falls:
www.nyfalls.com
Ruth's Waterfalls:
http://naturalhighs.net/waterfalls/default.htm
Western NY Waterfall Survey:
http://falzguy.com
Waterfalls of NY state:
www.angelfire.com/ny4/waterfalls/NewYork.html

Roadside Waterfalls

Short Walks to Waterfalls

Longer Hikes to Waterfalls

Longer Hikes to Waterfalls

Creekwalks

Wheelchair Accessible Waterfalls

Waterfalls for Ice Climbers

Waterfalls for Swimmers

Waterfalls for Swimmers

Waterfalls for Boaters / Rafters

Waterfalls by Level of Difficulty

1 Boot:

1 Boot:

2 Boots:

2 Boots:

3 Boots:

4 Boots:

4 Boots:

Word Index

Word Index

Word Index

Word Index

Word Index

Word Index